WOMEN IN MINISTRY

"Rise up, ye women that are at ease; hear my voice,
ye careless daughters; give ear unto my speech."
Isaiah 32:9

Samuel N. Greene, *Ph. D.*

Glory Publishing, Inc.

Glory Publishing, Inc
GloryPublishingInc.com

About the Author:
www.nwmin.org

Printed in the United States of America
ISBN 978-1-937199-60-9
Copyright © 2015. All Rights Reserved

All Scriptures used in this book were taken from the King James Version.

WOMEN IN MINISTRY

Foreword

In these days when we are about to witness that last great move of the Spirit of God and the coming of the Lord Jesus, we need to have clarified for us in a Scriptural manner the truth about women and their role in church ministry. To do this, we must approach the Word of God with an open (unveiled) face (II Corinthians 3:18). The time for bias and closed-mindedness is over! We must search the Scriptures to see about this principle.

The purpose of this manual is to consider how many women there were in the Scriptures whom God used in a marvelous way. We will look at their contribution to the Kingdom of God, and how their ministry and lives affected so many people. My hope is that it will leave us with a true Biblical account of women and their ministry, how important they are and were to God's dealings of women and their ministry, and how important they are and were to God's dealings with His people. By seeing how, why, how many, and how often they were used, it will leave no doubt in anyone's mind that it is and always has been God's desire for women to be used in ministry, as well as consider what life would have been like without them and their ministry! Hopefully sisters, as you see these women at work, it will encourage you in your own distinct calling and ministry. As we see how God used them so voluminously and how important their lives and ministries were, we will be left with no doubt concerning God's will for women. As we see these truths so obviously laid out in Scripture, it will confirm once and for all God's will and desire for women to be used mightily by God in the earth. It will put an end to skepticism, erroneous prejudices, and hindrances to women ministering, as well as expose the bias of the translators and the deep insecurities in men regarding keeping women in bondage. May God grant us eyes to see, ears to hear, and boldness to stand up for truth so that the other half of God's creation will be once and for all loosed into God's call. We will see what the Scriptures say they did, and will receive revelation not only from the Word in the circumstances of their stories, but by the definitions of their names, will open to us great and precious hidden truth, especially when we see them as types of God's church and kingdom.

Finally, when we consider women in ministry, I believe the only conclusion we can come to (Scripturally speaking) is that women are free to minister. The world is waiting to hear the Gospel. Maybe the reason we haven't reached them yet is because half of the body of Christ has been held in bondage! If we are going to experience His fullness, we need everyone that He has called to be fulfilling his or her ministry. *"Rise up, ye women that are at ease;* (not fulfilling your call) *hear my voice, ye careless daughters..."* (Isaiah 32:9-20). *"The Lord gives the word of power: The women who bear and publish the news are a great host."* (Psalms 68:11-Amplified Version)

To this end, that women might rise up without fear or condemnation, and that they may know they are standing on solid Biblical ground, this book has been written.

That the Gospel might be preached!

Samuel N. Greene, Ph.D.

WOMEN IN MINISTRY

Table Of Contents

Foreword...3
Lesson 1 - Overwhelming Evidence Women Should Minister.....................................7
Lesson 2 - Women In Ministry: The Controversy 13
Lesson 3 - I Timothy 2:7-15 21
Lesson 4 - I Corinthians 14:34-37 25
Lesson 5 - Submission, Headship, And Covering 27
Lesson 6 - Satan Hates Women 30
Lesson 7 - A Closer Look At The Fall 37
Lesson 8 - Ought Not This Woman 47
Lesson 9 - Let Her Alone 51
Lesson 10 - Worship & Women 61
Lesson 11 - Notable Women In Scripture 62
Lesson 12 - Daughters Of Zelophehad 76
Lesson 13 - The Story Of Anna 79
Lesson 14 - Elisabeth, Mother Of A Prophetic Company 87
Lesson 15 - Abishag...91
Lesson 16 - Abigail..97
Lesson 17 - Rahab 99
Lesson 18 - Leah 103
Lesson 19 - The Story Of Naomi - Ruth 1 107
Lesson 20 - Delilah - Stealer Of The Anointing 114
Lesson 21 - The Story Of Jael 144
Lesson 22 - The Great Woman..150
Lesson 23 - The Virtuous Woman 154
Lesson 24 - Jesus And Women..164
Lesson 25 - The Principle Of Barrenness In Women 169
Lesson 26 - Rise Up Ye Women 177
About The Author..179

Lesson 1
Overwhelming Evidence Women Should Minister

I.   A Personal and Scriptural Look

    A.   Personal Testimony

There have been several women who've been a great influence to me all throughout my life. They have shepherded me, counseled me, taught me, ministered deliverance to me, and have served as prophets to me. When I was newly saved, there were two teachers at my high school who became my pastors. One of the teachers taught me the Bible during my study hour every day. Without that initial foundation, I would have backslidden. Thinking back even further, it was the witness of my grandmother all through my early childhood years that eventually led to my salvation and baptism in the Holy Ghost. All through my young life before salvation, it was the testimony of women and their Christian lives that spoke to me about Jesus. I can't recall one single man ever telling me about Jesus and the importance of living the life of Jesus. Without the testimony of my grandmother, teachers, and other women from my early years, I don't think I would have been saved.

Upon moving to Florida several years later, I was pastored by Dan and Marti Duke. They BOTH birthed me into my present ministry and were the ones instrumental in my coming forth in God. Marti had much to do with my spiritual growth by encouraging, teaching, praying, and being an example of one pressing toward the mark. After that, I was introduced to a sister who I considered to be one of the greatest prayer warriors and Bible teachers ever; her name was June Lewis. Just watching that woman pray and worship, hearing her overcoming testimony, and receiving her powerful and anointed teaching, truly challenged, encouraged, and changed my life. Last but not least, I need only look to my helpmate and wife, Katie Greene, for a testimony of faithfulness, grace, and mercy, all the fruits of the Spirit, as well as an anointing to minister. After my salvation and subsequent entering into ministry, it was always the lives and testimonies of women that kept me in the grace of God, or showed me the way of God more perfectly. I'm sure all of us have had mothers, grandmothers, aunts, and friends who were the main Christian influence in our lives.

Time would not permit me to tell of all the other God-called, anointed women who have had great influence upon my life spiritually. One thing is absolutely certain, I've had enough to convince me of the undeniable fact that women can, do, and should be operating in ministry. How I thank God for these women and their ministries! All any of us would have to do is look at any local church, and we will find that women make up most of every church. They seem to always be there serving as intercessors, fasters, praisers, Sunday school teachers, or missionaries. I doubt that the church could have ever continued without the dedication of those precious women.

If one would be truly honest, they must admit, women make up the largest percentage of all churches. They also seem to be the most faithful. They certainly provide the background, service, and support of most churches. Truly, God has used them time and again for His glory. Praise God for these precious saints. I think it is way past time that they were recognized for all their achievements. It is also time to take off the bondage men have placed on them and set them free to minister. It is not right that over half of the body of Christ has been kept from moving in their divine calling and ministry.

    B.   Scriptural Examples

       1.   Psalm 68:11 – *"The Lord gives the word of power, the women who bear and publish the news are a great host."* (Amplified Old Testament)
       2.   I Corinthians 11:5 – *"But every woman that prayeth or prophesieth..."*
       3.   Isaiah 40:9 – *"O woman, that publishest good tidings to Zion, get thee up into the high mountain; O woman, that publishest good tidings to Jerusalem, lift up thy voice with strength; lift it up, be not afraid; say unto the cities of Judah, behold your God..."* (Literal Hebrew)

4. Acts 2:17-18 (Joel 2:28) – "*And it shall come to pass in the last days, saith God, I will pour out my Spirit upon all flesh; and your sons and your daughters shall prophesy...and on my servants and handmaidens I will pour out my Spirit and they shall prophesy.*"

5. Matthew 28:7-10 – The two Mary's – "*...go quickly and tell his disciples that He is risen from the dead...*" – Here we see that women were the first evangelists. I don't believe that this was done by accident, but it has set forth a principle that women should minister.

6. II Corinthians 5:20 – "*Now then we are ambassadors for Christ.*" – This means all of us are His ambassadors, whether we are male or female.

7. I Corinthians 14:26 – "*How is it then, brethren?* (The Greek word for brethren, when spoken in the plural as it is here, means a community based on identity or origin of life. We can therefore conclude that brethren here means the community of the redeemed, both male and female) *when ye come together, everyone of you hath a psalm, hath a doctrine* (a teaching), *hath a tongue* (moving in the gifts in a public service), *hath a revelation* (a disclosure, an uncovering of the heart and mind of God), *hath an interpretation.*"

8. I Corinthians 14:31 – "*For ye all* (male and female) *may prophesy one by one, that all may learn, and all may be comforted.*" – This is the great chapter in Scripture where Paul gives us the true order of ministry in the local church, and it certainly seems women are a large part of that ministry. God does not speak out of both sides of His mouth, nor is He double minded. It seems very clear that women are supposed to have a great part in the ministry and in the life of the local church. It is time to truly search the Scriptures about their place in ministry. Let us allow the Bible to speak for itself and let us stop letting creeds, denominational statements, and men's ideas shape what we believe.

9. All of the women prophetesses in the Old and New Testaments
10. Women deacons
11. Women elders

We will look at the above three in greater detail in another lesson. We will define all the women who have ministered in the Bible. Believe me, there is a great host, and everyone testifies to the fact that women are to be in ministry. We should always follow the weight of Scripture, not the biased opinions of men. We must search both the true languages in which the Bible was written because it seems that even the translators of the Bible had petty biases and prejudices against women. We must let God be true and every man a liar.

12. Titus 2:3-4 – "*The aged women likewise, that they be teachers of good things; that they may teach the young women...*"

13. Mark 16:7-18 – "*And these signs shall follow them that believe* (male or female)*... cast out devils... speak with new tongues... take up serpents... lay hands on the sick...*"

14. Revelation 1:6 – "*And hath made us* (male and female) *kings and priests unto God...*"

15. Galatians 3:26-28 – "*For ye are all the children of God by faith in Christ Jesus. For as many of you as have been baptized into Christ have put on Christ. There is neither Jew no Greek, there is neither bond nor free, there is neither male nor female; for ye are all one in Christ Jesus.*"

Jesus brought in a new era of ministry. He claims we should not consider gender anymore as it regards Christians, but that we should see all of us as the sons of God, members of one another, all free to minister and fulfill our calling in God. These Scriptures clearly declare that both men and women can minister to and through God. In the realm of the Spirit, we are not men and women, but rather we are all the sons of God. My hope is that as we see the innumerable times God uses women in Scripture and clearly calls for them to minister, the scales will fall from our eyes and we will see that half of the body of Christ has been in bondage. Is it any wonder then that the world has not come to salvation in Jesus?

16. Matthew 26:7-13 (John 12:1-8) – This is the story of Mary anointing Jesus in preparation for His sacrifice. This woman ministered to Jesus more than any other person in the New Testament. When no one else had the revelation of what the Lord was about to do, she did! She performed a tremendous work (verse 10) for the Lord, so much so that the Lord said whenever the gospel was

preached, she would be remembered for this one service. He certainly did not say this about any man or group of men!

17. John 4:28-30, 39 – *"The <u>woman</u> then left her waterpot, and went her way into the city, and saith <u>to the men</u>, Come, see a man, which told me all things that ever I did: <u>is not this the Christ?</u> Then they went out of the city, and came unto him…And many of the Samaritans of that city <u>believed on him for the saying of the woman</u>, which testified…"* – This passage certainly blows out the lie that women cannot or should not minister to men.

18. II John 1:4-5 – *"The elder unto the <u>elect lady</u> and <u>her children</u> (Spiritual children)…I rejoiced greatly that I found of thy children walking in truth… and now I beseech thee, lady, not as though I wrote a new commandment…"* John was writing to a woman elder. This also seems to disannul the theory that women can't be pastors or elders in the local church.

19. I Chronicles 25:1,5-7 (Exodus 15:20-21) – *"And God gave to Heman fourteen sons and <u>three daughters</u>. <u>All these</u> were under the hands of their father <u>for song</u> in the house of the Lord, with cymbals, psalteries, and harps, <u>for the service</u> of the House of God… so the number of them with their brethren that were instructed in the songs of the Lord…"*, *"And Miriam the prophetess, the sister of Aaron, took a timbrel in her hand and all the women went out after her with timbrels and with dances…"* – Here we see beyond a shadow of doubt <u>that women are called to be worship leaders</u>. This once again reminds us we must always let the Scriptures speak for themselves. We must rightly divide the Word of God (II Timothy 2:15). We must compare Scripture with Scripture. The Word is very clear that we are not to build a doctrine on just one isolated passage of Scripture (II Peter 1:20 – *"Knowing this first, that no prophecy of the scripture is of any private interpretation."*) and as it declares, *"In the mouth of two or three witnesses shall every word be established"* (II Corinthians 13:1). Far too much of what we believe has come down through church history based on Roman Catholic doctrine, and other erroneous determinations written by biased men or theologians or biased translators. We must search the Scriptures for ourselves so that our faith does not stand on the reasoning of men but by true revelation of Scripture.

20. Romans 16:1-2 – *"<u>I commend</u> unto you Phoebe <u>our sister</u>, which is a servant* (the Greek word here for servant is *diakonos* or <u>deacon</u>) *of the church…that ye received her in the Lord, as becometh saints, and that <u>ye assist her</u> in whatsoever business she hath need of you; for <u>she hath been a succourer</u>* (helper) <u>of many</u> *and of myself also."* – Here we discover women deaconesses.

21. Philippians 4:2-3 – *"I beseech Euodias and beseech Syntyche, that they be of the same mind in the Lord. And I entreat thee also true yokefellow…"* The Concordian Version translated the rest this way, *"to help them for they <u>strive earnestly in the work of the glad tidings</u> with me."* Another translation reads, *"to help them, remembering that they toiled by my side in spreading the Good News."* – These were two precious women who aided Paul greatly as he ministered. Not only did they aid him but were obviously known ministers themselves.

22. Romans 16:3 – Acts 18:26 – *"Greet Priscilla and Aquila my helpers* (Greek – co-laborer) *in Christ Jesus.",* *"And He* (Apollos) *began to speak boldly in the synagogue; who when Aquila and Priscilla had heard, they took him unto them and expounded unto him the way of God more perfectly."* <u>Priscilla was equal with Aquila in their teaching</u> and <u>pastoral ministry</u> (Romans 16:5). Here once again we see women <u>as pastors and teachers</u>. We see them ministering even to great men of God and instructing them in the way of God more perfectly.

23. Romans 16:7 – *"Salute Andronicus and Junia my kinsmen and fellow prisoners, who are of note among the apostles who also were in Christ before me."* This woman Junia was an apostle. There is some disagreement among scholars about whether Junia was a man or woman, but many early church fathers believed she was female. Thayers Lexicon of Greek and Hebrew words says the name is a variant of Julia. This was obviously a woman apostle. It seems it is just very hard for men to acknowledge this, perhaps because of insecurity, or just tradition, or simply the refusal to believe that a woman could be an <u>apostle</u>. Nevertheless, Paul himself calls her one.

24. Romans 16:12 – *"Salute Trypena and Tryphosa <u>who labor in the Lord</u>. Salute the beloved Persis, <u>which labored much in the Lord</u>…"* – All three of these women are extolled for their labor and service in the ministry. When you think about it, where would the church be today without the faithfulness and dedication of women to Jesus and His people.

25. Isaiah 32:9-14 and 15-20 – "*Rise up ye women that are at ease* (the Hebrew root word for *ease* means to loll, to secure in a bad sense) *hear my voice, ye careless daughters; give ear to my speech. Many days and years shall be troubled ye careless women; for the vintage* (crop or fruit) *the gathering shall not come. Tremble ye women that are at ease, be troubled ye careless ones; strip you and make bare, and gird sackcloth upon your loins.*"

This Scripture is the most important one of all. Women have been lulled to sleep with the false teaching that says they aren't allowed to minister. God wants women to hear His voice, and rise up to fulfill His call. If they don't, the gathering (the coming of the Lord, and our gathering together unto Him - II Thessalonians 2:1) will not come! Much of the fruit in the vineyard of the Lord will fail. We need to lay aside the traditions of men, and step out in faith to do what He has called us to do.

This is really just a sampling of Scriptures to whet our appetite concerning the truth of women in ministry. We are going to do a thorough and exhaustive study on this subject so as to leave no question concerning women and their role in the putting forth of the Gospel. We truly must, however, lay aside petty prejudices, human bias and reasonings, and approach God's Word with an unveiled face (II Corinthians 3:18). We also must be willing to let God's truth speak. Jesus said, "*If any man will do his will, he shall know of the doctrine, whether it be of God, or whether I speak of myself*" (John 7:17). We must set aside personal opinions and ideas that don't have Scriptural foundations. We have lived in the dark long enough! Especially as we see the end of all things drawing near. We must not let our own insecurities or fears dominate what we believe, nor should we let others dictate to us what we should believe, but let our trust and faith be in the Lord and His Word. As Paul declared in Romans 13:11, "*...now it is high time to awake out of sleep: for now is our salvation nearer than when we believed.*" Let each one of us "*study to shew thyself approved unto God, a workman that needeth not to be ashamed, rightly dividing the word of truth*" (II Timothy 2:15), and let us be like those noble Bereans who "*searched the scriptures daily, whether those things were so*" (Acts 17:11). May our faith not stand in the wisdom of men, but in God and His revealed Word. As God through His Word makes these truths real to us, then let us take the shackles off women and let them rise up and fulfill their calling and destiny in God and by doing so usher in that great and marvelous "day of the Lord"!

II.   Other Aspects To Consider About Women and Ministering

A.   I Corinthians 15:21-22 – "*[21]For since by man came death, by man came also the resurrection of the dead. [22]For as in Adam all die, even so in Christ shall all be made alive.*"

Both men and women were in Adam. Now both men and women are in Christ. We now shall consider the contrast between the two. We must remember we are no longer in Adam and all the bondage it brought. We are all now in Christ. With all the redemption and recovery it brought.

B.   In Adam – what does this mean?

1.   Romans 5:19 – "*For as by one man's disobedience many were made sinners, so by the obedience of one shall many be made righteous.*" – sin of disobedience brought the fall
2.   Romans 5:12 – "*Wherefore, as by one man sin entered into the world, and death by sin; and so death passed upon all men, for that all have sinned:*" – sin came into the world and death came on the human race

3.   The soul became the prominent factor in man's threefold existence; in the beginning, it was the spirit that was prominent.

    a.   Hebrews 4:12 – "*For the word of God is quick, and powerful, and sharper than any twoedged sword, piercing even to the dividing asunder of soul and spirit, and of the joints and marrow, and is a discerner of the thoughts and intents of the heart.*"
    b.   I Thessalonians 5:23 – "*And the very God of peace sanctify you wholly; and I pray God your whole spirit and soul and body be preserved blameless unto the coming of our Lord Jesus Christ.*"

      c.   I Corinthians 15:45 – "*And so it is written, The first man Adam was made a living soul; the last Adam was made a quickening spirit.*"

      d.   Genesis 2:7 – "*And the LORD God formed man of the dust of the ground, and breathed into his nostrils the breath of life; and man became a living soul.*"

4.   I Corinthians 15:46-47 – "[46]*Howbeit that was not first which is spiritual, but that which is natural; and afterward that which is spiritual.* [47]*The first man is of the earth, earthy: the second man is the Lord from heaven.*" – First the natural (earthy – flesh), then the spiritual (the Lord from heaven)

5.   In Adam, all are sinners.

6.   Galatians 3:28 – "*There is neither Jew nor Greek, there is neither bond nor free, there is neither male nor female: for ye are all one in Christ Jesus.*" - In Adam, there was the separation of people (Jews and Gentiles), separation of classes (slaves and free), and gender (male and female).

7.   In Adam, we are under the curse, doomed through the fall, where man is the head of the woman, the woman being in a subordinate role.

8.   In Adam, we are under the law, circumcision.

9.   Adam is the old man, unrighteous, having no peace.

C.   Praise God – we are now one, both male and female, in Christ

1.   II Corinthians 5:17 – "*Therefore if any man be in Christ, he is a <u>new creature</u>: old things are passed away; behold, all things are become new.*"

2.   Galatians 6:15 – "*For in Christ Jesus neither circumcision availeth anything, nor uncircumcision, but a <u>new creature</u>.*"

3.   Galatians 3:26-29 – "[26]*For ye are all the children of God by faith in Christ Jesus.* [27]*For as many of you as have been baptized into Christ have put on Christ.* [28]*There is neither Jew nor Greek, there is neither bond nor free, there is <u>neither male nor female</u>: for ye are <u>all one in Christ Jesus</u>.* [29]*And if ye be Christ's, then are ye Abraham's seed, and heirs according to the promise.*"

4.   Colossians 3:11 – "*Where there is neither Greek nor Jew, circumcision nor uncircumcision, Barbarian, Scythian, bond nor free: but <u>Christ is all</u>, and <u>in all</u>.*"

D.   In Christ – what does this means?

1.   Jesus' obedience delivered us from judgment.

2.   Jesus brought life into the world though his death.

3.   The human spirit now is God's dwelling place.

4.   The first was the natural, in Christ the spiritual is awakened.

5.   In Christ – heavenly, not earthly

6.   No more separation of peoples, races, classes (Galatians 3:28)

7.   In Christ, we are justified by grace.

8.   Christ is now the head of all.

9.   Men and women are equal in their place (women no more are subjugated)

10.   In Christ, there is no need for circumcision; we are now all born again.

11.   In Christ Jesus, we are no longer the old man but are the new man.

12.   In Christ, we are no longer unrighteous but have been made righteous (II Cor. 5:21)

13.   In Christ, we have peace with God (Romans 5:1)

14.   In Christ, we are not under the Law, but under grace

      a.   John 1:17 – "*For the law was given by Moses, but grace and truth came by Jesus Christ.*"

      b.   Romans 10:4 – "*For Christ is the end of the law for righteousness to every one that believeth.*"

      c.   Galatians 3:13 – "*Christ hath redeemed us from the curse of the law, being made a curse for us: for it is written, Cursed is every one that hangeth on a tree:*"

E.   Male and Female in the Body of Christ

1. Body of Christ typified by a man (sons of God)

   a. Ephesians 4:13 – *"Till we all come in the unity of the faith, and of the knowledge of the Son of God, unto a perfect man, unto the measure of the stature of the fulness of Christ:"*
   b. I John 3:1 – *"Behold, what manner of love the Father hath bestowed upon us, that we should be called the sons of God: therefore the world knoweth us not, because it knew him not."*

2. Body of Christ typified as a bride

   a. Ephesians 5:22-23 – *"Wives, submit yourselves unto your own husbands, as unto the Lord. For the husband is the head of the wife, even as Christ is the head of the church: and he is the saviour of the body."*
   b. Revelation 19:1-7 – *"...⁷Let us be glad and rejoice, and give honour to him: for the marriage of the Lamb is come, and his wife hath made herself ready."*
   c. II Corinthians 11:2-3 – *"For I am jealous over you with godly jealousy: for I have espoused you to one husband, that I may present you as a chaste virgin to Christ. But I fear, lest by any means, as the serpent beguiled Eve through his subtilty, so your minds should be corrupted from the simplicity that is in Christ."*

F. We are all now in Christ, both male and female

   1. All saved by grace (Ephesians 2:8)
   2. All new creatures (II Corinthians 5:11-21)
   3. All baptized in the Holy Ghost (Acts 2, 8, 10)
   4. All have been baptized into Christ (Galatians 3:27, I Corinthians 12:13)
   5. All kings and priests (Revelations 1:6, 5:9-10, I Peter 2:5-9)
   6. All have been given gifts (I Corinthians 12, Romans 12:1-8, Ephesians 4:18)
   7. All children of God through faith (Galatians 3:26)

Lesson 2
Women In Ministry: The Controversy

As with all Biblical principles, the subject of women in ministry has so many different schools or theories of thought. Can a woman preach or teach in the church? Or should she always be silent and learn at home from her husband? Can a woman have a leadership role in the church? Or is she simply to stay home and raise her children? Can a woman pastor? Can a woman prophesy? Can a woman teach? Can a woman be an evangelist? Can a woman be an apostle? Can she be an elder or deacon? Can she be a worship leader? Or should she always defer to a man? And what about the home life of Christian women, are they to always submit to their husbands in everything, or just some things? What does the term "headship" mean? Is she to be under authority always, except when it comes to other women? Should she just teach the younger women? Is it true that women must watch out so as not to be possessed by a "Jezebel" spirit? Are most women controlling and devious, always looking to usurp man's authority? Was Paul a women hater as some proclaim? And what about our Lord Jesus? What was His interaction and attitude towards women? Are all things of God to be male-dominated? What is a woman to do if she feels a distinct call of God upon her life? What if she has obvious giftings of the Holy Ghost? Should she just ignore them? And what if the greatest passion of her life is to tell people about Jesus? Is she to restrain this desire? Or is it true she can just be a Sunday school teacher, or be a missionary, without an ascension gift ministry? Can she move in the gifts of the Holy Spirit? And is she just a subordinate part of the human species? What if she has served the Lord for years, studied His Word diligently, prayed fervently, worshipped passionately, and has gained great wisdom and counsel - Should she just keep it to herself, or share these glorious truths with only women? Did God truly create her just to stand beside her husband, and be quiet in the background? Could it possibly be true that God created her as an inferior one? And what are we to say when most of our churches are made up of way more women than men? And why does it seem they are always the better prayer warriors, servants, doing anything and everything that is needed at the local church? Why does it seem that in general they are more faithful, certainly more spiritual, and far more sensitive to the things of God than men? Most of all, why does it seem that most people come into the Kingdom of God due to the testimony of women and their godly lives? All these and many more questions must be answered. We will hope to do so in this book.

The question remains, how shall we do it? The answer to this is simple. We will let the Bible speak for itself. We will study the original languages in which the Bible was written and compare Scripture with Scripture. We will draw on history to find the true context of what a passage might mean. But most importantly we want to hear what God Himself says on this subject. We will have to lay aside petty prejudices and bias, and come with a true heart as we study. We must be willing to bow to the truth, no matter where it leads. And once we have searched the Scriptures, prayed earnestly about this matter, considered all theories and ideas on this subject, and have come to an obvious conclusion, we should not let fear of man keep us from walking in the truth.

We must not let our faith or beliefs stand in the wisdom of men. We must know we live in a male oriented society, where men seem to rule. We must also consider that the Jewish religion did not have a good outlook on women, as is the case with most other major religions. We must study to see if there was any gender bias in the translating of Scripture, and also other ancient texts that have formed the belief about women from the beginning.

I believe that if we, in a true heart, an unveiled face, free of predetermined ideas, free of denominational traditions, even free of familial attitudes, and our own personal biases, come to God seeking Him and His Word for the answers, we will find them. For He hath said, "*And ye shall seek me, and find me, when ye shall search for me with all your heart*" (Jeremiah 29:13), "*Ask, and it shall be given you; seek, and ye shall find; knock, and it shall be opened unto you*" (Matthew 7:7). Jesus said, "*If any man will do his will, he shall know of the doctrine, whether it be of God, or whether I speak of myself*" (John 7:17), as well as in Proverbs 25:2 it says, "*It is the glory of God to conceal a thing: but the honour of kings is to search out a matter.*" Our goal is to search out and seek with all our hearts, in order to find, be opened to us, and know of the doctrine, concerning the truth about women.

I.   Differing Schools of Thought Concerning Women In Ministry

A. Listed by theory

1. A women's place is in the home as a wife, mother and house keeper. Also, she should have no role at all in church life. She is to be silent and learn at home from her husband.
2. Women may be allowed to pray, sing in the choir, teach Sunday school, and have a help ministry, but she is not permitted to serve in any leadership capacity in churches. She is always to be submitted and subordinate to men.
3. Women can participate in music ministry, prayer, Sunday school teaching, be involved in church social services, teach other women, and go to the mission field, but they are not allowed to function in any leadership roles or move in the gifts of the Spirit.
4. Women are allowed to function in any role God has called or gifted them in, with the exception that they cannot pastor, be an elder, or an apostle.
5. Women and men are equal before God. In the Spirit realm there is neither male nor female (Galatians 3:28). They can move in any five-fold office or spiritual gifting (I Corinthians 12), or in any other special ministry found in Romans 12. These believe all that are called by God are free to function in the gifting God has given them, in whatever measure and grace they are called to walk in, all under the headship of Christ Jesus our Lord. Obviously, this is the one that I personally embrace as the truth of God's Word.

II. What Created This Controversy, Other Than The Scriptures I Will Mention Later?

A. The Oral Law of the Jews called the Talmud

In the Jewish religion of which Christianity came out of, women were subjugated and subordinate to men, believing that women were the original sinners and that the fall is based solely on Eve's sin. After the Babylonian captivity, the Jews feared that their people would forget their Law given by God to Moses. So certain Rabbis and scholars decided to form a collection of writings about the Pentateuch. This became known as the Talmud. After a while, it was elevated as just as important as the Law itself, however only being men's interpretation of the Law. A negative attitude towards women come forth in these writings, but this was not found in the Scriptures. The Talmud was just these men's opinions about the Scriptures.

During the second century after Christ, this oral law was compiled into a book called the Talmud. It consisted of fourteen large volumes in Hebrew and Aramaic.

During Jesus' time on the earth, the religious leaders that adhered to these teachings constantly complained to Jesus that He did not conform to the traditions of the elders. Even the early church was besieged by these writings since most Christians had been former Jews. These religious leaders became known as the Judaizers. These were the ones who suborned Peter in his ministry to the Gentiles and greatly opposed the Apostle Paul. They stirred up trouble throughout the early church, trying to make Christians abide by not only the Law of Moses, but the oral law as well. They brought great confusion to the church, and Paul in his epistles to the Romans, Galatians, and Corinthians taught and fought against them. They fought with Paul, even signing a covenant to destroy him and his teachings. Many times Paul referred to the "Law" in the Bible, but it was not the Law of Moses, but this oral law of the Jews, the Talmud.

B. What some of these writings had to say about sin and women

1. Eve was the one who brought death and sin into the world.
2. Therefore women are forever guilty before God and the human race.

C. Some of what is found in this Law

1. All wickedness is but little to the wickedness of a woman, let the portion of a sinner fall on her.
2. Of the woman came the beginning of sin, and through her we all die.

3. A shameless woman shall be counted as a dog.
4. The whoredom of a woman may be known in her haughty looks and eyelids.
5. From a garment cometh a moth and from a woman cometh wickedness.
6. Women may bequeath on death to her children, their brothers and husbands, but cannot inherit from them.
7. One must not accept bailments from women, slaves, or children.
8. A woman should not read in the Torah (the Law) for the honor of the synagogues.
9. Rather have the roll of the Law burned than have it taught to women.
10. The testimony of 100 women is not equal to that of one man.
11. The evidence of a woman cannot be taken under oath.
12. A man's corpse may be laid in the street over which to hold an oration, but not a woman's. The greatest man in the city may accompany a man's corpse, but he is not to be troubled over a women's corpse.
13. It is a shame for a woman to let her voice be heard among men.
14. A local congregation consisted of 10 men. A woman could not be counted along with nine men.
15. In the Oral Law, a woman was dishonored in life and death.
16. Contempt was always heaped upon her.
17. She was counted as a non-person.
18. A 100 women are not better than two men.
19. When a boy comes into the world, peace comes into the world, when a girl comes nothing comes.
20. A woman is a pitcher of filth, with its mouth full of blood, yet all run after her.
21. Let the words of the Law be burned rather than they should be delivered to a woman.
22. Women were prohibited from teaching the Law to their children.
23. The wise men have commanded that no man should teach his daughter the Law for this reason, that the majority of them have not got a mind fitted for study, but pervert the words of the Law on account of the poverty of their minds.
24. Men come to learn, and women come just to hear.
25. Whoever teaches his daughter the Law is like one who teaches her lasciviousness.

26. The prayer of a devout Jewish male every morning was:

    Blessed be He that did not make me a Gentile
    Blessed be He who did not make me a woman
    Blessed be He who did not make me a slave

27. Women were allowed no part in the synagogue services.
28. Women were separated from men so they couldn't see.
29. They were not allowed to participate in worship.
30. Rabbis would not talk to a woman in public.
31. He could not even speak to His wife, daughter, or sister.
32. Some would even close their eyes when they saw a woman.

II. The Controversy

There has been, and there continues to be, a great controversy over whether women should be allowed to speak, teach, pastor, etc. We want to discover what kind of submission God really requires of a woman. We also want to look at what the Scriptures declare about the way a woman should dress. It is a very true statement to say women have been treated unfairly throughout history. As with all error, there is a root. We want to discover that root, then examine it in the light of Scripture, and by the grace of God bring forth truth to the matter.

A. Main Scriptures

1. I Corinthians 14:34-35 – "*Let your women keep silence in the churches: for it is not permitted unto them to speak; but they are commanded to be under obedience, as also saith the law. And if they will learn any thing, let them ask their husbands at home: for it is a shame for women to speak in the church.*"

2. I Timothy 2:11-12 – "*Let the woman learn in silence with all subjection. But I suffer not a woman to teach, nor to usurp authority over the man, but to be in silence.*"

3. I Peter 3:1-6 – "¹*Likewise, ye wives, be in subjection to your own husbands; that, if any obey not the word, they also may without the word be won by the conversation of the wives; ²While they behold your chaste conversation coupled with fear. ³Whose adorning let it not be that outward adorning of plaiting the hair, and of wearing of gold, or of putting on of apparel; ⁴But let it be the hidden man of the heart, in that which is not corruptible, even the ornament of a meek and quiet spirit, which is in the sight of God of great price. ⁵For after this manner in the old time the holy women also, who trusted in God, adorned themselves, being in subjection unto their own husbands: ⁶Even as Sara obeyed Abraham, calling him lord: whose daughters ye are, as long as ye do well, and are not afraid with any amazement.*"

4. I Corinthians 11:3-16 – "³*But I would have you know, that the head of every man is Christ; and the head of the woman is the man; and the head of Christ is God. ⁴Every man praying or prophesying, having his head covered, dishonoureth his head. ⁵But every woman that prayeth or prophesieth with her head uncovered dishonoureth her head: for that is even all one as if she were shaven. ⁶For if the woman be not covered, let her also be shorn: but if it be a shame for a woman to be shorn or shaven, let her be covered. ⁷For a man indeed ought not to cover his head, forasmuch as he is the image and glory of God: but the woman is the glory of the man. ⁸For the man is not of the woman; but the woman of the man. ⁹Neither was the man created for the woman; but the woman for the man. ¹⁰For this cause ought the woman to have power on her head because of the angels. ¹¹Nevertheless neither is the man without the woman, neither the woman without the man, in the Lord. ¹²For as the woman is of the man, even so is the man also by the woman; but all things of God. ¹³Judge in yourselves: is it comely that a woman pray unto God uncovered? ¹⁴Doth not even nature itself teach you, that, if a man have long hair, it is a shame unto him? ¹⁵But if a woman have long hair, it is a glory to her: for her hair is given her for a covering. ¹⁶But if any man seem to be contentious, we have no such custom, neither the churches of God.*"

5. Ephesians 5:22-24 – "²²*Wives, submit yourselves unto your own husbands, as unto the Lord. ²³For the husband is the head of the wife, even as Christ is the head of the church: and he is the saviour of the body. ²⁴Therefore as the church is subject unto Christ, so let the wives be to their own husbands in every thing.*"

   a. Colossians 3:18 – "*Wives, submit yourselves unto your own husbands, as it is fit in the Lord.*"

6. Ecclesiastes 7:26 – "*And I find more bitter than death the woman, whose heart is snares and nets, and her hands as bands: whoso pleaseth God shall escape from her; but the sinner shall be taken by her.*"

   a. Proverbs 7:24-27 – "²⁴*Hearken unto me now therefore, O ye children, and attend to the words of my mouth. ²⁵Let not thine heart decline to her ways, go not astray in her paths. ²⁶For she hath cast down many wounded: yea, many strong men have been slain by her. ²⁷Her house is the way to hell, going down to the chambers of death.*"

7. Genesis 3:16 – "*Unto the woman he said, I will greatly multiply thy sorrow and thy conception; in sorrow thou shalt bring forth children; and thy desire shall be to thy husband, and he shall rule over thee.*"

III. Some Seemingly Contradictory Scriptures – Main Scriptures and Assertions

   A. Many women Prophetesses

1. Miriam – Exodus 15:20-21
2. Huldah – II Kings 22:13-20
3. Anna – Luke 2:36-38
4. Phillip's daughters – Acts 21:8-9

B. Women as Preachers and Evangelists

1. Woman at Samaritan well – John 4:4-39
2. Two Mary's first to speak of the resurrection – Matthew 28:1-10
3. Ambassadors – II Corinthians 5:19-20 – all of us are ambassadors.
4. Psalms 68:11 – *"The Lord gives the word [of power]; the women who bear and publish [the news] are a great host."* (Amplified Version)

C. Women as Deacons

1. Phebe – Romans 16:1-2
2. Tryphena, Tryphosa, Persis – Romans 16:12
3. Exodus 38:8 – *"And he made the laver of brass, and the foot of it of brass, of the lookingglasses of the women assembling, which assembled at the door of the tabernacle of the congregation."*

D. Women as Elders (Pastors)

1. II John 1 – *"The elder unto the elect lady and her children, whom I love in the truth; and not I only, but also all they that have known the truth;"*
2. Deborah was a judge (to govern); she was the leader – Judges 4:4-5

E. Women as Teachers

1. Priscilla – Acts 18:26
2. Titus 2:3-5
3. Psalms 68:11 – *"The Lord giveth the word: the women that publish the tidings are a great host."* (ASV)

F. Women as Priests

1. Revelation 1:5-6 – *"And from Jesus Christ, who is the faithful witness, and the first begotten of the dead, and the prince of the kings of the earth. Unto him that loved us, and washed us from our sins in his own blood, And hath <u>made us</u> kings and priests unto God and his Father; to him be glory and dominion for ever and ever. Amen."*

G. Women as Worship Leaders

1. Heman's three daughters – I Chronicles 25:1, 5-7
2. Miriam – Exodus 15:20
3. Deborah – Judges 5:1-3, 7
4. Isaiah 12:6 – *"Cry aloud and shout joyfully, you women and inhabitants of Zion, for great in your midst is the Holy One of Israel."* (Amplified Version)

H. Women Anointed by the Spirit of God

1. Joel 2:28 – *"And it shall come to pass afterward, that I will pour out my spirit upon all flesh; and your sons and <u>your daughters shall prophesy</u>, your old men shall dream dreams, your young men shall see visions:"*

2. I Corinthians 14:26 – *"How is it then, brethren? when ye come together, <u>everyone of you</u> hath a psalm, hath a doctrine, hath a tongue, hath a revelation, hath an interpretation. Let all things be done unto edifying."*
3. I Corinthians 14:31 – *"For <u>ye may all prophesy</u> one by one, that all may learn, and all may be comforted."*
4. I Corinthians 11:5 – *"But every woman that prayeth or prophesieth with her head uncovered dishonoureth her head: for that is even all one as if she were shaven."*

I. Women As Apostles

   1. Miriam – Micah 6:4
   2. Junia – Romans 16:7

J. Neither Male nor Female Anymore

   1. Galatians 3:28 – *"There is neither Jew nor Greek, there is neither bond nor free, <u>there is neither male nor female</u>: for ye are all one in Christ Jesus."*

K. Women as judges and military leaders – Judges 4:4, 6-9, 5:7-15
L. Women could take the Nazarite vow – Numbers 6:1-27

M. Women mentioned in the hall of fame of faith

   1. Sarah – Hebrews 11:11, Genesis 21:2
   2. Rahab – Hebrews 11:31
   3. Other Women – Hebrews 11:33-40

N. Women participate in the destruction of Satan

   1. Judges 4:17-24, 5:24-27
   2. Genesis 3:13-15
   3. Revelation 12:1-8

O. Women used in order to save God's people

   1. Deborah – Judges 4-5
   2. Wise women delivered the city from the attack of Joab – II Samuel 20:15-22
   3. Esther – Esther 4:11

P. Both Israel and the Church spoken of as a woman

   1. Jeremiah 3:1-11
   2. Ephesians 5:23-32
   3. Revelation 19

Q. Women needed to bring in the harvest of the last days

   1. Isaiah 32:9-15

R. Wisdom is personified as a woman

   1. Proverbs 1:20-21, 2:13-18
   2. Proverbs 4:5-9, 7:4
   3. Proverbs 8:1-12, 9:1-3

IV. Reasons for the Controversy

    A.   Misunderstandings concerning certain Scriptures – Any Scripture can be misinterpreted, but there is a proper way to rightly divide the Word of God.

        1.   We must consider the historical context of the book, people to whom it was written, etc.

        2.   Never take one Scripture and build a doctrine on it. Principles and doctrines are formed when we find many witnesses to what we are searching out. The principles and doctrines of God are woven throughout the entire Bible.

            a.   II Peter 1:20 – *"Knowing this first, that no prophecy of the scripture is of any private interpretation."*

            b.   Matthew 18:16 – *"...that in the mouth of two or three witnesses every word may be established."*

        3.   We must compare Scripture with Scripture and rightly divide it. Every Scripture and every principle therein has a mate.

            a.   I Corinthians 2:13 – *"Which things also we speak, not in the words which man's wisdom teacheth, but which the Holy Ghost teacheth; <u>comparing spiritual things with spiritual</u>."*

            b.   II Timothy 2:15 – *"Study to shew thyself approved unto God, a workman that needeth not to be ashamed, rightly dividing the word of truth."*

            c.   Isaiah 34:16 – *"Seek ye out of the book of the LORD, and read: no one of these shall fail, none shall want her mate: for my mouth it hath commanded, and his spirit it hath gathered them."*

        4.   We should check the original Greek or Hebrew words for proper translation as well as several other translations (not just the King James Version).

        5.   We must approach all passages with a right heart, an unbiased attitude, and a meek spirit.

            a.   II Corinthians 3:18 – *"But we all, with <u>open</u>* (Greek – unveiled) *face beholding as in a glass the glory of the Lord, are changed into the same image from glory to glory, even as by the Spirit of the Lord."*

            b.   Psalms 25:9 – *"The meek will he guide in judgment: and the meek will he teach his way."*

        6.   There must be in us a willingness to search deeper than just a casual reading. We must seek the Lord for answers.

            a.   (Psalms 34:10 – *"...they that seek the LORD shall not want any good thing."*

            b.   Acts 17:11 – *"These were more noble than those in Thessalonica, in that they received the word with all readiness of mind, and searched the scriptures daily, whether those things were so."*

            c.   Proverbs 25:2 – *"It is the glory of God to conceal a thing: but the honour of kings is to search out a matter."*

        7.   It may only come by supernatural revelation, so we must allow the Holy Spirit to speak.

            a.   Matthew 16:17 – *"And Jesus answered and said unto him, Blessed art thou, Simon Barjona: for flesh and blood hath not revealed it unto thee, but my Father which is in heaven."*

            b.   I Corinthians 2:9-10 – *"But as it is written, Eye hath not seen, nor ear heard, neither have entered into the heart of man, the things which God hath prepared for them that love him. But God hath revealed them unto us by his Spirit: for the Spirit searcheth all things, yea, the deep things of God."*

            c.   Job 32:8 – *"But there is a spirit in man: and the inspiration of the Almighty giveth them understanding."*

8. We should hear the counsel of other men and women. We need the wisdom of other learned men and women because we don't have the whole counsel of God in our being nor does our church or the group we are part of.

   a. Proverbs 1:5-6 – *"A wise man will hear, and will increase learning; and a man of understanding shall attain unto wise counsels: To understand a proverb, and the interpretation; the words of the wise, and their dark sayings."*
   b. Ecclesiastes 12:11 – *"The words of the wise are as goads, and as nails fastened by the masters of assemblies, which are given from one shepherd."*

B. Traditions of men

There are so many things we do that even we ourselves have no idea why we are doing them. We do them because those before us did them. Let's see first if God wants us to believe and do certain things rather than the blind leading the blind with both falling into a ditch! This includes our parents, grandparents, our church, or denomination, or the initial ones who bring us into the things of God. It is amazing how many times those who lead us to Jesus will later hinder us from going on with God because of their own inability to see or hear the deeper things of God. If a doctrine or belief does not line up with the Word of God, we should not receive or walk in it. Good, sincere pastors and Christian friends have been wrong. We must make sure we are not in bondage to men.

   1. Colossians 2:8 – *"Beware lest any man spoil you through philosophy and vain deceit, after the tradition of men, after the rudiments of the world, and not after Christ."*
   2. Matthew 15:2-3 – *"Why do thy disciples transgress the tradition of the elders? for they wash not their hands when they eat bread. But he answered and said unto them, Why do ye also transgress the commandment of God by your tradition?"*
   3. Matthew 15:6 – *"...Thus have ye made the commandment of God of none effect by your tradition."*

C. Sexual bias

Some men simply feel superior to women. Not only is this unscriptural, but it is vain and foolish. A true understanding of the Word of God shows us that in Jesus there is neither male nor female. We are all sons of God (Galatians 3:28). We know by historical fact and record that the Hebrew Rabbis were very biased concerning women. Even the King James translators were biased in their translations of certain passages. Even now in fundamental circles, we find prejudices against women. In many Fundamental, Charismatic, and Pentecostal churches, women have been controlled, mistreated, and not allowed to come forth into ministry. It is time for this to stop! I'm not talking about women's lib or the feminist movement or any such thing, only that the other half of the body of Christ must be set free to fulfill their calling in God.

D. Insecurity concerning women in some men

Some men have a problem with strong women. All of us should have a problem with someone who is domineering or who operates with a controlling, usurping spirit. But I am speaking of women who know and love God with all their hearts, and who have been given God's authority, His blessing, and His anointing. Why would anyone fear a woman like this? Rather, we should be convicted to rise up off the lees we've settled on and press on into the things of God ourselves! We must be willing to bow down our ears to hear God and His wisdom from whatever vessel God is flowing through. Oh, that we might grow up into God in all things.

E. Male dominated society in religion

Because of misunderstanding about the fall in the garden, women have had to take a subservient role all throughout history.

Lesson 3
I Timothy 2:7-15

I. I Timothy 2:7-15 –*"7Whereunto I am ordained a preacher, and an apostle, (I speak the truth in Christ, and lie not;) a teacher of the Gentiles in faith and verity.8 I will therefore that men pray every where, lifting up holy hands, without wrath and doubting.9 In like manner also, that women adorn themselves in modest apparel, with shamefacedness and sobriety; not with broided hair, or gold, or pearls, or costly array;10 But (which becometh women professing godliness) with good works.11 Let the woman learn in silence with all subjection.12 But I suffer not a woman to teach, nor to usurp authority over the man, but to be in silence.13 For Adam was first formed, then Eve.14 And Adam was not deceived, but the woman being deceived was in the transgression.15 Notwithstanding she shall be saved in childbearing, if they continue in faith and charity and holiness with sobriety."*

We must first be very careful that we make no hard and fast rules that would lead to legalism. There are many explanations for this difficult passage of Scripture. As we consider once again the context, topical setting, Greek words and comparing it with other Scripture, we will come to a proper, Biblical conclusion and understanding. As teachers we must be honest and objective. There is no place for personal bias in interpreting the Word of God.

    A. Things We Must Consider

        1. Paul was writing to Timothy, the young pastor of the church at Ephesus. Timothy was having a struggle with people who were teaching "strange doctrines" (I Timothy 1:3-8). There were obviously some women teaching other doctrines. They were ministering confusion, wanting to be in authority as teachers, but they weren't prepared or ready, and didn't seem to be willing to wait until God promoted them. They usurped authority unlawfully.

        2. Paul is writing addressing these women in the church at Ephesus. Not all the women would be defined in this way, nor would they need to be addressed this way.

        3. Ephesus was a Gentile metropolis. Most of the church was made up of Gentiles, many of them whom had been delivered from paganism. Some were involved in Gnosticism, claiming to have a "secret knowledge" and using this knowledge to lord over people. Paul told Timothy to avoid these people –(I Timothy 6:20-21). Many of the women had been prostitutes in their former religion and were unskilled in godly speech and dress. They were still learning the ways of God.

        4. Timothy was a young man, and perhaps some tried to intimidate him (I Timothy 4:12). He was instructed not to back off from moving in the gift God had bestowed on him because of outspoken, overzealous teachers of false doctrine, or those with domineering spirits. Paul was writing to assist and encourage this brother.

II. Verse By Verse Explanation

    A. I Timothy 2:7-15

        1. Verse 7 – Paul explains his position of authority. He is a preacher (evangelist), apostle and teacher. The Amplified Version says "...*in the realm of faith and truth*". He was their apostle, therefore he was qualified to bring order and to teach guidelines.

        2. Verse 8 – He begins to teach. He says men should be in the habit of praying and worshipping (lifting hands) without anger or doubt.

        3. Verse 9 – Other Translations:

            a. Rotherham: *"in the same way"*
            b. Berkely: *"In similar spirit"*
            c. Knox: *"So, too, with the women"*

This is a direct reference to women praying and worshipping (not being silent) everywhere (including church services). He confirms women are to do this, and then begins to speak to certain attitudes carried by some women in that church.

4. Verse 9

He addresses another troubling situation. It seems some of the women were outlandish in their dress, appearance, and attitude. He is not saying women cannot wear attractive clothes, make up etc; he is saying they should use wisdom, be modest, and godly. A woman's beauty is determined by what kind of person she is on the inside. There is nothing wrong with dressing nice and looking good. If makeup helps you feel better about your appearance, there is no command against it. Let your moderation be known to all.

    a. Philippians 4:5 –*"Let your moderation be known unto all men. The Lord is at hand."*
    b. I Peter 3:1-6 –*"1Likewise, ye wives, be in subjection to your own husbands; that, if any obey not the word, they also may without the word be won by the conversation of the wives;2 While they behold your chaste conversation coupled with fear.3 Whose adorning let it not be that outward adorning of plaiting the hair, and of wearing of gold, or of putting on of apparel;4 But let it be the hidden man of the heart, in that which is not corruptible, even the ornament of a meek and quiet spirit, which is in the sight of God of great price.5 For after this manner in the old time the holy women also, who trusted in God, adorned themselves, being in subjection unto their own husbands:6 Even as Sara obeyed Abraham, calling him lord: whose daughters ye are, as long as ye do well, and are not afraid with any amazement."*
    c. Psalms 45:13 –*"The king's daughter is all glorious within: her clothing is of wrought gold."*
    d. Proverbs 31:30 –*"Favour is deceitful, and beauty is vain: but a woman that feareth the LORD, she shall be praised."*

    e. Greek Definitions

        1) Modest apparel – orderly, well arranged, decent
        2) Shamefacedness – reverence
        3) Sobriety – soundness of mind and judgment

From the above definitions we see that these women were obviously not modest or decent or shy about the way they looked. They weren't using wisdom or soundness of mind. They were also trying to impress the men and other women with their gold and costly array (I Timothy 6:5). Gain is not godliness, beauty is not godliness, but a woman who walks with God and has fruit to prove it, she is the one who professes godliness.

5. Verse 10 – A correct understanding of this verse brings confirmation to the fact that women are permitted to minister publicly.

    a. Professing – The Greek word *Epaggello* means to announce, to proclaim.
    b. Godliness – The Greek word *Theosebeia* means to be devout, piety. In other words if a woman is going to preach, teach, prophesy, etc., she must consider how she handles herself. As we carry this through into the next verse, we gain understanding.

6. Verse 11

    a. Silence – The Greek word for "silence" is *Hesuchia*, meaning stillness, quietness, peaceable. By implication, it means not to disturb. It does not mean absolute silence. Just as in I Corinthians 14:34, it doesn't mean women cannot speak or minister. It means they needed to learn in quietness, not disturbing by babbling or asking questions out of order. They needed to be still while someone else was speaking.

b. Subjection – The Greek word *Hupotasso* means arrange under. This is speaking of the marriage relationship. It means to put yourself in a place of submission or subjection, or one who yields. Obviously there were certain women who were having a problem learning and submitting. Other translations of verse 11:

"*A woman should learn quietly and humbly.*" (Phillips)
"*Let a woman learn in quietness, be learning in all submission.*" (Rotherham)

So, when are women allowed to speak, preach etc.? While someone else is ministering, they are to be quiet and submissive.

7. Verse 12 – Other translations:

"*I do not permit a married woman to practice teaching or domineering over a husband*" (Williams)
"*...to teach, neither to domineer over a man*" (Berkley)
"*...to teach, and issue commands to her husband*" (Knox)

a. We see from the above translations that this is speaking about a husband and wife (i.e verses 13-14 which speak of Adam and Eve). The Greek word for man here is *aner* meaning fellow or husband. Paul used the word *aner* 59 times. The King James Version translates it **husband** 34 times, and 25 other places it occurs where the text is clearly speaking of a **husband**. A wife is to be subject to her **godly husband**. She is not to usurp his authority.

b. Usurp Authority – The Greek word for "usurp" is *authenteo*, meaning to act of oneself, to dominate or to seize and hold in possession by force, without right. Paul is not forbidding women to teach; he is saying a married woman should not try to seize her husband's authority. If she will be at peace God will promote her and make room for her gifts. Proverbs 18:16 –"*A man's gift maketh room for him, and bringeth him before great men.*" She can teach, preach, prophesy, etc., under authority.

c. A woman is to have a covering or head. That covering is to be her husband, father or pastor. We will look at the aspect of leadership later.

1) I Corinthians 11:3 –"*But I would have you know, that the head of every man is Christ; and the head of the woman is the man; and the head of Christ is God.*"
2) Ephesians 5:22-23 –"*Wives, submit yourselves unto your own husbands, as unto the Lord. For the husband is the head of the wife, even as Christ is the head of the church: and he is the saviour of the body.*"
3) Colossians 3:18 –"*Wives, submit yourselves unto your own husbands, as it is fit in the Lord.*"

d. Objections to this are why some women cannot minister at all. Obviously, it refers to something else.

1) Paul is correcting a problem that existed there. He is dealing with women who were unruly, disobedient, and ignorant of the Scriptures and the ways of God.
2) Paul would not contradict himself when in other places he encourages women to pray, prophesy, teach, etc.

a) I Corinthians 14:25-31 –"*And thus are the secrets of his heart made manifest; and so falling down on his face he will worship God, and report that God is in you of a truth. 26How is it then, brethren? when ye come together, everyone of you hath a psalm, hath a doctrine, hath a tongue, hath a revelation, hath an interpretation. Let all things be done unto edifying. 27If any man speak in an unknown tongue, let it be by two, or at the most by three, and that by course; and let one interpret. 28But if there be no interpreter, let him keep silence in the church; and let him speak to himself, and to God.*"

²⁹Let the prophets speak two or three, and let the other judge. ³⁰If any thing be revealed to another that sitteth by, let the first hold his peace. ³¹For ye may all prophesy one by one, that all may learn, and all may be comforted."

    b) I Corinthians 11:5 –"But every woman that prayeth or prophesieth with her head uncovered dishonoureth her head: for that is even all one as if she were shaven."

    c) Titus 2:3-4 –"The aged women likewise, that they be in behaviour as becometh holiness, not false accusers, not given to much wine, teachers of good things; That they may teach the young women to be sober, to love their husbands, to love their children,"

    d) Romans 16:1-3 –"I commend unto you Phebe our sister, which is a servant of the church which is at Cenchrea: ²That ye receive her in the Lord, as becometh saints, and that ye assist her in whatsoever business she hath need of you: for she hath been a succourer of many, and of myself also. ³Greet Priscilla and Aquila my helpers in Christ Jesus."

8. The Holy Ghost and the Word of God do not contradict

    a. Jesus - Matthew 28:9-10 – "And as they went to tell his disciples, behold, Jesus met them, saying, All hail. And they came and held him by the feet, and worshipped him. Then said Jesus unto them, Be not afraid: go tell my brethren that they go into Galilee, and there shall they see me."

    b. Luke 2:36-38 –"And there was one Anna, a prophetess, the daughter of Phanuel, of the tribe of Aser: she was of a great age, and had lived with an husband seven years from her virginity;³⁷ And she was a widow of about fourscore and four years, which departed not from the temple, but served God with fastings and prayers night and day.³⁸ And she coming in that instant gave thanks likewise unto the Lord, and spake of him to all them that looked for redemption in Jerusalem."

    c. Acts 18:24-26 –"And a certain Jew named Apollos, born at Alexandria, an eloquent man, and mighty in the scriptures, came to Ephesus.²⁵ This man was instructed in the way of the Lord; and being fervent in the spirit, he spake and taught diligently the things of the Lord, knowing only the baptism of John.²⁶ And he began to speak boldly in the synagogue: whom when Aquila and Priscilla had heard, they took him unto them, and expounded unto him the way of God more perfectly."

    d. Acts 21:9 –"And the same man had four daughters, virgins, which did prophesy."

    e. Acts 2:16-18 –"But this is that which was spoken by the prophet Joel;¹⁷ And it shall come to pass in the last days, saith God, I will pour out of my Spirit upon all flesh: and your sons and your daughters shall prophesy, and your young men shall see visions, and your old men shall dream dreams:¹⁸ And on my servants and on my handmaidens I will pour out in those days of my Spirit; and they shall prophesy:"

    f. Judges 4:5 –"And she dwelt under the palm tree of Deborah between Ramah and Bethel in mount Ephraim: and the children of Israel came up to her for judgment."

    g. II Kings 22:12-20

    h. Exodus 38:8 –"And he made the laver of brass, and the foot of it of brass, of the lookingglasses of the women assembling, which assembled at the door of the tabernacle of the congregation."

    i. Exodus 15:20 –"And Miriam the prophetess, the sister of Aaron, took a timbrel in her hand; and all the women went out after her with timbrels and with dances."

    j. Psalms 68:25 –"The singers went before, the players on instruments followed after; among them were the damsels playing with timbrels.

    k. Numbers 6:1-27

Lesson 4
I Corinthians 14:34-37

I Corinthians 14:34-37 – *"³⁴Let your women keep silence in the churches: for it is not permitted unto them to speak; but they are commanded to be under obedience, as also saith the law. ³⁵And if they will learn any thing, let them ask their husbands at home: for it is a shame for women to speak in the church. ³⁶What? came the word of God out from you? or came it unto you only? ³⁷If any man think himself to be a prophet, or spiritual, let him acknowledge that the things that I write unto you are the commandments of the Lord."*

I. The Explanation – Line upon Line

    A. Why Did Paul Write This Book?

        1. To correct the confusion in the Corinthian church.
        2. To share the basic Biblical order of things including lifestyles, public services in the church, gifts of the Spirit, resurrection, death, etc.
        3. This book is actually a letter written by Paul in response to a letter the Corinthians had written him. He deals with one subject after another, as if he had their letter beside him as he wrote.

            a. I Corinthians 7:1, 25 –*"¹Now concerning the things whereof ye wrote unto me: It is good for a man not to touch a woman...²⁵ Now concerning virgins I have no commandment of the Lord: yet I give my judgment, as one that hath obtained mercy of the Lord to be faithful."*
            b. I Corinthians 8:1 – *"Now as touching things offered unto idols, we know that we all have knowledge. Knowledge puffeth up, but charity edifieth."*
            c. I Corinthians 12:1 –*"Now concerning spiritual gifts, brethren, I would not have you ignorant."*
            d. I Corinthians 10:1 –*" Moreover, brethren, I would not that ye should be ignorant, how that all our fathers were under the cloud, and all passed through the sea;"*

    B. In understanding a difficult passage of scripture we must:

        1. Compare Scripture with Scripture.
        2. Look at the historical setting.
        3. Evaluate the context.
        4. Look at the grammar and original meaning for words.
        5. Never throw away a principle that is supported by hundreds of passages because of one or two that seem contrary to it. Hold steady, wait on the Lord, and He will bring revelation and understanding.

    C. The Corinthian church was made up of a lot of new Christians. Many of the women had been prostitutes, serving in the temple of their religion. Their understanding of holiness and proper Biblical doctrine was limited.

    D. Chapter 14 is entirely devoted to what happens in a public church service.
    E. The overwhelming evidence of scripture contradicts the fact that women should be silent in church.

    F. Paul would not contradict himself.

        1. I Corinthians 11:5 –*"But every woman that prayeth or prophesieth with her head uncovered dishonoureth her head: for that is even all one as if she were shaven."*
        2. I Corinthians 14:5, 15, 31 –*"I would that ye all spake with tongues, but rather that ye prophesied: for greater is he that prophesieth than he that speaketh with tongues, except he interpret, that the church may receive edifying...¹⁵ What is it then? I will pray with the spirit, and I will pray with the understanding also: I will sing with the spirit, and I will sing with the understanding also...³¹ For ye may all prophesy one by one, that all may learn, and all may be comforted."*

3. I Corinthians 14:24, 26 –*"But if all prophesy, and there come in one that believeth not, or one unlearned, he is convinced of all, he is judged of all:²⁶ How is it then, brethren? when ye come together, everyone of you hath a psalm, hath a doctrine, hath a tongue, hath a revelation, hath an interpretation. Let all things be done unto edifying."*

G. In their church, men sat on one side, women on the other. It seemed they yelled questions to their husbands during the service.

H. If we truly believe women should be silent in church, then:

    1. No women singers or worshippers.
    2. No women choir directors.
    3. No women missionaries.
    4. No women teaching Sunday school.
    5. No friendly women.

I. Verse 34 should more correctly be translated: *"let your wives keep silence."* So what about single women?
J. The Greek word for "silence" means to hush or hiss. It is also used in verses 28 and 30. The context seems to mean silence in that the meeting is not interrupted, disrupted or brought to confusion.
K. The Greek for "speak" in verse 34 means to chatter, to babble. It does not indicate ministering at all, but idle or improper talking.
L. *"...as also saith the Law..."* – there is no Scripture anywhere in the Old Testament that hinders women from speaking.
M. The Law here is referring to the Oral Law of the Jews, the Rabbinical teaching (interpretation) of the Law.

N. The Oral Law said:

    1. A woman is a pitcher of filth.
    2. A woman is inferior to man.
    3. Let the words of the Law be burned rather than given to a woman.
    4. The testimony of one hundred women is not equal to the testimony of one man.
    5. It is a shame for a woman to let her voice be heard among men.
    6. Women are made to bear children.
    7. He that talks with women brings evil and will inhabit hell.

O. Did Paul teach that we should be governed by the Law? No, but rather that we have been made free from the Law.

    1. Romans 8:2 –*"For the law of the Spirit of life in Christ Jesus hath made me free from the law of sin and death."*
    2. Galatians 5:15 –*"But if ye bite and devour one another, take heed that ye be not consumed one of another."*
    3. Romans 10:4 –*"For Christ is the end of the law for righteousness to every one that believeth."*

P. Paul didn't say, "I don't permit it", but rather, "it is not permitted", indicating that someone else made this rule. It was the men who were trying to hush the women and subject them to the oral law.

Q. Verse 36, *"What?"* Paul rejects this.

Lesson 5
Submission, Headship and Covering

I. Submission

    A. There Are Many Aspects of Submission

        1. James 4:7 –*"Submit yourselves therefore to God. Resist the devil, and he will flee from you."*

This is the basis of all submission. We must be submitted to God first. All other submission or rebellion is related to whether you are submitted to God. When we are totally submitted to God, we will have no problem submitting to others. There have been cases of abuse of authority against God's people that I believe is due to lack of submission to God. The leader not submitted to God operates in a spirit of domination and control.

            a. I Samuel 15:23 –*"For rebellion is as the sin of witchcraft, and stubbornness is as iniquity and idolatry. Because thou hast rejected the word of the LORD, he hath also rejected thee from being king."* People try to control others in an ungodly way, because they are in rebellion themselves. When leadership is truly submitted to God, there is a divine flow of authority with no need for force or cruelty.

        2. I Peter 3:1-7

"¹Likewise, ye wives, be in subjection to your own husbands; that, if any obey not the word, they also may without the word be won by the conversation of the wives;²While they behold your chaste conversation coupled with fear. ³Whose adorning let it not be that outward adorning of plaiting the hair, and of wearing of gold, or of putting on of apparel;⁴ But let it be the hidden man of the heart, in that which is not corruptible, even the ornament of a meek and quiet spirit, which is in the sight of God of great price. ⁵For after this manner in the old time the holy women also, who trusted in God, adorned themselves, being in subjection unto their own husbands: ⁶Even as Sara obeyed Abraham, calling him lord: whose daughters ye are, as long as ye do well, and are not afraid with any amazement. ⁷Likewise, ye husbands, dwell with them according to knowledge, giving honour unto the wife, as unto the weaker vessel, and as being heirs together of the grace of life; that your prayers be not hindered."

            a. Ephesians 5:22-33

"²²Wives, submit yourselves unto your own husbands, as unto the Lord.²³ For the husband is the head of the wife, even as Christ is the head of the church: and he is the saviour of the body.²⁴ Therefore as the church is subject unto Christ, so let the wives be to their own husbands in every thing.²⁵ Husbands, love your wives, even as Christ also loved the church, and gave himself for it;²⁶ That he might sanctify and cleanse it with the washing of water by the word,²⁷That he might present it to himself a glorious church, not having spot, or wrinkle, or any such thing; but that it should be holy and without blemish. ²⁸So ought men to love their wives as their own bodies. He that loveth his wife loveth himself.²⁹ For no man ever yet hated his own flesh; but nourisheth and cherisheth it, even as the Lord the church:³⁰ For we are members of his body, of his flesh, and of his bones. ³¹For this cause shall a man leave his father and mother, and shall be joined unto his wife, and they two shall be one flesh.³² This is a great mystery: but I speak concerning Christ and the church. ³³Nevertheless let every one of you in particular so love his wife even as himself; and the wife see that she reverence her husband."

            b. Colossians 3:18 – *"Wives, submit yourselves unto your own husbands, as it is fit in the Lord."*

        3. We must see submission in a Biblical way

            a. James 4:7 – *Submit yourselves therefore to God. Resist the devil, and he will flee from you."* – Submission to God
            b. Ephesians 5:2 –*"Submitting yourselves one to another in the fear of God."* – Submission to one another

       c.   I Peter 5:5 –*"Likewise, ye younger, submit yourselves unto the elder. Yea, all of you be subject one to another, and be clothed with humility: for God resisteth the proud, and giveth grace to the humble."*
Hebrews 13:17 –*"Obey them that have the rule over you, and submit yourselves: for they watch for your souls, as they that must give account, that they may do it with joy, and not with grief: for that is unprofitable for you."* – Submission to leadership

       d.   Romans 10:3 –*"For they being ignorant of God's righteousness, and going about to establish their own righteousness, have not submitted themselves unto the righteousness of God."* – Submission to the righteousness of God

B.   Greek Words – Submission and subjection are the same words in Greek. They both mean "to arrange under, to rank under, to obey."

C.   Women to be submissive

    1.   She was created to be a helpmate
    2.   Taken from the side of man
    3.   God does not respect one over another
    4.   Heirs TOGETHER

D.   I Peter 3:1-6 (See Section A)

    1.   Verses 1-2 – Be submissive so that your husbands will see the Jesus in you and be won by your godly lifestyle.
    2.   Verse 3 – Make up does not make a woman.
    3.   Verse 4 – A humble, precious spirit. This means your life is within your heart, not what can be seen of man
    4.   Verses 5-6 – Women need to recognize the authority God has given them

    5.   Verse 7 – Warning to husbands

       a.   Dwell with knowledge
       b.   Give honor
       c.   Treat her as an heir together with you and God
       d.   That your prayers be not hindered

E.   Ephesians 5:22-33 – Colossians 3:18 (See Section A) – The context is first submit yourselves to each other

    1.   Wives obey your own husbands, not everyone else's.
    2.   Colossians 3:18 – as is fit in the Lord; don't disobey your conscience.
    3.   Ephesians 5:23-24 – He gives the divine order for marriage and home (I Corinthians 11:3, 7-10) – The Greek word for head basically means authority or direction.

       a.   Head of Christ – God
       b.   Head of man – Christ
       c.   Head of woman – Man

    4.   Ephesians 5:23, 28 and 33 – Warning to husbands

F.   Balance to submission

    1.   Ephesians 5:31 –*"For this cause shall a man leave his father and mother, and shall be joined unto his wife, and they two shall be one flesh."*

2. I Corinthians 11:11-12 –*"Nevertheless neither is the man without the woman, neither the woman without the man, in the Lord. For as the woman is of the man, even so is the man also by the woman; but all things of God."*

II. Headship – Covering

    A. I Corinthians 11:3 –*"But I would have you know, that the head of every man is Christ; and the head of the woman is the man; and the head of Christ is God."*

        1. Genesis 3:16 –*"Unto the woman he said, I will greatly multiply thy sorrow and thy conception; in sorrow thou shalt bring forth children; and thy desire shall be to thy husband, and he shall rule over thee."* – "Ruled" in the Hebrew means to govern, to have authority, covering

        2. Headship and covering then basically relates to authority or rulership in God's government or order of things.

        3. Man –"covered" in Greek – down or joined to someone else.
Woman –"covered" in Greek – same root word as above

        4. I Corinthians 11:10 – "power" in the Greek –authority (*exousia*)

Lesson 6
Satan Hates Women

In this chapter I hope to uncover why women have been silenced, abused, and thwarted from ministry. We could certainly put the blame on ignorance, male chauvinism, false teaching, misinterpretation of the Word of God, or simply put the blame on men's deep held insecurities and fears about women. However I want to unmask the real perpetrator of the silencing and abuse of women in ministry or just life in general. The answer is satan himself. He hates women because Eve was the first to expose him and his treachery.

I trust with all my heart that all of us now will approach this subject with an open or unveiled face (II Corinthians 3:18); one that comes with no preconceived ideas or traditions of men or bias of any kind! Let us allow God's Word to speak for itself, and not be dogmatic or unreasonable or unwilling to receive the truth of God concerning women. Nor should we fear what the Word declares as truth. Remember John 8:32, "*And ye shall know the truth, and the truth shall make you free.*" This should be our desire. As we discover who has been behind all of the repression, abuse, subjugation, and mistreatment of women down through history, we can then fight, pray, fast, and attack this adversary in an enlightened way. Sisters, as you read and study, let God deliver you and make you free from the long held chains of satan, religion, male superiority, and finally see and enter into God's great call upon your life. Believe it or not, the body of Christ desperately needs your ministry. If Jesus is ever going to come back, and the harvest reached, women must be released into ministry.

Through the ages, men, the one God purposed to be as a protection for women, be it as father or husband, has often been the one the enemy has used to express his hatred toward women. All we need do is read a newspaper or watch television to hear the multiple examples of wives being abused. This is so prevalent in our society today. Four times in Ephesians 5:25-33 God commanded the man to love his wife (see verses 25, 28, 33). He is told in I Peter 3:7, "*Likewise, ye husbands, dwell with them according to knowledge, giving honour unto the wife, as unto the weaker vessel, and as being heirs together of the grace of life; that your prayers be not hindered.*" Also in Colossians 3:19, "*Husbands, love your wives, and be not bitter against them.*" Nevertheless, even in many Christian homes this is not true. And men, both fathers, husbands, brothers, etc., have become tools of satan. This must stop and men need to receive the truth about women and rejoice, encourage, and help them fulfill their calling. Religion also has been the biggest abusers of women with their misinterpreted doctrines on submission, headship, and covering. History has shown us religion has been women's greatest enemy, but behind all this is satan working to destroy, hold back, and keep women silent. I believe it is because he fears them and knows if they are ever released into ministry, it will spell his doom. I pray this lesson brings that about, especially when one just looks in the natural at women. Who is more gifted at multi-tasking and getting a job done? Women have been given unique and special gifts from God that men simply do not have. We need them to help us get the job done of reaching the world for Jesus and bringing in the harvest. It is in our best interest to see them loosed!

I.   The Beginning Of Satan's Hatred Toward Women

    A.   Genesis 3:13-15 – "*13And the LORD God said unto the woman, What is this that thou hast done? And the woman said, The serpent beguiled me, and I did eat. 14And the LORD God said unto the serpent, Because thou hast done this, thou art cursed above all cattle, and above every beast of the field; upon thy belly shalt thou go, and dust shalt thou eat all the days of thy life: 15And I will put enmity between thee and the woman, and between thy seed and her seed; it shall bruise thy head, and thou shalt bruise his heel.*"

        1.   Verse 13 – Eve, unlike Adam, who blamed God and the woman for his sin (verse 12), boldly admits, "*The serpent beguiled me, and I did eat.*" Notice how she clearly points out that it was the serpent who was behind their whole affair.

            a.   Other translations:

                "*the serpent <u>tricked</u> me*"
                "*the serpent <u>beguiled, cheated, outwitted,</u> and <u>deceived</u> me*"

"the serpent hath <u>caused me to forget</u>, and I do eat"
"the serpent <u>deceived</u> me, and I ate"
"the serpent <u>seduced</u> me, she said, and I ate"
"the snake tricked me, so I ate the fruit"
"I was tricked by the <u>deceit of the snake</u>"
"It was the serpent. He deceived me, and I ate"

    b.   Definition of beguiled in Hebrew, *nasha* – to lead stray, to mentally delude, to morally seduce – This word defines for us satan according to Scripture.

    c.   From this we see that the woman was the first one to expose satan and his tricks.

2.   Satan defined in Scripture

    a.   Psalms 43:2 – *"For thou art the God of my strength: why dost thou cast me off? why go I mourning because of the oppression of the enemy?"* – enemy in Hebrew, *oyeb* – to hate as an adversary or foe

    b.   Psalms 143:3 – *"For the enemy hath persecuted my soul; he hath smitten my life down to the ground; he hath made me to dwell in darkness, as those that have been long dead."*

    c.   Matthew 13:24-30, 39 – *"24Another parable put he forth unto them, saying, The kingdom of heaven is likened unto a man which sowed good seed in his field: 25But while men slept, his enemy came and sowed tares among the wheat, and went his way. 26But when the blade was sprung up, and brought forth fruit, then appeared the tares also. 27So the servants of the householder came and said unto him, Sir, didst not thou sow good seed in thy field? from whence then hath it tares? 28He said unto them, An enemy hath done this. The servants said unto him, Wilt thou then that we go and gather them up? 29But he said, Nay; lest while ye gather up the tares, ye root up also the wheat with them. 30Let both grow together until the harvest: and in the time of harvest I will say to the reapers, Gather ye together first the tares, and bind them in bundles to burn them: but gather the wheat into my barn. 39The enemy that sowed them is the devil; the harvest is the end of the world; and the reapers are the angels."*

    d.   Mark 1:13 – *"And he was there in the wilderness forty days, tempted of Satan; and was with the wild beasts; and the angels ministered unto him."*

    e.   Mark 8:33 – *"But when he had turned about and looked on his disciples, he rebuked Peter, saying, Get thee behind me, Satan: for thou savourest not the things that be of God, but the things that be of men."*

    f.   Luke 13:16 – *"And ought not this woman, being a daughter of Abraham, whom Satan hath bound, lo, these eighteen years, be loosed from this bond on the sabbath day?"*

    g.   Luke 22:31 – *"And the Lord said, Simon, Simon, behold, Satan hath desired to have you, that he may sift you as wheat:"*

    h.   Acts 5:3 – *"But Peter said, Ananias, why hath Satan filled thine heart to lie to the Holy Ghost, and to keep back part of the price of the land?"*

    i.   II Corinthians 2:11 – *"Lest Satan should get an advantage of us: for we are not ignorant of his devices."*

    j.   II Corinthians 11:14 – *"And no marvel; for Satan himself is transformed into an angel of light."*

    k.   II Corinthians 12:7 – *"And lest I should be exalted above measure through the abundance of the revelations, there was given to me a thorn in the flesh, the messenger of Satan to buffet me, lest I should be exalted above measure."*

    l.   I Thessalonians 2:18 – *"Wherefore we would have come unto you, even I Paul, once and again; but Satan hindered us."*

    m.   II Thessalonians 2:9 – *"Even him, whose coming is after the working of Satan with all power and signs and lying wonders,"*

    n.   Revelation 2:20-25 – *"20Notwithstanding I have a few things against thee, because thou sufferest that woman Jezebel, which calleth herself a prophetess, to teach and to seduce my servants to commit fornication, and to eat things sacrificed unto idols. 21And I gave her space to repent of her fornication; and she repented not. 22Behold, I will cast her into a bed, and them that commit adultery with her into great tribulation, except they repent of their deeds. ²³And I will kill her children with death; and all the churches shall know that I am he which searcheth the reins and hearts: and I will give unto every one of you according to your works. ²⁴But unto you I say, and unto the rest in Thyatira, as many as have not this doctrine, and which have not known the depths of Satan, as they speak; I will put upon you none other burden. ²⁵But that which ye have already hold fast till I come."*

o. Revelation 12:9 – *"And the great dragon was cast out, that old serpent, called the Devil, and Satan, which deceiveth the whole world: he was cast out into the earth, and his angels were cast out with him."*

p. I Samuel 1:6 – *"And her adversary also provoked her sore, for to make her fret, because the LORD had shut up her womb."*

q. I Peter 5:8 – *"Be sober, be vigilant; because your adversary the devil, as a roaring lion, walketh about, seeking whom he may devour:"*

r. I Timothy 4:1 – *"Now the Spirit speaketh expressly, that in the latter times some shall depart from the faith, giving heed to seducing spirits, and doctrines of devils;"*

s. Matthew 4:1-11

t. John 13:2 – *"And supper being ended, the devil having now put into the heart of Judas Iscariot, Simon's son, to betray him;"*

u. Ephesians 6:11 – *"Put on the whole armour of God, that ye may be able to stand against the wiles of the devil."*

v. I Timothy 3:7 – *"Moreover he must have a good report of them which are without; lest he fall into reproach and the snare of the devil."*

w. I John 3:8 – *"He that committeth sin is of the devil; for the devil sinneth from the beginning. For this purpose the Son of God was manifested, that he might destroy the works of the devil."*

x. John 8:44 – *"Ye are of your father the devil, and the lusts of your father ye will do. He was a murderer from the beginning, and abode not in the truth, because there is no truth in him. When he speaketh a lie, he speaketh of his own: for he is a liar, and the father of it."*

y. Ephesians 4:26-27 – *"Be ye angry, and sin not: let not the sun go down upon your wrath: Neither give place to the devil."*

z. Daniel 7:25 – *"And he shall speak great words against the most High, and shall wear out the saints of the most High, and think to change times and laws: and they shall be given into his hand until a time and times and the dividing of time."*

3. Verse 14 – *"And the LORD God said unto the serpent, Because thou hast done this, thou art cursed above all cattle, and above every beast of the field; upon thy belly shalt thou go, and dust shalt thou eat all the days of thy life:"*

a. Because of Eve exposing him, satan is cursed.

b. The serpent represents the devil in Scripture (Revelation 12:9 – *"And the great dragon was cast out, that old serpent, called the Devil, and Satan, which deceiveth the whole world: he was cast out into the earth, and his angels were cast out with him.",* Revelation 20:2 – *"And he laid hold on the dragon, that old serpent, which is the Devil, and Satan, and bound him a thousand years,"*)

c. He has now been judged and cursed because of the woman; no wonder he is so angry with her.

4. Verse 15 – *"And I will put enmity between thee and the woman, and between thy seed and her seed; it shall bruise thy head, and thou shalt bruise his heel."*

a. Hebrew for enmity, *eybah* – hostility, hatred; from a root, *ayab* – to hate, to be hostile towards, to be an enemy

b. Also, the promise of the Messiah's coming and bruising satan is promised. We see this fulfilled in Jesus' death and victory at Calvary, and in Romans 16:20, *"And the God of peace shall bruise Satan under your feet shortly. The grace of our Lord Jesus Christ be with you. Amen."*

Eve did not blame God or reject Him. She did not hide what had happened or side with satan, but made a choice and sided with God against satan. Yes, Eve sinned by eating the forbidden fruit, but she did not reject God. She even knew the serpent had deceived her. Her husband had been no help and He had been expressly told by God to guard the garden (Genesis 2:8, 15-17 – "*8And the LORD God planted a garden eastward in Eden; and there he put the man whom he had formed…15And the LORD God took the man, and put him into the garden of Eden to dress it and to keep it. 16And the LORD God commanded the man, saying, Of every tree of the garden thou mayest freely eat: 17But of the tree of the knowledge of good and evil, thou shalt not eat of it: for in the day that thou eatest thereof thou shalt surely die.*"). So how did this beguiling, anti-God serpent get in the garden anyway? The answer can only be that Adam had at some time allowed him in. Also, why didn't it seem strange to him that the serpent spoke? Maybe it is because he had spoken to him before.

5. Adam is the culprit here, not Eve

    a. Job 31:33 – "*If I covered my transgressions as Adam, by hiding mine iniquity in my bosom:*"
    b. Hosea 6:7 – "*But they like <u>men</u>* (Hebrew – <u>*Adam*</u>) *have transgressed the covenant: there have they dealt treacherously against me.*"

Maybe that is why Eve was created to help him recover himself. The word helper in Hebrew is used in the Bible as a designation for someone who rescues or saves from difficult situations, rather than a subordinate assistant. He certainly didn't protect his wife. He blames God and Eve and refuses to accept his responsibility. Why did satan address her anyway? Maybe it was because he had already spoken to Adam and had convinced him about taking the forbidden fruit. Moreover, she was the stronger of the two and if Satan could get her to respond, then Adam would too. It certainly seems apparent that Adam was not surprised by any of this. It could be that he wanted Eve to do the dirty work and then she would be the one God blamed. When you think about this logically, it appears to be the only real answer. It is obvious to me that Adam had had contact with the serpent beforehand, and by not trying to prevent Eve or warn her of the consequences, it seems he wanted to eat from that forbidden tree. His silence here speaks very loudly that this theory is true. He didn't offer any resistance to her. He simply took the fruit and ate it. Also, Adam shielded satan and blamed God and the woman. Perhaps he had formed a friendship with the serpent long before Eve came. Future Scripture puts the blame solely on Adam and not Eve. She had been deceived. He knew full well what he was doing.

6. A look at what the Scripture says about who was to blame

    a. Adam

        1) I Timothy 2:14 – "*And Adam was not deceived, but the woman being deceived was in the transgression.*"
        2) I Corinthians 15:22 – "*For as in Adam all die, even so in Christ shall all be made alive.*"
        3) Romans 5:12, 15-19 – "*12Wherefore, as by one man sin entered into the world, and death by sin; and so death passed upon all men, for that all have sinned…15But not as the offence, so also is the free gift. For if through the offence of one many be dead, much more the grace of God, and the gift by grace, which is by one man, Jesus Christ, hath abounded unto many. 16And not as it was by one that sinned, so is the gift: for the judgment was by one to condemnation, but the free gift is of many offences unto justification. 17For if by one man's offence death reigned by one; much more they which receive abundance of grace and of the gift of righteousness shall reign in life by one, Jesus Christ.) 18Therefore as by the offence of one judgment came upon all men to condemnation; even so by the righteousness of one the free gift came upon all men unto justification of life. 19For as by one man's disobedience many were made sinners so by the obedience of one shall many be made righteous.*"

    b. Eve

1) I Timothy 2:14 – *"And Adam was not deceived, but the woman being deceived was in the transgression."* – The Greek here reads, *"...was thoroughly deceived and so became involved."*

2) II Corinthians 11:3 – *"But I fear, lest by any means, as the serpent beguiled Eve through his subtilty, so your minds should be corrupted from the simplicity that is in Christ."* – Once again the Greek *"thoroughly deceived"* is used.

The Scriptures are plain on this matter. Adam was to blame. He was the culprit, not Eve. Eve, however, had now become satan's main enemy, because to her was promised the Messiah. Satan has turned his attention on her, to stop her at any cost!

II. Satan Hates Women and Especially Women In Ministry

   A. Scriptures

   1. Daniel 11:17, 37 – *"17He shall also set his face to enter with the strength of his whole kingdom, and upright ones with him; thus shall he do: and he shall give him the daughter of women, corrupting her: but she shall not stand on his side, neither be for him...37Neither shall he regard the God of his fathers, nor the desire of women, nor regard any god: for he shall magnify himself above all."* – This is speaking of the antichrist, and his desire to corrupt women, however they refuse.

      a. Exodus 1:15-22 – *"15And the king of Egypt spake to the Hebrew midwives, of which the name of the one was Shiphrah, and the name of the other Puah: 16And he said, When ye do the office of a midwife to the Hebrew women, and see them upon the stools; if it be a son, then ye shall kill him: but if it be a daughter, then she shall live. 17But the midwives feared God, and did not as the king of Egypt commanded them, but saved the men children alive. 18And the king of Egypt called for the midwives, and said unto them, Why have ye done this thing, and have saved the men children alive? 19And the midwives said unto Pharaoh, Because the Hebrew women are not as the Egyptian women; for they are lively, and are delivered ere the midwives come in unto them. 20Therefore God dealt well with the midwives: and the people multiplied, and waxed very mighty. 21And it came to pass, because the midwives feared God, that he made them houses. 22And Pharaoh charged all his people, saying, Every son that is born ye shall cast into the river, and every daughter ye shall save alive."*

   2. Luke 13:16 – *"And ought not this woman, being a daughter of Abraham, whom Satan hath bound, lo, these eighteen years, be loosed from this bond on the sabbath day?"*

   3. I Samuel 1:1-7, 10-11 – *"1Now there was a certain man of Ramathaim-zophim, of mount Ephraim, and his name was Elkanah, the son of Jeroham, the son of Elihu, the son of Tohu, the son of Zuph, an Ephrathite: 2And he had two wives; the name of the one was Hannah, and the name of the other Peninnah: and Peninnah had children, but Hannah had no children. 3And this man went up out of his city yearly to worship and to sacrifice unto the LORD of hosts in Shiloh. And the two sons of Eli, Hophni and Phinehas, the priests of the LORD, were there. 4And when the time was that Elkanah offered, he gave to Peninnah his wife, and to all her sons and her daughters, portions: 5But unto Hannah he gave a worthy portion; for he loved Hannah: but the LORD had shut up her womb. 6And her adversary also provoked her sore, for to make her fret, because the LORD had shut up her womb. 7And as he did so year by year, when she went up to the house of the LORD, so she provoked her; therefore she wept, and did not eat...10And she was in bitterness of soul, and prayed unto the LORD, and wept sore. 11And she vowed a vow, and said, O LORD of hosts, if thou wilt indeed look on the affliction of thine handmaid, and remember me, and not forget thine handmaid, but wilt give unto thine handmaid a man child, then I will give him unto the LORD all the days of his life, and there shall no rasor come upon his head."*

   4. The church is seen in the Scriptures as a woman; notice satan's attack against her:

a. Revelation 12:3-4, 13-17 – "*3And there appeared another wonder in heaven; and behold a great red dragon, having seven heads and ten horns, and seven crowns upon his heads. 4And his tail drew the third part of the stars of heaven, and did cast them to the earth: and the dragon stood before the woman which was ready to be delivered, for to devour her child as soon as it was born...13And when the dragon saw that he was cast unto the earth, he persecuted the woman which brought forth the man child. 14And to the woman were given two wings of a great eagle, that she might fly into the wilderness, into her place, where she is nourished for a time, and times, and half a time, from the face of the serpent. 15And the serpent cast out of his mouth water as a flood after the woman, that he might cause her to be carried away of the flood. 16And the earth helped the woman, and the earth opened her mouth, and swallowed up the flood which the dragon cast out of his mouth. 17And the dragon was wroth with the woman, and went to make war with the remnant of her seed, which keep the commandments of God, and have the testimony of Jesus Christ.*"

b. Matthew 16:18 – "*And I say also unto thee, That thou art Peter, and upon this rock I will build my church; and the gates of hell shall not prevail against it.*"

B. Judaism

Men and women were separated from one another in the temple and in synagogues, and women were to be silent. Women were separated and silenced in their homes as well. They were not allowed to eat meals with their husbands, when there were guests present.

The oral law of the Jews is now called the Talmud. This oral law came into existence after the exile of the Jews. The Hebrews had lost their way, so to keep the Jews in remembrance of God's law (the Torah, the books of Moses) men began to make laws of their own from their interpretation of the true law of God. This led to a massive amount of laws or "traditions" that bound the Jewish people, especially women.

1. What Jesus/Apostles said about these traditions

a. Matthew 15:1-6 – "*1Then came to Jesus scribes and Pharisees, which were of Jerusalem, saying, 2Why do thy disciples transgress the tradition of the elders? for they wash not their hands when they eat bread. 3But he answered and said unto them, Why do ye also transgress the commandment of God by your tradition? 4For God commanded, saying, Honour thy father and mother: and, He that curseth father or mother, let him die the death. 5But ye say, Whosoever shall say to his father or his mother, It is a gift, by whatsoever thou mightest be profited by me; 6And honour not his father or his mother, he shall be free. Thus have ye made the commandment of God of none effect by your tradition.*"

b. Mark 7:3-9, 13 – "*3For the Pharisees, and all the Jews, except they wash their hands oft, eat not, holding the tradition of the elders. 4And when they come from the market, except they wash, they eat not. And many other things there be, which they have received to hold, as the washing of cups, and pots, brasen vessels, and of tables. 5Then the Pharisees and scribes asked him, Why walk not thy disciples according to the tradition of the elders, but eat bread with unwashen hands? 6He answered and said unto them, Well hath Esaias prophesied of you hypocrites, as it is written, This people honoureth me with their lips, but their heart is far from me. 7Howbeit in vain do they worship me, teaching for doctrines the commandments of men. 8For laying aside the commandment of God, ye hold the tradition of men, as the washing of pots and cups: and many other such like things ye do. 9And he said unto them, Full well ye reject the commandment of God, that ye may keep your own tradition...13Making the word of God of none effect through your tradition, which ye have delivered: and many such like things do ye.*"

c. Colossians 2:8 – "*Beware lest any man spoil you through philosophy and vain deceit, after the tradition of men, after the rudiments of the world, and not after Christ.*"

d. I Peter 1:18-19 – "*Forasmuch as ye know that ye were not redeemed with corruptible things, as silver and gold, from your vain conversation received by tradition from your fathers; But with the precious blood of Christ, as of a lamb without blemish and without spot:*"

This oral law (Talmud) was written by Jewish scholars interpreting the Pentateuch. It came to be seen as of equal authority with the Old Testament Scriptures. Just after the second century these oral laws were compiled in a book, The Talmud. It consists of fourteen large volumes. The Judaisers in the New Testament wanted to bind the Gentile believers with this law. Paul became their arch enemy. (See lesson 2 for statements found in the oral law.)

These traditions were made by men and not by God. They are not found in Holy Scripture. This is just one of the many ways satan uses men and religion to persecute women. Consider John 8:3-11 – "*3And the scribes and Pharisees brought unto him a woman taken in adultery; and when they had set her in the midst, 4They say unto him, Master, this woman was taken in adultery, in the very act. 5Now Moses in the law commanded us, that such should be stoned: but what sayest thou? 6This they said, tempting him, that they might have to accuse him. But Jesus stooped down, and with his finger wrote on the ground, as though he heard them not. 7So when they continued asking him, he lifted up himself, and said unto them, He that is without sin among you, let him first cast a stone at her. 8And again he stooped down, and wrote on the ground. 9And they which heard it, being convicted by their own conscience, went out one by one, beginning at the eldest, even unto the last: and Jesus was left alone, and the woman standing in the midst. 10When Jesus had lifted up himself, and saw none but the woman, he said unto her, Woman, where are those thine accusers? hath no man condemned thee? 11She said, No man, Lord. And Jesus said unto her, Neither do I condemn thee: go, and sin no more.*" Notice that only the woman was brought, not the man.

Lesson 7
A Closer Look At The Fall

Turn to the book of Genesis. I want to take time and look more closely at the fall of man. Let me begin by saying many times when God reveals truth to us, we must know He always speaks the word as we are able to hear it. All of us today are at different levels of light, revelation, glory, and understanding. As such, I always ask the Lord that whatever word He gives me, there will be milk for babes, bread for children, meat for men, strong meat for the aged, and if there happens to be any overcomers in the midst, let there be some hidden manna. I trust that no matter whatever spiritual level of maturity you are in, God would minister something to your heart. If there is something written on these pages that you don't understand, that doesn't necessarily mean it is wrong. It could be wrong, but as with everything you hear or read, I encourage you to search the Scriptures to see if these things are so (Acts 17:11). If it is too much for you to receive right now, put it on a shelf and wait. Don't be critical. Give God time. I can look back over 38 years now and see many truths that I initially thought to be heretical and that I would never have believed them, but now I embrace them as if they were the best truths in the world. Age and experience has a lot to do with this. Also, I believe satan has tried everything he could do to keep this word from coming forth. He is afraid of what is written here. He is and was a liar from the beginning. We have seen previously that he hates women because the first woman exposed him in the garden. In this lesson, I want to take a closer look at the fall of man.

Up to this point in Genesis 1, God had been creating the heavens, the earth, the animals, the trees, the sea, etc. Genesis 1:26 begins by saying, "*And God said...*" This is the triune God speaking. The word "God" here is *Elohiym* and it is a plural noun. Even when the first time God's name is mentioned in Genesis 1:1, it is used as a plural noun, "*In the beginning, God (Elohiym)*". Moreover, every time the word "one" is used to describe God, it is used in the plural sense as well. So the threefold God said, "*...Let us make man in our image...*" We see in the next chapter that when God created man, He caused a mist to fall over the earth (Genesis 2:6-7). It hadn't rained up to this point. It was a mist, and He caused a mist to come over the earth. He "*formed man*" out of the ground, but the Hebrew Word for "formed" means "molded", which speaks of a process. "*Let us make man in our image, after our likeness*". The Hebrew word for "likeness" means an <u>exact duplicate in kind</u>. I like this! The Lord is the only God, but we are like Him. Psalms 82:6 says, "*Ye are gods; and all of you are children of the most High*", meaning we were intended to be god-like, an exact duplicate in kind of the most High God. We can't even comprehend this with our soulish man, but just as God would speak and it will come to pass, that is what waits for a people. Jesus spoke to the fig tree and it did immediately what He commanded it to do. The disciples were amazed, and He made a statement to them, if you believe what you're saying, this will happen to you. Jesus wants us to walk in what He walked in. He wants us to be an exact duplicate in kind.

Continuing in Genesis 1:26-28:

> "*...26And let <u>them</u> have dominion over the fish of the sea, and over the fowl of the air, and over the cattle, and over all the earth, and over every creeping thing that creepeth upon the earth...28And God blessed them, and God said unto them, Be fruitful, and multiply, and replenish the earth, and <u>subdue</u> it: and have dominion over the fish of the sea, and over the fowl of the air, and over every living thing that moveth upon the earth.*"

I want to quickly say something about the word "subdue" here. The Bible says we are kings and priests on this earth and we've been called to subdue it (Revelation 5:10). The one thing many have forgotten is that as Christians, we have the ability to subdue in the spirit the things around us, "*for we wrestle not against flesh and blood, but against principalities, against powers, against the rulers of the darkness of this world, against spiritual wickedness in high places*" (Ephesians 6:12). For example, concerning the subject of politics, it ultimately does not matter who is elected president. Christians seem to be concentrating more on getting people to vote, getting people more involved in the political process than they do with spiritual matters. Jesus never ran for mayor. That was immaterial to Him. He said, "*My kingdom is not of this world...*" (John 18:36). Pilate tried to invoke His own governing power by saying to Jesus he can set Him free. But Jesus essentially said to Pilate, you have nothing to do with this. We are God's ambassadors on this earth and when God brings His last great glory, the former and latter rain in the earth, into a many membered son, the earth is going to see again the real ministry, not in just one man, but in millions of sons and daughters walking in dominion in His nature and likeness, as an exact duplicate in kind on the earth. Not in heaven, but on the earth. On the earth is where we need it. There is a 3½ year ministry of Jesus that is yet to be fulfilled and I anticipate breathlessly for that moment to begin, when God releases this ministry, when He says, "*Arise, shine; for thy light is come, and the glory of the LORD is risen upon thee.*" (Isaiah 60:1). People will literally see the glory of God in your life. They will feel it and know. When Jesus walked into the room, everyone knew it because the atmosphere changed. This is the way it should be in every one of our lives that we are so in tune with the intimacy and glory of God that when we come into a room that same glory follows us. The local church is supposed to be a powerful thing. As individual people grow in the things of God and come together, it will be a glorious and earth shattering thing.

Next, notice the word them in verse 26 of chapter one as well as in Genesis 5:1-2 which says, "*¹This is the book of the generations of Adam. In the day that God created man, in the likeness of God made he him; ²Male and female created he them; and blessed them, and called their name Adam, in the day when they were created.*" We see the word "them" used again. Also it says God created them "male and female". The initial man, created in the image and likeness of God, was both male and female, that is having both the male and female characteristics. It was only later that God took the female part out of man to create woman. If God created us in His image and in His likeness, and He created them "male and female", then this simply tells us that God has both male and female characteristics in His being. The name "God Almighty" in the Hebrew is "*El Shaddai*" which means the "breasty one; the nourishing one". Also, there are a multitude of Scriptures talking about God reaching out to us as children, cradling us in His arms, which are the female characteristics of God. There is nothing weird about this at all. Every one of us should try to nourish these characteristics in our own life. For men, this is hard because later on in creation, God took out of man the female characteristics. That is why we need the woman to be complete. Women are not subordinate at all. They are an absolute necessity because of the ingredients, the instincts, and the characteristics God gave her are absolutely essential for walking in this earth and having dominion. A man cannot have dominion by himself.

So God created man in His own image; in the image of God. He repeats that statement in verses 26-27. Anything God mentions twice, doubly confirms its truth. In Genesis 41:32, God gave Pharaoh a dream twice, "*And for that the dream was doubled unto Pharaoh twice; it is because the thing is established by God, and God will shortly bring it to pass.*" We need to have a revelation in our hearts that we are in the image of God. I believe that revelation would stop a lot of sin; if we kept a constant consciousness that we are the image of God on the earth because we don't want to dishonor His name or bring shame to His character, it would prevent many of our sins from being committed.

Finishing Genesis 1, it says, "*³¹And God saw every thing that he had made, and, behold, it was very good. And the evening and the morning were the sixth day.*" Up to this point in creation, even after creating man, there is nothing but harmony and absolute goodness in God's creation. Nothing was created wrong.

Everything God created up to this point was good, which brings us into Genesis chapter 2. At the end of verse 5 it says, "*there was not a man to till the ground*". This tells us that man had a purpose. God had created this beautiful world, but there needed to be somebody there to cultivate it, nurture it, and bring it forth. That is why we should take care of the environment. We are to be caretakers of the earth. But as verses 6-7 continue, it reads, "*⁶But there went up a mist from the earth, and watered the whole face of the ground. ⁷And the LORD God formed (Hebrew – "molded") man of the dust of the ground (this is man's physical body), and breathed into his nostrils the breath of life; and man became a living soul.*" God breathed into the original man the essence of life itself, which is in God. Every human being, whether Christian or not, carries the breath of God in them. Even those that curse and hate God, they breathe today because of His grace. This is man's spirit. The body without the spirit is dead, but once the spirit came into man, birthed of God's Spirit, man then "became a living soul". God's creative breath was breathed into man and as this breath hit man's body, man became a living soul. There is nothing wrong with touching, tasting, hearing, seeing, all the senses. They were created by God. It was only after the fall that we have to be concerned about these things. Everything up to this point was very good and right, the spirit was in control. The spirit of man was ruling and reigning before the fall of man; everything else was subordinate to it.

Genesis 2:8, "*And the LORD God planted a garden eastward in Eden; and there he put the man whom he had formed.*" Eden in Hebrew means "paradise, a place of delight, pleasantness". Now what makes this so important is this: Eden wasn't enough for Adam. It takes us back to the age old question where Peter asked Jesus, "*We have forsaken all, and followed thee; what shall we have therefore?*" (Matthew 19:27). And though the Lord answered him, it should never be about what we are going to get. You see, some people want the Lord for what He does for them. Some people's whole prayer life is about getting something and having their needs met. Furthermore, if the truth be told, many people's worship isn't really worship at all. So many of the songs we sing now are about us, our blessings, our deliverance, etc. I try not to sing too many of those songs. When I come to worship, I come to worship, give thanks, honor, and give adoration to Him alone. There is a big difference between being someone who just praises the Lord and one who is a true worshipper (John 4:23). Never forget this. You and I want to be worshippers.

So God plants this garden, a place of pleasantness, delight, a paradise. The question that my heart asks is: *what else could Adam have wanted*? Was God enough for him? That is the thing about the soul, the mind, the emotions, the intellect and the affections; it is always looking for something more than what it has right in front of it. The grass always seems greener on the other side. Solomon says, "*The eye is not satisfied with seeing, nor the ear filled with hearing*" (Ecclesiastes 1:8). Our soul always seems to want more. We never seem to find contentment if we let our minds wander, but Paul teaches us from his own life and says, "*I have learned, in whatsoever state I am, therewith to be content.*" (Philippians 4:11). Contentment is something you have to learn to obtain. Paul goes on to say in I Timothy 6:6, "*Godliness with contentment is great gain*", and in Hebrews 13:5, "*Be content with such things as ye have: for he hath said, I will never leave thee, nor forsake thee.*"

The reason why many are not content is that God is not enough for them and what God has given and blessed them with is not enough; they want something else. This is all coming from the soulish realm. However, our spirit is a partaker of the divine nature. It is not going to want more because it is God's. All of the poetry that has been written, all of the great stories, dramas, and pathos of life are great, but it is in the soulish realm. "*The carnal mind is enmity against God*" Romans 8:7 tells us. After the fall, our carnal mind has become an enmity against God. John put it this way, "*Love not the world, neither the things that are in the world. If any man love the world, the love of the Father is not in him*" (I John 2:15). What is in the world? Well, John defines it in the next verse, "*For all that is in the world, the lust of the flesh, and the lust of the eyes, and the pride of life, is not of the Father, but is of the world.*" (I John 2:16). The soul always wants to see something more or feel something more. Nothing is ever enough.

Ask yourself this question tonight. Are you content? What if it was just you and Jesus for the rest of your life? Could you live and be content? Our dreams and our goals and our desires must be like David's, Moses', or Paul's, who said respectively, groaning in their hearts to the Lord, "*One thing have I desired of the LORD, that will I seek after*" (Psalms 27:4), "*Shew me now thy way, that I may know thee*" (Exodus 33:13), and "*...That I may know him*" (Philippians 3:10). We have a nation and generation of people now trying to know themselves. Do you not know that once you get to know yourself that you will find out who you are, as Paul wrote, "*For I know that in me (that is, in my flesh,) dwelleth no good thing*" (Romans 7:18). Solomon talks about a people that only desire to find themselves. I found myself at an early age and realized that I wasn't that good. I don't know what you think about yourself, but everything good in me is Jesus. When Paul said, I am chief above sinners, I believe he really meant it. And so, man became a living soul.

Genesis 2:8-9, "*8And the LORD God planted a garden eastward in Eden; and there he put the man whom he had formed. 9And out of the ground made the LORD God to grow every tree that is pleasant to the sight, and good for food; the tree of life also in the midst of the garden, and the tree of knowledge of good and evil.*" So then God put man in the garden and caused all the trees to grow. There He also put the tree of life and the tree of the knowledge of good and evil. God purposely put both trees in there for one purpose: to give man a choice. You see, long before man was ever created, sin had happened in the universe through Lucifer the archangel, and the heavens were not pure in His sight. So God had to give man a choice. He had to do it. You see satan was Lucifer who had walked up and down the stones of fire. Lucifer lived in the glory and was the worship leader in heaven, but think about it - that wasn't enough for him. He ended up falling. This is the same problem with many men, especially those with big souls. It is hard for them to be grateful for what they have. They can't acknowledge

God and be content with what He has given them. They spend their whole lives searching, only to find they've left a trail of misery for all the people they've betrayed. If they would have just stopped way back when and said, *Wait a minute, God gave me this*, then maybe all would have been different.

Reading on in Genesis 2:15, "*And the LORD God took the man, and put him into the garden of Eden to dress it and to keep it.*" Another translation of this verse reads, "*...To work, and to watch it*". Man was put into the garden to watch it. This is very important. Man's job was to guard this garden. And then the Lord commanded the man and said, "*Of every tree of the garden thou mayest freely eat: But of the tree of the knowledge of good and evil, thou shalt not eat of it: for in the day that thou eatest thereof thou shalt surely die*" (verses 16-17). Have you ever considered this? Adam was allowed to eat of any tree except one. Why did he never take of the tree of life? He is told he could eat of any tree including the tree of life. Once someone eats of the tree of life, that's it, no more knowledge of good and evil and you can't go back. Adam chose not to do that and that was the beginning of the weakness in Adam. He did not take of the tree of life! Because once you eat of the tree of life, you are in the same condition forever, and for some reason, his condition in the place of paradise, wasn't enough for him.

At the creation of man, even when things seemed to be precious and good, all of a sudden the Lord God says in verse 18, "*It is not good that the man should be alone; I will make him an help meet for him.*" Doesn't that seem odd? So many good things have happened and all of a sudden the Lord says, "*It is not good that man should be alone*". Verse 31 of chapter 1 said, "*It was very good*". So the question needs to be asked, what was the problem and what had transpired since chapter 1? I believe the problem was not with Eden or with God, but the problem was with Adam.

Many scholars believe there was a reason Adam did not take of the tree of life and that somehow, when God said that it isn't good that man should be alone, Adam had already stumbled in some form or fashion. I believe this to be true because he refused to take of the tree of life, when given the choice. The Word "alone" here should be translated "separation", or "in his separation". So another translation could be, "*It is not good for man to be <u>in his separation</u>*". Separated from what? There's only one thing that he could have been separated from and that is God Himself. Something had separated him and the only thing that could fix it in God's eyes was, "*I will make him an help meet for him*": a woman! Amen!

Before we look into "help meet", I want to look at reasons why Adam could've had some problems at this point in the story. First of all, as we continue in Genesis 3, what do we find? We find the serpent is in the garden (serpent being satan – Revelation 12:9, 20:2) who had already been kicked out of the third heaven. Adam was put in the garden, as we saw previously, to guard it. Evidently he didn't guard it enough. What does Ecclesiastes 10:8 tell us? "*He that diggeth a pit shall fall into it; and whoso breaketh an hedge, a serpent shall bite him.*" How did the serpent get in the garden anyway? God did not let him in the garden. The garden was a paradise, pleasant and a delightful place. That is definitely not true about any place that satan is in. There is nothing pleasant and delightful about satan. It seems Adam had let him in.

Not only did Adam let him in, but Adam just let the serpent talk to Eve without any warning. If Satan started talking to your wife, as a man and as her husband, wouldn't you say something? Why didn't Adam say something? I believe Adam already heard the same thing and had previously talked to satan himself. I can't prove this, but there seems to be no other revelation that satisfies me. I can't imagine a man just standing there as satan talks to his wife. There must have been something in Adam that liked what he was hearing, possibly because he had similar discussions with the serpent. And consider this, Adam didn't refute anything the serpent said, even when the serpent told a bold face lie and said "You shall not die". This is a big thing because satan is defaming the character of God. Adam should have immediately stood up and said something! But if you are not right with God, or you are separated from God, you would be in a condition where you would let something like that go. He didn't refute anything the serpent said - nothing. I believe Adam wanted to eat of the tree, but was afraid and wanted the woman to do it, so that she could take the blame. God wasn't enough for Adam. Adam wanted to be a god himself. Also, when Eve handed Adam the fruit, he didn't say anything or give a refusal, but simply took the fruit and ate it. Adam didn't even say, "Are you sure we shouldn't do this honey?" He just took it immediately and then he encouraged Eve to hide from God's presence. When God came looking He came looking for Adam first. How come God didn't say, "Adam and Eve, where are you?" No, He said to Adam *"Where art thou?"* Adam didn't know where he was anymore. Adam should've known better.

Later, when God challenged them, Adam said, *"I heard thy voice in the garden, and I was afraid, because I was naked; and I hid myself"* (Genesis 3:10). Never does he use the word we. Women have one weakness and it isn't a bad thing. She is too faithful when she doesn't need to be. Eve, because she loved him, just went where he went. Later we will see that God warns her about doing that. He then, when God asked what happened, responded oddly. God's first two questions were, *"Who told thee that thou wast naked? Hast thou eaten of the tree, whereof I commanded thee that thou shouldest not eat?"* (Genesis 3:11). God gave Adam every opportunity to put the blame where it really belonged. But look what Adam said, *"And the man said, The woman whom thou gavest to be with me, she gave me of the tree, and I did eat."* (Genesis 3:12). Adam blamed God and the woman and he hid satan. This reminds me of an important principle: if you are in a counseling session with someone, just listen to what they say. If you have a true discerning spirit, you can read more into what they don't say than of what they do say.

I read in Adam's voice that he was protecting satan. How could he have not at least mentioned him, when God Himself was asking him? The first thing I would have told God would be that the devil tempted me. Instead Adam blamed God and the woman. She didn't make Adam eat of the fruit. No, he was there and she gave it to him and he did eat. So not only was he hiding satan, but Adam himself also had secrets. If you have secrets, you are out of the will of God. If you have secrets, it doesn't matter what you say or justify, you are not living in the light, but in darkness and you need to repent.

I was ministering the other day saying we should want to have a life with no secrets: no side hidden doors, no compartments or no places with a do not enter sign containing a lock on it that only you know the combination to. If there are areas in your life that are like this, then you have secrets and are hiding something. The stupidity of it with Adam is that God knows everything. You can say all day that this isn't happening or that you are not doing this and blame it on God or another person, but anybody who has any discernment would know immediately that it is what you didn't say that's important.

We are to have no more secrets! Did you do something today that you would be ashamed of if your wife or husband saw you do it? Is there something in your thought life that you would keep hidden from Jesus if He were to ask you about it? We have to stop living double lives. James 1:8 says, *"A double minded man is unstable in all his ways."* If you lie in a little thing you will lie in a big thing.

So we clearly see that Adam didn't take any personal responsibility for what happened. He just blamed others. How hard is it for you to say, "I'm sorry, the devil tempted me, but I did it"? I Samuel 2:3 says, *"Talk no more so exceeding proudly; let not arrogancy come out of your mouth: for the LORD is a God of knowledge, and by him actions are weighed."* In this story, I see Adam having a weakness, not satisfied with his lot in life, wanting to be godlike, always looking for something more, and a willingness to hide and deceive. We always have said the woman was the deceiver, but the only truthful person in this story was the woman.

Now let us look at the woman and in God creating her. Back to Genesis 2:18, *"And the LORD God said, It is not good that the man should be alone; I will make him an help meet for him."* I want to take a closer look at the word "help" here in the Hebrew. Most bibles that contain references in the margins will define "help" as "support or an "aid". This is absolutely not the complete definition of help at all. This is where we not only see biases in translators but in bible makers as well. They perpetuate bad doctrine. Listen to what the full definition of "help" means. First of all it means "aid", but it comes from a root word that means to "surround, to protect". What is the normal image of a man? Isn't it to surround and protect a woman? It is completely opposite in the eyes of God. The word implies superior help. And the root means someone who rescues you in a time of crisis or from difficult situations. Two things here, first, Eve was created because Adam was in a difficult situation and needed to be restored. Second, Adam needed Eve to protect him. Twenty one times this word "help" is used in the Old Testament, and most of the time it is used to describe God supernaturally helping Israel or being delivered from her enemies. "Meet" in the Hebrew means to "stand boldly out, the opposite, the counterpart, a front". Now this is very important. She is the opposite of Adam, but she is the one that is standing boldly out. She's the stronger of the two, but she is also his counterpart, and everyone who is in a harmonious marriage knows that your spouse is the counterpart to you. That is the way. Eve was created out of Adam's rib, or the side of Adam. Eve was created at Adam's side, meaning she was his equal. She was not created under his feet, but at his side. Galatians 3:28 says, "*There is neither male nor female: for ye are all one in Christ Jesus.*" So this is the "help meet" God gave Adam.

Genesis 2:21-22, "*21And the LORD God caused a deep sleep to fall upon Adam and he slept: and he took one of his ribs, and closed up the flesh instead thereof; 22And the rib, which the LORD God had taken from man, made he a woman, and brought her unto the man.*" It is interesting that Eve is called three things in the story. First she is the woman, then she is the wife, and then she is called Eve, the mother of all living. Three different titles were given to her. The word "rib" in Hebrew really means "a side, a chamber, a corner". One scholar believes it means "alter ego". She came from Adam's side. This means that she is to stand equal with him and she is just like him, nothing less.

When Adam sees Eve, the Hebrew bible reads, "This is it." I wonder what she looked like. Adam knew in his heart that he was already shifted and separated. By the time God brought Eve to him, he really looked at her in the proper way, that is, "this is it," not meaning I've found someone who will really help, protect, and guard me. He really didn't have her help him at all during the temptation. He used her, which is another trait of men. He used her to accomplish what he wanted accomplished so that he wouldn't have to take the blame for it..

Chapter 3 begins, "*Now the serpent was more subtil than any beast of the field which the LORD God had made. And he said unto the woman, Yea, hath God said, Ye shall not eat of every tree of the garden?*" Remember, the serpent doesn't even belong in the garden. He is the adversary, the old serpent. Adam had let him in and when the serpent asked the woman his first question: "Yea, hath God said?" Adam should have immediately said, "Don't question the Word of God!" But he said nothing. Why? Because obviously he had already received what the serpent said and questioned God himself in his separateness state. The woman answered the serpent by saying, "*2...We may eat of the fruit of the trees of the garden: 3But of the fruit of the tree which is in the midst of the garden, God hath said, Ye shall not eat of it, neither shall ye touch it, lest ye die.*" Give her credit, what she said is what God said. But the serpent responded and said unto the woman, "*Ye shall not surely die*". This is a lie. He is a liar and has been a liar since the beginning. Everything Satan says to us is always a lie. How is satan to presume what God knows? This isn't even reasonable. That is why we have to read the Bible slowly and meditate on it. The word "meditate" in the bible means to chew like a cow chews their cud. A cow will chew, swallow, burp the food back up, and chew some more. This is meditation. You have to not think while you read, but listen while you read.

Genesis 3:5, "*For God doth know that in the day ye eat thereof, then your eyes shall be opened, and ye shall be as gods, knowing good and evil.*" This surely does not speak of your natural eyes, but of the eyes of your soul. Luke 11:34 says, "*The light of the body is the eye: therefore when thine eye is single, thy whole body also is full of light; but when thine eye is evil, thy body also is full of darkness.*" Even the world says the eye is the window to the soul. Satan is basically saying to her, "I want your soul to be pre-eminent Eve". This is the tempting thing about it. In the soulish realm, there is so much pathos, romanticism, drama, and overall, stuff that appears to be so interesting and great that it appeals to you. "*6And when the woman saw that the tree was good for food, and that it was pleasant to the eyes, and a tree to be desired to make one wise, she took of the fruit thereof, and did eat, and gave also unto her husband with her; and he did eat.*" Now Adam has not said anything at all to protect her. It doesn't say Eve wanted to be as God, but that the tree was pleasant and to be desired. Adam wanted it, I believe, because he wanted to be as God. "*7And the eyes of them both were opened, and they knew that they were naked; and they sewed fig leaves together, and made themselves aprons.*" This was when their soulish eyes opened. Neither shame, nor condemnation had ever been in the earth until then. So they sewed fig leaves together. Religion started on that day. Religion is nothing more than fig leaves, or our trying to cover something only God can cover. "*8And they heard the voice of the LORD God walking in the garden in the cool of the day: and Adam and his wife hid themselves from the presence of the LORD God amongst the trees of the garden.*"

"*9And the LORD God called unto Adam, and said unto him, Where art thou?*" God knew where Adam was. God wanted Adam to know where he was. Adam responded by saying, "*10I heard thy voice in the garden, and I was afraid, because I was naked; and I hid myself."* The Lord followed up by asking him, *"11And he said, Who told thee that thou wast naked? Hast thou eaten of the tree, whereof I commanded thee that thou shouldest not eat?"* God was giving Adam every opportunity to repent, but instead of repenting, Adam blamed the woman and God (verse 12). Continuing in verse 13, *"And the LORD God said unto the woman, What is this that thou hast done? And the woman said, The serpent beguiled me, and I did eat."* Now we've been pretty hard on men up to this point, but one of the weaknesses in women is this very thing. The difference between Adam and Eve is this: Adam knew what he was doing, whereas Eve really believed and was deceived. Every time the word "deceived" is mentioned in the Greek, it means thoroughly deceived, or completely convinced that it was right. If there is anything a woman needs to watch out for, and it is the greatest characteristic she has, it is her intuition and her ability to sense and discern things. I thank God that He has given me a level of discernment. I feel everything. I can feel something happening a mile away from where I'm standing. I'm sensitive. This is rare in men, but it is a gift of God given to women.

Having the gift of sensitivity makes you extremely vulnerable, not only vulnerable to yourself, but also to the many voices in the world, which none are without significance. You see, God has made it to where neither the man nor the woman can make it by themselves. We need the other. The greatest problem for the woman is her greatest asset. She must be careful and what she really needs in her life is not someone subjugating or ruling her, but she needs a father ministry, be it as a father naturally, a husband, a pastor, or a brother, etc. She needs an objective influence in her life to be at least a check and balance to her. There is great freedom in this, sisters. There is no need to be upset or feel bound by this. In the multitude of counselors there is safety. Eve would have listened if Adam would have just spoken up. That is the problem we have. We have a bunch of mealy-mouthed men who either will not speak up or have ulterior motives. Sadly, some men won't warn their wives because they want their wives to sin, so there might be an opportunity they might get a divorce. Don't assume that God doesn't know of all your thoughts and of the tricks you try to play.

Upon being asked by the Lord what happened, Eve exposed Satan right out, and notice the Lord doesn't say anything more to her. This satisfied God because He immediately turned to the serpent, *"14And the LORD God said unto the serpent, Because thou hast done this, thou art cursed above all cattle, and above every beast of the field; upon thy belly shalt thou go, and dust shalt thou eat all the days of thy life: 15And I will put enmity between thee and the woman, and between thy seed and her seed; it shall bruise thy head, and thou shalt bruise his heel."* The word "enmity" means hatred and hostility. There is enmity between satan and the woman because the woman exposed satan. There is enmity between satan's seed and woman's seed. This represents all of mankind and also the seed of the messiah which shall bruise satan's head.

"16Unto the woman he said, I will greatly multiply thy sorrow and thy conception; in sorrow thou shalt bring forth children..." Let me say a few things about this before I continue. Having a baby is not a curse. Please don't say anything stupid when you find out you are pregnant, like "I don't want this baby". Please don't do this. The little spirit inside that baby will hear everything we say. You have to be very careful about that. The bible says, *"Children are an heritage of the LORD: and the fruit of the womb is his reward"* (Psalms 127:3), and *"Happy is the man that hath his quiver full of them"* (Psalms 127:5). So having a baby is not a curse. The sorrow spoken of in Genesis is that the children you birth in the world are going to be birthed now as sinners. The sorrow is going to be knowing that the fall has taken place and everything that comes out of you now is under the law or the curse. This is the sorrow.

The Lord continued in verse 16 speaking to the woman, *"...and thy desire shall be to thy husband, and he shall rule over thee."* Most scholars are so ridiculous with this part of the verse. They try to make this a sexual thing. I'm telling you, most theologians, especially rabbis, say that you will have sexual desire toward your husband. I don't think it means this but something else. The phrase, *"And thy desire shall be to thy husband"*, means in the actual Hebrew, *"You are turning away from God and turning to your husband"*. This is absolutely phenomenal. When God said to her about the sorrow in conception and the promise of the Messiah, Eve became the first believer. When He said it shall come forth, it shall bruise, etc. she believed God. How do I know this? Because in the next chapter when she bore her first son, she actually believed it was the Messiah. She thought Cain was the seed. She actually believed what the Lord said and became the first believer in the Messiah. So in actuality, God was warning her here because He knew what was going to happen. She was not out with God.

43

She was not separated. She told the truth. She exposed satan, and God did not curse her. He simply told her the facts. He told her that she will be sad when the children that she would bring in the world will be born in sin and then He said to her that her desire shall be to her husband and he shall rule over her. One can translate that as follows, *"If you do this, you are basically turning away from God and to your husband, and as a result, he will rule over you"*. We interpret that to mean that a woman is supposed to desire her husband and that he is to rule over her. This is the way we've always been taught. Actually, God is saying this is a bad thing. You are never supposed to put a man over God. In that statement God said to Eve, "You are alright with me. You are fine. Don't do this, because if you do this, he will rule over you". God was warning Eve! Hasn't this happened over our history?

As the story continued, God dealt with Adam and then, *"20And Adam called his wife's name Eve; because she was the mother of all living."* Notice how her name was changed from woman, to wife, to Eve, the mother of all living. All of mankind is going to flow out of her, but also the promise seed, the Messiah, will come from her.

"21Unto Adam also and to his wife did the LORD God make coats of skins, and clothed them." This was the first sacrifice, the first blood shed for the remission of sin.

> *"22And the LORD God said, Behold, the man is become as one of us, to know good and evil: and now, lest he put forth his hand, and take also of the tree of life, and eat, and live for ever: 23Therefore the LORD God sent him forth from the garden of Eden, to till the ground from whence he was taken. 24So he drove out the man; and he placed at the east of the garden of Eden Cherubims, and a flaming sword which turned every way, to keep the way of the tree of life."*

Now read this again closely. In verse 22 it says, *"The man is become as one of us, to know good and evil."* I do not see the words "she" or "the woman" involved here. This is important. Yes, Eve did eat of the tree of the knowledge of good; she did eat and her soul was opened and she did follow her husband and hid, but when God questioned her, like her name "help meet" means, she boldly stood out and said, "The serpent did this. He's the one who made me do this." Many people say this all the time, "The devil made me do it", but in Eve's case this was really true. Eve was completely and thoroughly deceived and she thought it was right to eat and she didn't get any help from Adam telling her differently. So yes, Eve did partake of the sin, but there is a difference between what Adam did and what she did because everywhere else in the bible in which the fall is mentioned, it doesn't say Eve brought sin into the world. Moreover, it is Adam's name that is mentioned over and over again. *"By one man sin entered into the world, and death by sin"* Romans 5:12 says. Because of one man's sin, death entered the earth. When Eve said that the serpent beguiled her and that she did eat, and when God prophesied to her and warned her about Adam ruling over her, she wasn't out with God. She was still in with God. That is why God says in verse 22, *"The man is become as one of us"*. Adam, when he took of the tree, was consumed with the knowledge of good and evil, but once Eve exposed satan, the prophecy came about the messiah and Eve literally became a believer right on the spot. And so she could partake of the tree of life right then. But Adam was lost in the knowledge of good and evil, having blamed God and the woman. Adam was very corrupt. So God had to kick Adam out , *"Lest he put forth his hand, and take also of the tree of life, and eat, and live for ever"*, meaning live forever in the condition he is in, which wasn't good. Therefore the Lord God sent the man out. She isn't mentioned! The Lord God sent him out from the garden of Eden to till the ground from whence he was taken. So He drove out who? The man!

"24So he drove out the man; and he placed at the east of the garden of Eden Cherubims, and a flaming sword which turned every way, to keep the way of the tree of life." Eve did not really have to leave the garden. So earlier, when God said *"He shall rule over you"*, do you think God was really trying to put the man in charge over the woman? I don't think so. Adam really hadn't repented. So now when we read *"He shall rule over you"*, God was not saying the man is to rule over the woman, but it was God warning Eve, *"He shall rule over you"*. Now I will address in another section of this book the fact that Ephesians 5:23 says, *"For the husband is the head of the wife, even as Christ is the head of the church"*, which is in this life and I will explain why that is in there. In Adam, this is the case, but in Christ, there is neither male nor female (Galatians 3:28). When we are in Adam, this is the way it is. When we are in Christ, we are all the children of God by faith.

So the man was told to leave. So what did Adam do next? We see in Genesis 4:1, "*And Adam knew Eve his wife; and she conceived, and bare Cain, and said, I have gotten a man from the LORD.*" The man she got from the Lord, she believed it was the Messiah. How sad it was when she realized this wasn't true. Pretty much, this is the last time her name is mentioned in the Bible. Eve had left the garden. She chose to go with her husband. This is another trait of a woman. Two of her greatest attributes, which are faithfulness and loyalty, are two of her greatest curses. How many women do you know who are staying with men who abuse them and are mean to them? These women stay with their abusive husbands anyway. The greatest asset of faithfulness and loyalty can become a curse to you. Eve left God and followed Adam out of loyalty. Why did she do that? Did Adam say anything to her to make her think that he loved her? Not really. This is the sense I got when I meditated on it. God warned her, if she did this, she would be turning from him and her husband would rule over her, but for the little time she had before the fall with him, the oneness she experienced was so precious to her, that she chose that. How many women are on a journey to find oneness with a man, true oneness? Let us be honest, it doesn't happen very often that a woman would find that true oneness. I'm not trying to discourage anyone. It can happen and does happen. She was hoping for the oneness she had known previously, but she knew she had the promise of the Messiah coming. So she thought to herself, okay, God created me to protect him in rough situations and he has been kicked out of the garden now and he can't get back in, so I think she just felt sorry for him and she went out with him.

The root of the whole premise of women having to be subjugated and subordinate to men is in this story. However, as we have taken a closer look, we find that it is really completely different than what we've been taught. It is all right there if you let the Holy Spirit show you. Sisters, you are not to be subjugated to or to be in bondage to men. You are no lesser of a human being than any man. The only thing that the Scriptures mention in that aspect is that women are naturally weaker than men. For the most part (there are always exceptions), men are physically stronger than women. In the Bible, this is the only weakness mentioned that women have in comparison to men.

Just think with me right now about the heart of God the Father. He loved her so much. The great thing about God the Father is what we see in the story of the Prodigal Son in Luke 15, in which the father let his son go, knowing he would come back. That is why Jesus came! Jesus did everything opposite of the tradition of that day in regards to treating women and He did it on purpose. He lived a constant lifestyle proving that the old Judaiser oral laws were a bunch of nonsense and he restored women to the place that they were originally created her to be. The very people who say Paul hated women are just so ignorant of the Scriptures. On the contrary, Paul is the biggest supporter of women's ministry in the Bible. Paul is the very one who proves women are free to minister.

What would you do with the choice? Sisters, does your husband mean more to you than Jesus? Brothers, does your wife mean more to you than Jesus? You need to love and cherish your spouse, but nobody can live on a pedestal. Sisters, stop judging your husband, putting him on a pedestal and a place of great expectation. Haven't you learned yet to stop this expectation foolishness? You learn that if you don't expect a lot, you don't get disappointed. It then always becomes a blessing when your spouse does something right when you stop from constantly expecting your husband or wife to do this or that or the other. Cut them some slack. Amen!

Men have inherent weaknesses that they just cannot seem to get over without the help of a woman, and sisters have one or two weaknesses where they absolutely need the covering aspect of the man. But the bottom line truth is, that our true head, who is both male and female, is the Lord Jesus Himself, and we don't turn from Him to anybody. We don't want anybody other than the Lord Jesus ruling over us. Jeremiah 5:30-31 says, "*A wonderful and horrible thing is committed in the land; The prophets prophesy falsely, and the priests bear rule by their means; and my people love to have it so*". Ezekiel says to the wicked shepherds of Israel "*With force and with cruelty have ye ruled them*" (Ezekiel 34:4). Why do people love to be ruled with force and cruelty? Look at an abused woman staying with her husband. Why does she stay? I believe it's because once you get beaten down long enough, you start to believe and become what your abusive husband may tell you about yourself over the years. You begin to believe him when he tells you that you are inferior, that you're a lesser human being and that you need someone to watch over you and protect you, and that you were the reason sin entered into the world. This is what has happened to women. I declare to you today, both men and women, to turn back to the

Father. Let us all turn back today, and let's all say, "Lord forgive me for turning away. The only person I want ruling over me is You, and Lord while You are at it, please remove any secrets or hidden places in me". Amen!

Sisters, never again will you be turned from the Lord. Brothers, never again will you be in His separateness, when you can be with the Lord. Is God enough for you? I pray the glory of God comes down upon you now, and the Spirit of the Lord would say unto you, come back my people. Come back. "*For thy Maker is thine husband; the LORD of hosts is his name; and thy Redeemer the Holy One of Israel; The God of the whole earth shall he be called.*" (Isaiah 54:5). Say this with me. "King Jesus, from this night on, I make this solemn vow that I will desire only You and I will not turn away from You. I want to be ruled only by You. The greatest oneness I seek is with You. I love You Jesus. Help thou my unbelief. Take the scales off from my eyes. Break the chains off from my soulish carnal mind and let the spirit within me rise up and take precedence in my life. I humble myself and ask You, have mercy on me for all the moments where You have not been my true head, where I've had an idol, or another lover besides thee. "*Whom have I in heaven but thee? and there is none upon earth that I desire beside thee. My flesh and my heart faileth: but God is the strength of my heart, and my portion for ever*" (Psalms 73:25-26). I look nowhere else, I'm here and I'm here for You. I love You Jesus. Seal this word to our hearts Father! Let a sweet refreshing presence flow over us now! Jesus, our true husband, will never fail!

Lesson 8
Ought Not This Woman

I. Scriptures Revealing Jesus' Ministry To Women

    A. Luke 13:10-17

"¹⁰And he was teaching in one of the synagogues on the sabbath. ¹¹And, behold, there was a woman which had a spirit of infirmity eighteen years, and was bowed together, and could in no wise lift up herself. ¹²And when Jesus saw her, he called her to him, and said unto her, Woman, thou art loosed from thine infirmity. ¹³And he laid his hands on her: and immediately she was made straight, and glorified God. ¹⁴And the ruler of the synagogue answered with indignation, because that Jesus had healed on the sabbath day, and said unto the people, There are six days in which men ought to work: in them therefore come and be healed, and not on the sabbath day. ¹⁵The Lord then answered him, and said, Thou hypocrite, doth not each one of you on the sabbath loose his ox or his ass from the stall, and lead him away to watering? ¹⁶And ought not this woman, being a daughter of Abraham, whom Satan hath bound, lo, these eighteen years, be loosed from this bond on the sabbath day? ¹⁷And when he had said these things, all his adversaries were ashamed: and all the people rejoiced for all the glorious things that were done by him."

        1. Eighteen is the number in Scripture for bondage
        2. She had a spirit of infirmity and was bowed over
        3. Jesus called her to Him which was not allowed by the Rabbis.
        4. Jesus looses her; Rabbis didn't even teach women
        5. The ruler of the synagogue is furious and uses the Sabbath for an excuse
        6. Jesus calls him a hypocrite
        7. By Jesus giving the example of loosing his ox on the Sabbath showed that the Pharisees cared more for animals than this woman.

        8. Other translations of *"ought not his woman..."*:

            "So why isn't it right for me to untie this daughter of Abraham and lead her from the stall where Satan has had her?"
            "Shouldn't she be freed?"
            "Surely it is not wrong for her to be freed"
            "Isn't it right to free her on the day of worship?"
            "Shouldn't she be untied?"

        9. She was a daughter of Abraham
       10. His adversaries are ashamed and the common people rejoice!

    B. Mark 5:25-34 – *"²⁵And a certain woman, which had an issue of blood twelve years, ²⁶And had suffered many things of many physicians, and had spent all that she had, and was nothing bettered, but rather grew worse, ²⁷When she had heard of Jesus, came in the press behind, and touched his garment. ²⁸For she said, If I may touch but his clothes, I shall be whole. ²⁹And straightway the fountain of her blood was dried up; and she felt in her body that she was healed of that plague. ³⁰And Jesus, immediately knowing in himself that virtue had gone out of him, turned him about in the press, and said, Who touched my clothes? ³¹And his disciples said unto him, Thou seest the multitude thronging thee, and sayest thou, Who touched me? ³²And he looked round about to see her that had done this thing. ³³But the woman fearing and trembling, knowing what was done in her, came and fell down before him, and told him all the truth. ³⁴And he said unto her, Daughter, thy faith hath made thee whole; go in peace, and be whole of thy plague."*

        1. Normally her disease would exclude her from all religious rituals.
        2. She was unclean and a defiled person according to the law.

3.   Jesus called her daughter
4.   Notice she fell down before Him worshipping Him
5.   Jesus healed this woman!

C.   Luke 18:1-8 – "*¹And he spake a parable unto them to this end, that men ought always to pray, and not to faint; ²Saying, There was in a city a judge, which feared not God, neither regarded man: ³And there was a widow in that city; and she came unto him, saying, Avenge me of mine adversary. ⁴And he would not for a while: but afterward he said within himself, Though I fear not God, nor regard man; ⁵Yet because this widow troubleth me, I will avenge her, lest by her continual coming she weary me. ⁶And the Lord said, Hear what the unjust judge saith. ⁷And shall not God avenge his own elect, which cry day and night unto him, though he bear long with them? ⁸I tell you that he will avenge them speedily. Nevertheless when the Son of man cometh, shall he find faith on the earth?*"

1.   This whole parable was teaching men to always pray
2.   A woman is asking for justice from a worldly judge
3.   The judge initially refuses her, but she would not let him alone; like a woman, she would not let go until justice was given.
4.   She had great faith
5.   Verse 7 says God will avenge His elect (which included women)

D.   Luke 7:11-15 – "*¹¹And it came to pass the day after, that he went into a city called Nain; and many of his disciples went with him, and much people. ¹²Now when he came nigh to the gate of the city, behold, there was a dead man carried out, the only son of his mother, and she was a widow: and much people of the city was with her. ¹³And when the Lord saw her, he had compassion on her, and said unto her, Weep not. ¹⁴And he came and touched the bier: and they that bare him stood still. And he said, Young man, I say unto thee, Arise. ¹⁵And he that was dead sat up, and began to speak. And he delivered him to his mother.*"

1.   Jews were not to touch a dead body
2.   Nain in Greek means – afflicted, beautiful
3.   Jesus had compassion and healed her son
4.   He delivers him back to his mother

E.   Luke 21:1-4 – "*¹And he looked up, and saw the rich men casting their gifts into the treasury. ²And he saw also a certain poor widow casting in thither two mites. ³And he said, Of a truth I say unto you, that this poor widow hath cast in more than they all: ⁴For all these have of their abundance cast in unto the offerings of God: but she of her penury hath cast in all the living that she had.*"

1.   In the temple there was a separate court for women, Gentiles, and priests and Jews
2.   Jesus obviously was in the court of the women
3.   He says this poor widow because of her penury cast in more; other translations of verse 4:

"*She has contributed out of her lack and her want*"
"*She out of her poverty put in all she had to live on*"
"*For they have given a tiny part of their surplus, but she, poor as she is, has given everything she has*"
"*She gave extravagantly what she couldn't afford, she gave her all*"
"*But she, even out of her need, has put in all her living*"

4.   He compares her to those who gave out of their abundance

F.   Mark 1:29-31 – "*²⁹And forthwith, when they were come out of the synagogue, they entered into the house of Simon and Andrew, with James and John. ³⁰But Simon's wife's mother lay sick of a fever, and anon they tell him of her. ³¹And he came and took her by the hand, and lifted her up; and immediately the fever left her, and she ministered unto them.*"

1. This was not allowed by the Jews
　　　2. It was not proper to touch any woman by the hand except your wife
　　　3. She also was not allowed to serve Him

G. Matthew 15:22-28 – "*22And, behold, a woman of Canaan came out of the same coasts, and cried unto him, saying, Have mercy on me, O Lord, thou Son of David; my daughter is grievously vexed with a devil. 23But he answered her not a word. And his disciples came and besought him, saying, Send her away; for she crieth after us. 24But he answered and said, I am not sent but unto the lost sheep of the house of Israel. 25Then came she and worshipped him, saying, Lord, help me. 26But he answered and said, It is not meet to take the children's bread, and to cast it to dogs. 27And she said, Truth, Lord: yet the dogs eat of the crumbs which fall from their masters' table. 28Then Jesus answered and said unto her, O woman, great is thy faith: be it unto thee even as thou wilt. And her daughter was made whole from that very hour.*"

　　　1. She was a Gentile and they were considered dogs
　　　2. Jesus was not to speak to her at all
　　　3. She overcame all this by faith
　　　4. This pointed to the fact that the Gentiles would ultimately be included
　　　5. Canaan means – low, humble, to be subdued, to be brought low, a servant
　　　6. She acknowledged Him as the Messiah (verse 22)
　　　7. Three times Jesus rejects her
　　　8. He says His people are the children, she is a dog (verse 26)
　　　9. Jesus commends her for her great faith

H. Luke 10:38-42 – "*38Now it came to pass, as they went, that he entered into a certain village: and a certain woman named Martha received him into her house. 39And she had a sister called Mary, which also sat at Jesus' feet, and heard his word. 40But Martha was cumbered about much serving, and came to him, and said, Lord, dost thou not care that my sister hath left me to serve alone? bid her therefore that she help me. 41And Jesus answered and said unto her, Martha, Martha, thou art careful and troubled about many things: 42But one thing is needful: and Mary hath chosen that good part, which shall not be taken away from her.*"

　　　1. Women were not supposed to learn
　　　2. Rabbis thought them incapable of learning
　　　3. The Jews saw women as simply slaves
　　　4. They were also not to serve Him
　　　5. Jesus helps both of these sisters

I. John 8:1-11

"*1Jesus went unto the mount of Olives. 2And early in the morning he came again into the temple, and all the people came unto him; and he sat down, and taught them. 3And the scribes and Pharisees brought unto him a woman taken in adultery; and when they had set her in the midst, 4They say unto him, Master, this woman was taken in adultery, in the very act. 5Now Moses in the law commanded us, that such should be stoned: but what sayest thou? 6This they said, tempting him, that they might have to accuse him. But Jesus stooped down, and with his finger wrote on the ground, as though he heard them not. 7So when they continued asking him, he lifted up himself, and said unto them, He that is without sin among you, let him first cast a stone at her. 8And again he stooped down, and wrote on the ground. 9And they which heard it, being convicted by their own conscience, went out one by one, beginning at the eldest, even unto the last: and Jesus was left alone, and the woman standing in the midst. 10When Jesus had lifted up himself, and saw none but the woman, he said unto her, Woman, where are those thine accusers? hath no man condemned thee? 11She said, No man, Lord. And Jesus said unto her, Neither do I condemn thee: go, and sin no more.*"

　　　1. By the Law, both the man and the woman should have been stoned
　　　2. Notice their hypocrisy by not bringing the man

3. If Jesus had not been there she would have been stoned
4. Grace and mercy came by Jesus (John 1:14-17)
5. Jesus by the Holy Ghost revealed their own sins
6. He doesn't condemn her and she leaves saved (verse 11)

J.   John 4:4-40

"*4And he must needs go through Samaria. 5Then cometh he to a city of Samaria, which is called Sychar, near to the parcel of ground that Jacob gave to his son Joseph. 6Now Jacob's well was there. Jesus therefore, being wearied with his journey, sat thus on the well: and it was about the sixth hour. 7There cometh a woman of Samaria to draw water: Jesus saith unto her, Give me to drink. 8(For his disciples were gone away unto the city to buy meat.) 9Then saith the woman of Samaria unto him, How is it that thou, being a Jew, askest drink of me, which am a woman of Samaria? for the Jews have no dealings with the Samaritans. 10Jesus answered and said unto her, If thou knewest the gift of God, and who it is that saith to thee, Give me to drink; thou wouldest have asked of him, and he would have given thee living water. 11The woman saith unto him, Sir, thou hast nothing to draw with, and the well is deep: from whence then hast thou that living water? 12Art thou greater than our father Jacob, which gave us the well, and drank thereof himself, and his children, and his cattle? 13Jesus answered and said unto her, Whosoever drinketh of this water shall thirst again: 14But whosoever drinketh of the water that I shall give him shall never thirst; but the water that I shall give him shall be in him a well of water springing up into everlasting life. 15The woman saith unto him, Sir, give me this water, that I thirst not, neither come hither to draw. 16Jesus saith unto her, Go, call thy husband, and come hither. 17The woman answered and said, I have no husband. Jesus said unto her, Thou hast well said, I have no husband: 18For thou hast had five husbands; and he whom thou now hast is not thy husband: in that saidst thou truly. 19The woman saith unto him, Sir, I perceive that thou art a prophet... 25The woman saith unto him, I know that Messias cometh, which is called Christ: when he is come, he will tell us all things. 26Jesus saith unto her, I that speak unto thee am he. 27And upon this came his disciples, and marvelled that he talked with the woman: yet no man said, What seekest thou? or, Why talkest thou with her? 28The woman then left her waterpot, and went her way into the city, and saith to the men, 29Come, see a man, which told me all things that ever I did: is not this the Christ? 30Then they went out of the city, and came unto him. 31In the mean while his disciples prayed him, saying, Master, eat. 32But he said unto them, I have meat to eat that ye know not of. 33Therefore said the disciples one to another, Hath any man brought him ought to eat? 34Jesus saith unto them, My meat is to do the will of him that sent me, and to finish his work. 35Say not ye, There are yet four months, and then cometh harvest? behold, I say unto you, Lift up your eyes, and look on the fields; for they are white already to harvest. 36And he that reapeth receiveth wages, and gathereth fruit unto life eternal: that both he that soweth and he that reapeth may rejoice together. 37And herein is that saying true, One soweth, and another reapeth. 38I sent you to reap that whereon ye bestowed no labour: other men laboured, and ye are entered into their labours. 39And many of the Samaritans of that city believed on him for the saying of the woman, which testified, He told me all that ever I did. 40So when the Samaritans were come unto him, they besought him that he would tarry with them: and he abode there two days."*

1. Jews had no dealing with Samaritans
2. Rabbis were not to be speaking to a woman in public
3. Woman were not allowed to be taught
4. She was also an unclean woman of ill repute
5. The woman gets saved (verse 29) and leads many to Jesus as an evangelist (verse 39)
6. The disciples were amazed that Jesus even talked with her (verse 27)
7. Samaria means – a place of watching, guardianship
8. Sychar means – drunken
9. He shouldn't have asked her to give Him a drink
10. This woman preached to men (verse 28)
11. Jesus also stayed two days with the Samaritans, which by Law He shouldn't have done.

Lesson 9
Let Her Alone

This lesson is taken from Mark 14. We've so far seen that the Bible translators were biased, the Jewish people subjugated their women, women were considered inferior, women were dominated, and were spoken of in the most horrible and unclean ways, even by Rabbis. And yet, in spite of all of this, Jesus comes and everything changes. Wherever Jesus comes, it upsets the apple cart of what has been before it. I am going to say that again. Anytime Jesus walks in a place, anything that has been going on before that is going to be changed. The Israelites were living in the tradition of the elders, not in the Word of God. They elevated the tradition, the Talmud, and considered it as holy as the Word of God. Where that came from is nonsense. It is obviously a manmade tradition.

One of the things we found in the book of Genesis is that man has an inherent weakness in him. When God created Eve for him, it was not to be the help mate we've been told. On the contrary, something had happened in Adam, because the word help-meet means someone that is very strong that will help you in a crisis situation and help you to return and protect. It does not mean a house wife doing the cooking and the washing of the clothes. God brought Eve to Adam because God said it was not good that man be alone. The word alone means separated. Adam had separated himself from God already. Adam had the right to eat of the tree of life, but did not do it. Why? There had to be a reason because if you eat of the tree of life, you remain in that condition forever. He did not choose to do that.

While the serpent was talking with Eve, Adam did not say a word, never trying to come against the serpent. Adam wanted Eve to take of the fruit because he wanted it himself and he wanted the blame to go on her. Adam ended up blaming Eve and God, whereas Eve just blamed the serpent. When she did that, God said she has now become the enemy of satan and satan hates women. The sorrow is not in birthing children, but from the fact that mankind that will come forth out of her womb will be born into sin. When it says that her desire shall be toward her husband, it doesn't mean something sexual, but it means that if her desire is toward her husband, he will rule over her. God is warning her here. He didn't tell Eve to leave the garden; He commanded the man to leave the garden. Eve, in a sense, had become the first believer. So when her desire went toward her husband, she was turning from God to Adam. But Eve is like most women. Two of their greatest assets can be their greatest hindrances; their faithfulness and their sensitivity. The woman's faithfulness became the thing that caused her to walk out of the garden and then turn to Adam instead of the Lord. And since that moment men have been subjugating, ruling, dominating, and controlling women throughout history.

But when Jesus came to the earth, He was different. He talked to a woman sitting at the well, which was not allowed. He let a woman touch Him which was not allowed. Everything He did you will find that there were women around Him constantly. Actually there were more women than men. And so Jesus upset the apple cart of religion. Everything we believe needs to be founded upon the Word of God and not tradition. We need to be like those noble Bereans who searched the Scriptures daily whether those things were so (Acts 17:11). At some point, even Jesus got tired of the attitude of men towards women, especially the religious hierarchy.

Now, let's read Mark 14, "*¹After two days was the feast of the passover, and of unleavened bread: and the chief priests and the scribes sought how they might take him by craft, and put him to death. ²But they said, Not on the feast day, lest there be an uproar of the people. ³And being in Bethany in the house of Simon the leper, as he sat at meat, there came a woman having an alabaster box of ointment of spikenard very precious; and she brake the box, and poured it on his head. ⁴And there were some that had indignation within themselves, and said, Why was this waste of the ointment made? ⁵For it might have been sold for more than three hundred pence, and have been given to the poor. And they murmured against her.*" Religious Pharisees and religious people strain at gnats and swallow camels. Why would anybody be indignant over Jesus receiving worship, especially the kind of worship typified here. She gave the most precious thing she had and anointed the Lord Jesus with it, all the while having the revelation of what was about to happen. None of the other disciples had the revelation before or even after Jesus' death, because in Luke 24 we find that when the sisters came and told the disciples that Jesus is risen, they didn't believe it and said they were speaking idle tales.

It even took Jesus appearing in the midst of them for them understand and believe what Jesus did, and these men walked with Jesus for 3 ½ years, all the time. This says to me that you can be with Jesus, around Jesus, in the presence of Jesus, hearing His Word, seeing His miracles, and yet be unchanged. It is like a rock that has been sitting in a river for thousands of years, but when you pull it out and break it open, inside the rock is dry as dust and the water had never penetrated it. In far too many churches there will be those like the disciples that did not prepare themselves that will say to Jesus, "we have eaten and drunk in your presence," but the Lord will say, "depart from me, I never knew you." Yes, we can be in His presence, hear His Word, be in glorious meetings, but only Jesus knows the condition of everyone's heart and who is really being changed by it. The condition of our heart is so much more important than how loud we shout, how much we dance, prophesy, etc. These things are necessary and important, but what God is after is our heart. Here in this story, these people are murmuring against this woman.

Before I continue, I want to mention to you that in this story, like all the other situations throughout the New Testament with Jesus interacting with women, Jesus always was against the rules. People around Jesus many times never said anything, but they were probably angry with Him all the time. This wasn't supposed to happen, especially a woman coming into a place where she wasn't welcome and taking the most precious thing to her and giving it to Jesus. It was costly. People always criticize that which they are not willing to do themselves. They murmur against other people to hide the fact that they don't have the same kind of passion, or they are in darkness.

So once these men began to murmur against the woman, "*6Jesus said, Let her alone...*" I don't believe Jesus said this quietly and in passing. I think Jesus had had enough and said directly to the brothers, "Let her alone!" Psalms 68:11 tells us clearly that "*The Lord gave the word: and great was the company of women that published it*" (Amplified). In these last days, women are going to be used mightily by God, but there is a spirit in men, particularly in leadership, that is similar to Nabal in the Bible, who are fools over the household of God. Solomon says, "*I have seen servants upon horses, and princes walking as servants upon the earth*" (Ecclesiastes 10:7). There are too many princes or princesses who should be on top of horses, in places of leadership, who are not because of some denominational creed, some manmade doctrine or thinking (even though they think it is the Bible). Many of these beliefs really came out of a distorted tradition that dates back to the early Roman Catholic Church. You and I have the original Hebrew and Greek to find these things out. I don't want my faith resting in the wisdom of men. I don't want my revelation to be that of another man's. I want my own, right from the Word of God.

"*6And Jesus said, Let her alone why trouble ye her? she hath wrought a good work on me. 7For ye have the poor with you always, and whensoever ye will ye may do them good: but me ye have not always.*" Religious people always seem to want to talk about the poor or about something to do or something we should be doing. This is just like Martha in Luke 10:38-42 where it says, "*...Martha was cumbered about much serving, and came to him, and said, Lord, dost thou not care that my sister hath left me to serve alone? bid her therefore that she help me.*" She is trying to get Jesus to tell Mary to stop sitting under the Word of God and to start doing something. I have been criticized a lot in my ministry that I am not doing this or not doing that, but Jesus answered Martha and "*...said unto her, Martha, Martha, thou art careful and troubled about many things: But one thing is needful: and Mary hath chosen that good part, which shall not be taken away from her.*"

Marthas always end up getting weary, cumbered about with much serving, coming back from the mission field worn out and beaten up, and ending up being a non-factor in the Kingdom of God. We are to only go when Jesus says go. But sitting at Jesus' feet is supposed to be a continual thing. There should not be a time in our life when we are not sitting at Jesus' feet, hearing His Word and worshipping Him intimately. We will then hear a Word from God to go out and do a job and when we are done, we come back, right there at His feet again until another Word comes. For a true disciple, this is forever. We are not to have the mentality that we only need a few years of Bible school in the beginning and then we are fine. We are to be students of the Word for the rest of our lives. The sad thing is, most people are just happy with having one meeting Wednesday night and one meeting Sunday morning. The thing we have to realize is that when we come to Jesus, it is no longer our life. The carnal (soulish) man cannot receive the things of the Spirit of God, neither can he know them. He that loves his life in this world (life meaning soulish life) shall lose it, but he that hates his soulish life in this world shall find it. Stop trying to find yourself and find Jesus. That is all you need to do.

"Let her alone." How many times have you been sitting in a meeting and some man is put there preaching and there is no anointing? Meanwhile you know there is a sister in the front row, who you get most of your spiritual substance from, who has the Word of the Lord! This is kind of like what Elijah did when he stopped by the widow woman's house. He had an apartment there where he could spend time there, get filled up, and go back out and minister. The woman that is more qualified to minister is not allowed to because of tradition and a misinterpretation of the Scriptures. Half the body of Christ has been in bondage. Brothers just can't get the job done. Adam already had turned from the Lord before Eve was created. Eve was created to restore Adam. That is the revelation and the truth that has been hidden by satan and religion to keep man in positions of authority. Women are far stronger than men. Men are beastial and weak. Men have a hard time hearing this, but that is just because they have insecurities and don't know who they are. I personally have no problem with strong women. Actually, I love them because they are the best workers and they can multi-task more than anything you know. As we joked the other night, women can have a baby on one arm, they can cook the bacon with the other arm, and the phone in one of their ears counseling somebody; and all men can barely do is rock on their recliner and push the remote.

"Let her alone why trouble ye her? she hath wrought a good work on me. 7For ye have the poor with you always, and whensoever ye will ye may do them good: but me ye have not always." People don't recognize it is an absolutely glorious thing that the manifest presence of God comes to you. Everything else fades into oblivion, even things like feeding the poor, clothing the naked. Moses fasted 80 days in the presence of God and you didn't hear him complaining. It is just religion. They are all about works and have no revelation of grace. Like Martha they are distracted with cares, even sincere good things like feeding the poor. Which is greater, feeding the poor or giving a costly sacrifice to Jesus? This is Jesus' answer in verses 8-9, "She hath done what she could: she is come aforehand to anoint my body to the burying. 9Verily I say unto you, Wheresoever this gospel shall be preached throughout the whole world, this also that she hath done shall be spoken of for a memorial of her." This woman had a revelation of Jesus' death and resurrection while the others did not.

Here are some other translations to verses 6-8: "Let her alone, why are you troubling her...she hath done a good and beautiful praiseworthy and noble thing to me", "Leave her alone, and why criticize her for doing such a good thing to me", "Let her alone, why are you giving her a hard time?...she's just done something wonderfully significant to me." The disciples didn't recognize the wonder and significance of what she was doing. Another reads, "She did what she could, when she could." Maybe she was saving up for years, who knows. All we know is that it was expensive and costly what she gave, and she did it when she could. Have you ever thought about saving your money and instead of buying yourself something, save up as much as you can so you can give a tremendous offering to the Lord? We don't think that way. We think people like that are fanatics, but I like what one brother said years ago, "A fanatic is someone who loves Jesus more than you".

Other translations also include, "Let her be, why are you bothering her? What she could do she did do", "The woman did the only thing she could do for me." Maybe some of us don't have good voices, we don't play instruments, and we don't have a lot of money, but we can sure love Jesus and prove it with our daily life. If you or I don't have anything else, we can sure prove our love for Jesus by loving our brothers and sisters. This woman did what she could, when she could. "Let her alone, why berate her for doing a good thing?", "Let her alone, why do you molest her? That which she had, she used." "Why are you annoying her?", "Why do you embarrass her?" In another account Jesus says, "And he turned to the woman, and said unto Simon, Seest thou this woman? I entered into thine house, thou gavest me no water for my feet: but she hath washed my feet with tears, and wiped them with the hairs of her head. Thou gavest me no kiss: but this woman since the time I came in hath not ceased to kiss my feet." (Luke 7:44-45). Men take it for granted. When you love somebody, you don't take it for granted that they know it. You tell them. You live the life for them. Many people can tell Jesus they love Him, but they don't ever really show it to Him by the way they live their lives.

"That which she had, she used." God only requires you use what you have. If you don't have a lot of money in your life right now, there is still a lot of other things you can do for the Kingdom of God.

Let me tell you a little story. Recently, some friends of mine told me that a person they knew went to a very large charismatic meeting with another woman. The first woman was not filled with the Holy Ghost and her friend was. The first person did something during the meeting; the man of God leading the meeting didn't like it very much. She did it innocently with no malice or forethought. What happened was this. The woman friend was up front getting prayed for; she apparently got slain in the Spirit and was laying on the ground. The first woman, because she had never seen anything like this before, ran down to the front because she thought her friend had fainted and tried to help her. Well the "man of God" didn't like this and began to berate her in front of everyone; it embarrassed her so badly she got up and began to walk out. Even after she was trying to leave, he wouldn't leave her alone. He yelled at her and said bad things to her all the way while she walked out. Where were the other men in the place? Somebody should have spoken up and helped this poor woman and spoken to this "man of God." The way this man of God acted is not the Spirit of God. Have you ever seen Jesus act like this, arrogant, haughty, full of pride, and having a know-it-all attitude? Never! Women have been embarrassed, ridiculed, put down, but sisters, hear the Word of the Lord. Jesus is stepping into the situation and He is telling all these men, "Leave her alone!"

In the last days, God is putting a stop to this. Even during Jesus' first coming 2000 years ago, so much of His ministry loosed women. What do you think is going to happen during Jesus' second coming? It is not going to be easy for men with ambition. They will have to have their ego checked and dealt with when women truly come forth with superior ministries. Men should rejoice when they see the anointing of God upon a woman. If a woman is a better preacher, sit down and be quiet, and let her go. You may just learn something. In the last days, Joel says, "*your sons and your daughters shall prophesy*" (Joel 2:28). God is saying this will surely happen.

Look at Song of Solomon 5 when religious leaders began tormenting this woman in the story. It is time to leave her alone. In this account in Song of Solomon, Jesus has come into His garden, that is, His bride's heart, and He wants to spend time with her. But she is asleep and has put off her coat and shoes; she really does not respond to Him at first. She finally gets up in verses 5, "*I rose up to open to my beloved; and my hands dropped with myrrh, and my fingers with sweet smelling myrrh, upon the handles of the lock. I opened to my beloved; but my beloved had withdrawn himself, and was gone: my soul failed when he spake: I sought him, but I could not find him; I called him, but he gave me no answer.*" She was too late.

The beautiful thing about this story is even when you don't respond to Him, the Lord will use that to draw you and get you to run after Him. Jesus uses everything for His glory. So this bride, even though she was a little lazy and didn't want to get up at first, she got up and went after Him. Watch what happens in verse 7, "*The watchmen that went about the city found me, they smote me, they wounded me; the keepers of the walls took away my veil from me.*" The watchmen always represent, in Scripture, leadership and look at what they did. She then says in verse 8, "*I charge you, O daughters of Jerusalem, if ye find my beloved, that ye tell him, that I am sick of love.*" They respond by saying in verse 9, "*What is thy beloved more than another beloved, O thou fairest among women? what is thy beloved more than another beloved, that thou dost so charge us?*" One good thing about this story is that even thou these men ridicule her, beat her, and wound her, she keeps on going. Don't be discouraged sisters if it doesn't seem like it is happening now. If you have a call of God on your life and God is anointing you, He will do it. Men do not have charge over the call of God.

Another translation reads, "*They slapped and beat and bruised me, ripping off my clothes.*" This means they made her naked and exposed her. How many woman have a call of God upon their lives and are passionately running after the Lord, only to be told they are ambitious and are put down? Another thing to be mentioned is they slapped and beat and bruised her. We all know the stories of abuse in households, and how women that are abused many times end up staying there and egetting killed by the man they should have left years ago. This is another trait of womankind, their loyalty and faithfulness (even when the jerk she is married to is as disloyal, dishonest, and as rotten as he can be, and takes delight in saying ugly things to her or talking behind her back or exposing her and uncovering her). The word of the Lord is, "Let her alone!" Every idle word that is spoken, God hears and will judge and everyone will be accountable for all things that they say.

Then she is asked, "*What is thy beloved more than another beloved?*" Two other translations state, "*What is so great about your lover?*", "*What's there so wonderful about Him that you would charge us and ask where He is?*" She begins in verses 10-16 explaining what Jesus means to her and it puts them to shame. How many times have we heard of stories even around where we live, of people being told in church they can't play their tambourine, or they are shouting too loud and they need to turn it down a little bit. We've moved into an atmosphere in many places that our churches are like businesses. We want to succeed by getting as many people in as we possibly can by not offending anybody. But all Jesus ever did His whole life, without a spirit of trying to, was offend people daily.

For the leadership even to ask, "*What is your beloved more than another beloved?*" reveals where they are coming from and where their heart is at. How many times have we heard preachers talk about intimacy with God but we never see them worship? You never see many in leadership break down weeping in the presence of God. You never see them fall on their face in the glory. You don't see them dance when the church is dancing. But rather, you see them standing stiff and not doing anything. You see, we are like little children and we receive more by what somebody doesn't do than what they do. So we are watching our leadership, watching our watchmen. If your leader doesn't worship, without his saying anything, your conscious tells you it's okay not to worship. You may feel you don't have to shout or dance and that it is just for the radical ones. However, leadership should be the first to get on their face and worship.

So what do we do when we are not really on fire for the lord, or we don't have passion for Jesus or His Word? When we get around people that do, the only thing we can do is judge and criticize and murmur about them so we appear spiritual. If you ever catch an elder beating on a woman, this is what you need to say, "Leave her alone" – even if she messes up. The new thing over the years in many charismatic churches is nobody is allowed to prophesy in the congregation during the meetings. If you want to prophesy, you have to write it down, and take it to one of the elders. They read it and pass it along to the pastor who reads it to finally decide if it is okay. This doesn't even make sense.

The Bible says, "*Thy people shall be <u>willing</u>* (Hebrew – <u>spontaneous</u>) *in the day of thy power*" (Psalms 110:3). Prophecy is a spontaneous utterance and means a "bubbling up". Why would leadership not want people to prophesy? Proverbs 14:4 states, "*Where no oxen are, the crib is clean: but much increase is by the strength of the ox.*" We can have a nice clean crib where nobody ever plays a tambourine, nobody ever shouts, dances, prophesies, or outright abandons themselves in worship, but nobody grows in this situation and there is no increase. My greatest desire is to abandon myself to the Lord every time I meet with Him. And if anybody tries to stop me from being with Jesus, I will say, "Leave me alone!" Amen! If sheep see me abandoning myself as a leader, then they will see and understand how someone is to respond to God. The leader ought to be prophesying and encouraging the people to do so, and giving them time to do it. If they do not allow the people to be free to prophesy and worship, they are in error. Why do churches that do not allow prophesying and liberty in the Holy Ghost always seem to overflow with people? Also, why is it that the places where there is liberty in worship and liberty to prophesy seem to be struggling in numbers and size? Jeremiah explains in Jeremiah 5:31, "*The prophets prophesy falsely, and the priests bear rule by their means; and my people love to have it so.*" There is something in all of us that loves to be manipulated and controlled. Not me!

As we are looking at men trying to hinder women of God, let us look now at Lamentations chapter 5, "*1Remember, O LORD, what is come upon us: consider, and behold our reproach. 2Our inheritance is turned to strangers, our houses to aliens...11They ravished the women in Zion, and the maids in the cities of Judah.*" Other translations of verse 11 are as follows, "*The enemy abused the women of Jerusalem and the girls in the cities of Judah*", "*They took by force the women in Zion the virgins in the houses of Judah*", "*They'll press the women in Zion*", "*Our wives have been raped in mount Zion itself and in every Judean village our daughters have been forced to submit*". Judah means praise. Psalms 137:1-4 says, "*1By the rivers of Babylon, there we sat down, yea, we wept, when we remembered Zion. 2We hanged our harps upon the willows in the midst thereof. 3For there they that carried us away captive required of us a song; and they that wasted us required of us mirth, saying, Sing us one of the songs of Zion. 4How shall we sing the LORD's song in a strange land?*"

The people of God were in Babylonian captivity. Zion is not just a physical mountain, but to us, it is the place where God is enthroned in the hearts of His people in worship. What was happening was the women in Zion were being abused. How many times has a sister, while worshipping the Lord or just caught up in the glory, been shut down and stopped? God likens it to rape and abuse. Women have been forced to submit. I will deal with headship and submission later. But in my 33 years of pastoring now, I have seen horrible incidences where men have tried to make women submit to them and the women, because they have been taught and engrained in their thinking to submit to anything a man wants to do, ended up becoming like their husband and losing out with God. I've seen this hundreds of times. Sisters, I'm telling you this, wives submit yourselves to your husbands, in the Lord. Whenever a man tries to make you do something that is not in the Lord, you don't have to do it. Peter says we ought to obey God rather than men. Paul himself told us to respect authority, and then said woe is me if I preach not the gospel. When somebody asks you to do anything that violates your conscious, don't do it. Why are we supposed to submit to people that don't even have a walk with God? Here's a woman that goes to church 15 times a week, reads her Bible, prays in the Holy Ghost, worships intimately, but she has to submit herself to somebody that hardly even has a walk with God, doesn't have any passion for Jesus, and he is supposed to know better what to do. That is why God said to Eve in Genesis 3:16, "*...thy desire shall be to thy husband, and he shall rule over thee*", meaning Eve, if you turn away from me and turn towards your husband, he is going to rule over you. God was trying to warn Eve, don't leave the garden, stay here! Nothing should ever make you turn your back on Jesus, nothing. Anybody that tries to tell you that something is more important than Jesus, His Word, His presence, and His Kingdom, the devil is speaking through them to you. I don't care how sincere they are or anything like that.

Notice I Peter 3:7 which says, "*Likewise, ye husbands, dwell with them according to knowledge, giving honour unto the wife, as unto the weaker vessel* (weaker only in the physical realm)*, and as being heirs together of the grace of life; that your prayers be not hindered.*" In too many households, husbands who are in sin, not in the Lord, are ruling over women who love Jesus and are called. At some point, the moment the former and latter rain come together and all the glory of God comes down, He says in Joel 2:28, "*your sons and your daughters shall prophesy.*" When the glory falls, it will be all over. Jesus will be saying through the anointing of women, "let her alone." John 8:36, "*If the Son therefore shall make you free, ye shall be free indeed.*" God has not called us to bondage but unto liberty. Where the Spirit is Lord, there is liberty, freedom for everybody to move and act. As it says in I Corinthians 14:31, "*For ye may all prophesy one by one, that all may learn, and all may be comforted.*"

Later on in I Corinthians 14 Paul goes on to say, "*Let your women keep silence in the churches: for it is not permitted unto them to speak; but they are commanded to be under obedience, as also saith the law* (this is not talking about the law from the Bible but the oral law or the traditions of the elders). *35And if they will learn any thing, let them ask their husbands at home: for it is a shame for women to speak in the church.*" There is no Scripture in the Old Testament where women are told to be silent in meetings. It was a tradition of the elders passed down from the Babylonish Talmud. It is disgusting what is written in the Talmud, as I brought out in another chapter. We learn from our fathers, from our authority figures, or from people we respect, are intelligent, or who we think have it all together, and subconsciously we believe what they say and act them out. Women who have to be subjected, dominated, and controlled, eventually just bow and believe this is the way it is supposed to be. That is why Isaiah 32:9 says, "*Rise up, ye women that are at ease.*" Women have been lulled to sleep because of a false teaching. Don't you ever let anybody cause your faith in God to be diminished. Don't you ever let anybody stop you from being free in your worship. Stop letting other people dictate to you who you are. When I walk into a meeting, I am not looking for someone else to get me going. I'm already going before I ever get there. Amen!

Now we know there is a big difference between some women and other women with controlling devils. Ecclesiastes 7:26 says, "*more bitter than death the woman, whose heart is snares and nets, and her hands as bands...*" There is a spirit which does more harm to women in ministry, which is controlling women who are pushy, don't have a submissive spirit, aren't submitted to anybody, and they run their mouths without thinking. Is it any wonder all religious men, when they see a women with this spirit, justify why they don't allow women to minister? One woman with this type of spirit seems to ruin it for all women. But the bride is not like that. Read Proverbs 31, "*The heart of her husband doth safely trust in her*" (verse 11), "*She will do him good and not evil all the days of her life*" (verse 12).

Let us now look at a story in II Samuel 13. In case you didn't know, David had many wives and he had a son by one of those wives whose name was Amnon. Amnon fell in love with Absalom's (another one of his half-brothers) sister (Tamar) and Amnon got so love sick that his servant said to him, "What's wrong with you, why are you acting so different?" Amnon responded by saying, "because I am so in love with Tamar." The servant then said, just like the devil whispering in his hear, "Go to your father king David, and say you're not well and could Tamar come and cook for me and make some cakes for me?" So David agrees and sends Tamar. Obediently she comes over to minister to Amnon. While she is there, Amnon wants her to feed him herself. Then when she gets close to him, he grabs her and rapes her. She pleads with him not to do it, but he does. You see, Tamar wore a coat of many colors. This is just like Joseph in the book of Genesis. This coat is a symbol of the bride, the sons of God, or someone who is special to God. And this man violated her. As soon as he is finished (and she is broken-hearted and weeping), he says get out. The Bible says, "*Then Amnon hated her exceedingly; so that the hatred wherewith he hated her was greater than the love wherewith he had loved her. And Amnon said unto her, Arise, be gone.*" (verse 15). Amnon wasn't loving, he was lusting. When he had finished with her, he literally just threw her out and locked the door. Now she is no longer a virgin. She's destroyed for the rest of her life. She can't marry because of this. The callousness and lack of concern from Amnon is unbelievable. How many men do this to women? They get what they want and then they dump them, not caring anything about her. A man in crisis thinks of himself, whereas a woman in crisis thinks about her household and her children. He just threw her out. Absalom's life job then is to kill Amnon, which he does. Then this destroys his own life and affects David's life. All because of one man's lust that he couldn't control and some servant, like satan, whispering into his ear and telling him to use trickery to get it done. This happens in the natural but also in the realm of the spirit. And God is saying, "Let her alone!"

The next story I want to look at is in I Samuel 1. The story goes like this. Elkanah had two wives, one named Hannah, and the other named Peninnah. Hannah means "grace, mercy, graciousness, favor, gracious gift." Peninnah means "coral or a place where dead fish live." Hannah couldn't have any children, but Peninnah had a bunch of them. The Bible says that Penninah "*provoked her* (Hannah) *sore.*" Now this is another level. Song of Solomon 2:2 says, "*As the lily among thorns, so is my love among the daughters.*" What is even worse is when women participate in the persecution, subjugation, and domination of other women, being used by satan all the while thinking they are doing God a service. The word provoked literally means "to trouble, to grieve, to rage, or to be indignant against." As Hannah had to live in the same household as Peninnah, so there are many women being provoked by other women in the household of faith. Hannah had no children, and since we seem to live in an arena where big is God, Hannah is condemned. Thank God for Elkanah being a man of God (a type of Jesus) and ministering to Hannah by telling her, "*why is thy heart grieved? am not I better to thee than ten sons?*" (verse 8).

Later, Hannah goes up to the sacrifice in Shiloh, which means peace. Even in a place of peace there are the Penninahs provoking the Hannahs. Religion strains at gnats and swallows camels, making a big deal about something that means nothing in the light of eternity. And Hannah is so upset because Peninnah keeps provoking her. It says Hannah poured out her heart in bitterness of soul to the Lord. Do you know Jesus wants you to pour out your heart? Don't think He is going to get mad at you for telling the truth about what is happening to you. He actually wants you to do that so He can start the process of helping you. Why do we lie to the Lord that everything is fine when everything is not alright? So next comes Eli, the priest. He looks at her and judges her with the outward appearance. He sees her mouth moving but doesn't hear her speaking and says to her, "When are you going to stop being a drunk?" This is leadership at its finest. Here is a woman pouring out her soul in desperation and Eli is rebuking her for being a drunk. She then has to explain to him what is wrong.

This reminds me of a time two years ago when I was in Hungary ministering. During one of the nights of ministry, every person in the church came forward to be ministered to. I could tell there was something amiss with the pastors of the church. I sensed something was not right. But the people came down to be ministered to. I was ministering on being in your place in a local church, finding a true covering, and being shepherded. I will never forget this as long as I live. Of the several pastors that were there, none of them came to the front to minister to the people. They were in the back talking to each other and sharing jokes, totally unaware of what was happening in the front.

What happened was this. One young man that was in line came forward and he was weeping. When I got in front of him, he literally screamed out, "I need a father", "I need a covering." And he fell into my arms. Well, the first thing I did was look at the pastor in the back and was wanting to turn this brother over to him, thinking that the pastor would have enough sense to come over and minister to the desperate cry of this brother. All the brother wanted was a father in the Lord, a leader in his life to guide him and show him what to do. And I waited, but all I saw was them standing, talking, and laughing, not even cognizant of what was going on. It was one of the hardest things I had to deal with in my life. I ministered the best I could to them, but within two days the leadership were meeting with me telling me they wanted me to leave. Though every night the glory of God fell and the altar calls were filled with everyone in the church, the pastors met with me and told me to leave. The sad thing about the situation was that night was to be our last meeting together and I promised all the people that during the last meeting we would let the spirit of prophecy fall and minister to each one of them individually. Believe me, every single person was planning on being there. You see, the pastor let his insecurity rule him. He made a decision in the flesh and had no awareness of the presence of God at all. This is the body of Christ. This wasn't the first time I was kicked out of a place and it won't be the last. I did nothing but preach the gospel and minister to the people with love. I wept most of the time I was ministering to the people.

What is emerging in the charismatic community is there is no real touch of God in the leadership. Many people in leadership don't have an intimate walk with God. They don't know the presence of God and they don't know Word of God. The people's lives that are sitting under them, are being destroyed and nobody seems to care. If you say something about it, you are considered radical. Wasn't John the Baptist a radical, and Elijah when he said "*How long halt ye between two opinions? If the Lord be God, follow him: but if Baal, then follow him.*" (I Kings 18). Pioneers always cause trouble and upset the apple cart. That is the way it is. Consider Jesus when He entered the temple and threw over the money changers and kicked out those selling doves using a whip! I do not fear men and if I can do something about it, I will not allow religion to bind the sheep of God. A revolution has to begin within the local churches where men of God really love the Lord, love His presence, love His Word, and really love their sheep. They have to press on in! I promise you that when their disciples come forth, then they will go and do the same thing. Then their disciples will come forth and do the same thing, and so on. This is what Paul taught and did. In his days, the whole known world heard the gospel without a television, radio, or a pamphlet. Paul told Timothy, "*And the things that thou hast heard of me among many witnesses, the same commit thou to faithful men, who shall be able to teach others also.*" (II Timothy 2:2).

Lastly, I want to look at John 8. This is the height of "let her alone." When we look at this in context, in John 7, it was the feast of Tabernacles and in the last day, the great day of the feast "*Jesus stood and cried, saying, If any man thirst, let him come unto me, and drink.*" (John 7:37). The feast of Tabernacles had just finished, and the place was still filled with worshippers. Nobody had gone home yet, and it was the next day after the feast.

During this time we see how the Pharisees responded and reacted. In verse 32 of John 7, it reads, "*The Pharisees heard that the people murmured such things concerning him; and the Pharisees and the chief priests sent officers to take him.*" Later on in verses 45-49 it says, "*44And some of them would have taken him; but no man laid hands on him. 45Then came the officers to the chief priests and Pharisees; and they said unto them, Why have ye not brought him? (They were supposed to arrest Jesus) 46The officers answered, Never man spake like this man. 47Then answered them the Pharisees, Are ye also deceived? 48Have any of the rulers or of the Pharisees believed on him? 49But this people who knoweth not the law are cursed.*"

Now we move to John 8 in verse 2, "*And early in the morning he came again into the temple, and all the people came unto him; and he sat down, and taught them.*" These were the people that hadn't gone home yet from the feast of Tabernacles. The scribes and Pharisees had brought soldiers earlier and they couldn't arrest Jesus so they went to take Jesus themselves. This is how they did it, as we keep reading in John 8, "*3And the scribes and Pharisees brought unto him a woman taken in adultery; and when they had set her in the midst, 4They say unto him, Master, this woman was taken in adultery, in the very act. 5Now Moses in the law commanded us, that such should be stoned: but what sayest thou? 6This they said, tempting him, that they might have to accuse him.*"

My first question before we move on immediately is, where was the man caught in the act? According to Jewish law, men don't get punished when adultery takes place. Actually a man that is married under the Jewish oral law can have sex with any women he wants too as long as they weren't married. It wasn't considered adultery. But if a woman was caught in the act of adultery, she was stoned. Talk about injustice. But they threw the woman at Jesus' feet wanting to know what He says to the intent to trick Him that they might arrest Him. But Jesus gives us a hint of what we're supposed to do. Jesus ignored them. He acted as if He never even heard them, *"But Jesus stooped down, and with his finger wrote on the ground, as though he heard them not."* So when they continued to ask Jesus, He lifted up and said to them something profound. Up to this point in history, nobody had ever heard these types of words before. The first time I heard these words, I remember how awestruck I was at the statement itself and the truthfulness of it. *"He that is without sin among you, let him first cast a stone at her."* There is nobody on the face of the earth that has a right to throw a stone. See, Jesus knew their motivation was not godly and that it was evil. The Pharisees could have cared less about the woman and catching her in adultery. They had an agenda.

Jesus *"again he stooped down, and wrote on the ground." "⁹And they which heard it, being convicted by their own conscience, went out one by one, beginning at the eldest, even unto the last: and Jesus was left alone, and the woman standing in the midst."* I believe Jesus was writing on the ground their own secret sins. He was writing the sins of those so-called elders. After they were convicted and left, Jesus was left alone with the woman. I believe this is the way it is always supposed to be where sin is concerned; Jesus alone with the person, Jesus and the person dealing with the sin. The soldiers couldn't arrest Jesus. The elders couldn't do it. This is the power of truth. Truth wields a mighty sword. Truth can cut through religious lies and foolishness. Truth caused them to back off and get away. I remember the day in my own life in my own type of situation where Jesus spoke to me to not justify myself. Isaiah 50:8 says, *"He is near that justifieth me; who will contend with me? let us stand together: who is mine adversary?"*

Finally, *"When Jesus had lifted up himself, and saw none but the woman, he said unto her, Woman, where are those thine accusers? hath no man condemned thee?"* Men condemn, God convicts. We can never deal with sin by screaming and pointing a finger and condemning. God always says He will meet us in mercy. He is after redemption and reconciliation first. Her response to Jesus was, *"She said, No man, Lord. And Jesus said unto her, Neither do I condemn thee: go, and sin no more."* What was Jesus saying to these men? Leave her alone! It is time all across the body of Christ that men leave women alone. Stop murmuring, stop troubling them, stop embarrassing them, stop annoying them, stop trying to get them to submit to absolute foolishness, and let them free! You will be surprised. Once you let women free and get them moving into their ministry, tremendous fruit comes. It is amazing that the Son of God had to come and say leave her alone. These people in Mark 14 couldn't recognize the good work this woman was doing for Jesus.

Wherever there is a sister who loves the Lord, loves the Word of God, and whose spirit cries out to be used of God, and she is in a place where she is not allowed to be free and she has been told to be quiet and submit, hear the voice of God. Leave her alone! For every sister that feels a tremendous call upon her life to lead worship, to evangelize, to prophesy, to preach, to teach the Word of God, etc., and you've been hindered and promises were made and never kept, and when you hear the murmuring and the things they say about you, hear the Word of the Lord. Leave her alone! Only Jesus can stop this religious foolishness. Only Jesus can stop the Judiazers. As they were so upset in Luke 13 that a woman had a spirit of infirmity and very mad that Jesus healed her, Jesus responded to them, *"And ought not this woman, being a daughter of Abraham, whom Satan hath bound, lo, these eighteen years, be loosed from this bond on the sabbath day?"* (Luke 13:16).

I'm saying to you, it is the will of God for women to minister. It is the will of God for you to find your calling and begin to run after it. Study the Scriptures and know this to be true so you can have an answer to every man that asks you of the hope that is in you. They will have nothing to say against you because it will be clear in the Scripture and they will be convicted by their own conscious. As long as you keep your spirit sweet, it will just be you and Jesus alone to do the will of God. The earth is waiting for the manifestation of the sons of God, but I fear that the sons of God don't recognize the daughters of Israel among them. Until they do, we will continue with half the world not coming to Jesus. Hear me, the hour is coming when that great anointing is going to fall and everyone will be loosed into their ministry. Now sisters, if you feel a distinct call from God, and there is a pull in your heart to be used of God but you've been confused, and you didn't know if women were to minister or you've been told that, be established today in the present truth. Never again let religion bind you and insecure men who are afraid of a woman filled with God stop you from ministering. If you've never acknowledged that you are called of God, do it today. Say to Jesus, Lord I've always sensed your call but nobody else has recognized it, help me. Spirit of the living God fall upon these sisters and sweep through and change every heart for the glory of God.

Lesson 10
Worship & Women

Since true worship is such an important part of a child of God's life, we want to search the Scriptures to see what they say women's relationship to it is. The fact is both Scripturally and naturally, or by simply judging what happens in most churches, you can't help but come to the conclusion that Jesus is adored and praised far more by women than men.

I.   Worship & Women In Scriptures

A.   Examples

1.   Exodus 15:1, 20-21 – "*¹Then sang Moses and the children of Israel this song unto the LORD, and spake, saying, I will sing unto the LORD, for he hath triumphed gloriously: the horse and his rider hath he thrown into the sea...²⁰And Miriam the prophetess, the sister of Aaron, took a timbrel in her hand; and all the women went out after her with timbrels and with dances. ²¹And Miriam answered them, Sing ye to the LORD, for he hath triumphed gloriously; the horse and his rider hath he thrown into the sea.*" (Micah 6:4 – "*For I brought thee up out of the land of Egypt, and redeemed thee out of the house of servants; and I sent before thee Moses, Aaron, and Miriam.*")

2.   I Samuel 1:28-2:11 – Hannah's song after the Lord gave her Samuel
3.   Psalms 45:9-11 – Bride of Christ
4.   Matthew 13:22-28 – Woman of Canaan
5.   Acts 16:14-15 – Lydia means – bending, brought forth, travailing, to firebrand
6.   Genesis 29:35 (17, 31) – Leah birthing Judah; Leah means – wearied, to be exhausted, to labor, faint
7.   Judges 5:1-3, 12

   a.   Awake – to open your eyes, to stir up yourself
   b.   Utter – to arrange, to speak, to subdue
   c.   Isaiah 32:9-18 – "*Rise up ye women that are at ease*"

8.   Psalms 102:16-18 – remnant worshippers in the last days; verse 18 in Hebrew, "*This shall be written for the last generation to come*".
9.   Psalms 150:6 – Everything includes women
10. Psalms 68:25
11. Psalms 87:2-7 – Women of Zion
12. Luke 1:41-45 – Song of Elisabeth; Elisabeth's name means – God is her oath, a worshipper of God.
13. Luke 1:46-55 – Song of Mary
14. Luke 2:36-38 – Song of Anna – her name means grace
15. Revelation 14:1-5 – Verse 2, some scholars suggest that these "treble voices" could be both men and women
16. II Samuel 6:12-22 – Women worshipping around the "ark", the manifest presence of God.
17. I Chronicles 25:1-7 – The Tabernacle of David
18. Restoration of the Temple

   a.   Ezra 2:1, 65
   b.   Nehemiah 7:67
   c.   Nehemiah 3:12

19. Psalms 46 – Alamoth means – a lass, damsel, a virgin
20. John 4:5-26
21. Genesis 4:17-20 – Adah means – ornament, to adorn, beauty, pleasure; it comes from a root that means – whom Jehovah adores (Ezekiel 28:11-19)

Lesson 11
Notable Women In Scripture

Throughout the Word of God, there are women who were notable for many different reasons. Many of them were used of the Lord in tremendous ways. Because the Scriptures seem to make a special mention of them, and since we are studying women In ministry, it would behoove us to at least take a brief look at them, proving again God's heart towards women and confirming women's place in Scripture, history, and ministry. By studying these women, we can understand more about women's role in ministry. We have looked and will continue to look at the women who made a significant impact Scripturally.

I. Noble Women In Scripture

    A. Women that the Scriptures declare were important – Many times in the Word we see this phrase, "His mother's name was..." This is given in many cases to show the godly influence of these women in their children's lives.

        1. **Azubah**

I Kings 22:42 – *"Jehoshaphat was thirty and five years old when he began to reign; and he reigned twenty and five years in Jerusalem. And his mother's name was Azubah the daughter of Shilhi."*
II Chronicles 20:31 – *"And Jehoshaphat reigned over Judah: he was thirty and five years old when he began to reign, and he reigned twenty and five years in Jerusalem. And his mother's name was Azubah the daughter of Shilhi."*

            a. She is the second Azubah found in Scripture.
            b. She was the daughter of Shilhi whose name means – Armed of the Lord, one armed with darts.
            c. She was the wife of Asa the third king of Judah and the mother of Jehoshaphat. Her influence is seen in the life of her husband, who was one of the good kings of Judah, as well as in the life of her son, who, though he did plenty wrong, still was somewhat of a good king.

        2. **Apphia** – Philemon 2 – *"And to our beloved Apphia, and Archippus our fellowsoldier, and to the church in thy house:"*

            a. Her name means – That which is fruitful, a dear one.
            b. She is called a fellow soldier in the Gospel.
            c. She was an integral part of her local church. She helped pastor.

        3. **Dorcas (Tabitha)** – Acts 9:36-43

"³⁶Now there was at Joppa a certain disciple named Tabitha, which by interpretation is called Dorcas: this woman was full of good works and almsdeeds which she did. ³⁷And it came to pass in those days, that she was sick, and died: whom when they had washed, they laid her in an upper chamber. ³⁸And forasmuch as Lydda was nigh to Joppa, and the disciples had heard that Peter was there, they sent unto him two men, desiring him that he would not delay to come to them. ³⁹Then Peter arose and went with them. When he was come, they brought him into the upper chamber: and all the widows stood by him weeping, and shewing the coats and garments which Dorcas made, while she was with them. ⁴⁰But Peter put them all forth, and kneeled down, and prayed; and turning him to the body said, Tabitha, arise. And she opened her eyes: and when she saw Peter, she sat up. ⁴¹And he gave her his hand, and lifted her up, and when he had called the saints and widows, presented her alive. ⁴²And it was known throughout all Joppa; and many believed in the Lord. ⁴³And it came to pass, that he tarried many days in Joppa with one Simon a tanner."

            a. Her name means – Gazelle, an emblem of beauty

b. She obviously was a women who cared because she did many good works.
c. Almsdeeds means works of mercy.
d. She also made many precious garments for people.
e. She is a great example of generosity.
f. God thought enough of her that He raised her from the dead.

4. **Eunice – Acts 16:1-3**

"*¹Then came he to Derbe and Lystra: and, behold, a certain disciple was there, named Timotheus, the son of a certain woman, which was a Jewess, and believed; but his father was a Greek: ²Which was well reported of by the brethren that were at Lystra and Iconium. ³Him would Paul have to go forth with him; and took and circumcised him because of the Jews which were in those quarters: for they knew all that his father was a Greek.*"
II Timothy 1:5 – "*When I call to remembrance the unfeigned faith that is in thee, which dwelt first in thy grandmother Lois, and thy mother Eunice; and I am persuaded that in thee also.*"
II Timothy 3:14-15 – "*But continue thou in the things which thou hast learned and hast been assured of, knowing of whom thou hast learned them; And that from a child thou hast known the holy scriptures, which are able to make thee wise unto salvation through faith which is in Christ Jesus.*"

a. Her name means – conquering, well, happy, victory.
b. She was a Jew who became a believer.
c. She was the mother of one of Paul's best disciples.
d. She was a woman of true, genuine faith, and obviously influenced her son in the Lord and in his ministry.
e. She was also a woman of the Word, teaching Timothy from birth the Holy Scriptures.

5. **Hephzibah**

II Kings 21:1 – "*Manasseh was twelve years old when he began to reign, and reigned fifty and five years in Jerusalem. And his mother's name was Hephzi-bah.*"
Isaiah 62:4 – "*Thou shalt no more be termed Forsaken; neither shall thy land any more be termed Desolate: but thou shalt be called Hephzi-bah, and thy land Beulah: for the LORD delighteth in thee, and thy land shall be married.*"

a. Her name means – my delight is in her, in whom is my delight.
b. She was the wife of the godly king Hezekiah.
c. She was the mother of Manasseh who reigned over Judah for 55 years. He however was the exact opposite of his father and mother.
d. Her name was chosen by God to be His symbolic name for Zion.
e. She certainly is a type of the bride of Christ.

6. **Jehosheba**

II Kings 11:2-3 – "*But Jehosheba, the daughter of king Joram, sister of Ahaziah, took Joash the son of Ahaziah and stole him from among the king's sons which were slain; and they hid him, even him and his nurse, in the bedchamber from Athaliah, so that he was not slain. And he was with her hid in the house of the LORD six years. And Athaliah did reign over the land.*"
II Chronicles 22:11-12 – "*But Jehoshabeath, the daughter of the king, took Joash the son of Ahaziah, and stole him from among the king's sons that were slain, and put him and his nurse in a bedchamber. So Jehoshabeath, the daughter of king Jehoram, the wife of Jehoiada the priest, (for she was the sister of Ahaziah,) hid him from Athaliah, so that she slew him not. And he was with them hid in the house of God six years: and Athaliah reigned over the land.*"

a. Her name means – Jehovah is her oath, the Lord's oath, Jehovah is the oath.
b. She was the daughter of king Joram (Jehoram) and half sister of king Ahaziah.

      c.   She rescued her nephew Joash from certain death at the hands of Athaliah, the wicked queen of Judah. When Ahaziah was killed in battle, his mother, Athaliah, attempted to kill all her grandsons and take the throne for herself.

      d.   She then hid him in the Temple for six years until he was old enough to be proclaimed king.

      e.   Because of her courageous act, she preserved the line of Judah which is the "house and lineage of David" (Luke 2:4), from which Jesus descended.

7. Joanna

Luke 8:1-3 – "*¹And it came to pass afterward, that he went throughout every city and village, preaching and shewing the glad tidings of the kingdom of God: and the twelve were with him, ²And certain women, which had been healed of evil spirits and infirmities, Mary called Magdalene, out of whom went seven devils, ³And Joanna the wife of Chuza Herod's steward, and Susanna, and many others, which ministered unto him of their substance.*"

Luke 23:55-56 – "*⁵⁵And the women also, which came with him from Galilee, followed after, and beheld the sepulchre, and how his body was laid. ⁵⁶And they returned, and prepared spices and ointments; and rested the sabbath day according to the commandment.*"

Luke 24:1-10 – "*¹Now upon the first day of the week, very early in the morning, they came unto the sepulchre, bringing the spices which they had prepared, and certain others with them. ²And they found the stone rolled away from the sepulchre. ³And they entered in, and found not the body of the Lord Jesus. ⁴And it came to pass, as they were much perplexed thereabout, behold, two men stood by them in shining garments: ⁵And as they were afraid, and bowed down their faces to the earth, they said unto them, Why seek ye the living among the dead? ⁶He is not here, but is risen: remember how he spake unto you when he was yet in Galilee, ⁷Saying, The Son of man must be delivered into the hands of sinful men, and be crucified, and the third day rise again. ⁸And they remembered his words, ⁹And returned from the sepulchre, and told all these things unto the eleven, and to all the rest. ¹⁰It was Mary Magdalene, and Joanna, and Mary the mother of James, and other women that were with them, which told these things unto the apostles.*"

      a.   Her name means – Jehovah has been gracious, Jehovah has shown favor, the Lord is grace, the Lord give graciously

      b.   She was the wife of Chuza, king Herod's steward.

      c.   She ministered to Jesus of her substance, which means she provided for the material needs of Jesus and His disciples from her own funds.

      d.   She proclaimed Jesus' resurrection.

      e.   She had received healing and deliverance from Jesus.

      f.   Jesus appeared to her.

8. Jochebed

Exodus 6:20 – "*And Amram took him Jochebed his father's sister to wife; and she bare him Aaron and Moses: and the years of the life of Amram were an hundred and thirty and seven years.*"

Exodus 2:1-10 – "*¹And there went a man of the house of Levi, and took to wife a daughter of Levi. ²And the woman conceived, and bare a son: and when she saw him that he was a goodly child, she hid him three months. ³And when she could not longer hide him, she took for him an ark of bulrushes, and daubed it with slime and with pitch, and put the child therein; and she laid it in the flags by the river's brink. ⁴And his sister stood afar off, to wit what would be done to him. ⁵And the daughter of Pharaoh came down to wash herself at the river; and her maidens walked along by the river's side; and when she saw the ark among the flags, she sent her maid to fetch it. ⁶And when she had opened it, she saw the child: and, behold, the babe wept. And she had compassion on him, and said, This is one of the Hebrews' children. ⁷Then said his sister to Pharaoh's daughter, Shall I go and call to thee a nurse of the Hebrew women, that she may nurse the child for thee? ⁸And Pharaoh's daughter said to her, Go. And the maid went and called the child's mother. ⁹And Pharaoh's daughter said unto her, Take this child away, and nurse it for me, and I will give thee thy wages. And the woman took the child, and nursed it. ¹⁰And the child grew, and she brought him unto Pharaoh's daughter, and he became her son. And she called his name Moses: and she said, Because I drew him out of the water.*"

Hebrews 11:23 – *"By faith Moses, when he was born, was hid three months of his parents, because they saw he was a proper child; and they were not afraid of the king's commandment."*

      a. Her name means – Lord of glory, glory of the Lord, Jehovah is glorious, Jehovah is her glory.
      b. A daughter of Levi
      c. Married a man of the tribe of Levi
      d. Mother of three important children – *Moses, Aaron, Miriam*
      e. She recognized Moses was a goodly child.
      f. She hid him to protect him from Pharaoh.
      g. She made an ark for him – For us this is spiritual. She covered him in an ark of intercession and worship.
      h. Pushed him out in the river – Gave him to God.

9. **Keturah**

Genesis 25:1-4 – *"¹Then again Abraham took a wife, and her name was Keturah. ²And she bare him Zimran, and Jokshan, and Medan, and Midian, and Ishbak, and Shuah. ³And Jokshan begat Sheba, and Dedan. And the sons of Dedan were Asshurim, and Letushim, and Leummim. ⁴And the sons of Midian; Ephah, and Epher, and Hanoch, and Abida, and Eldaah. All these were the children of Keturah."*
I Chronicles 1:32-33 – *"Now the sons of Keturah, Abraham's concubine: she bare Zimran, and Jokshan, and Medan, and Midian, and Ishbak, and Shuah. And the sons of Jokshan; Sheba, and Dedan. And the sons of Midian; Ephah, and Epher, and Henoch, and Abida, and Eldaah. All these are the sons of Keturah."*

      a. Her name means – incense, the smoke of incense.
      b. She became Abraham's wife in his old age.
      c. Some called her a concubine.
      d. She became the mother of Abraham's six other sons making him the father of many nations.

10. **Lois** – II Timothy 1:5 – *"When I call to remembrance the unfeigned faith that is in thee, which dwelt first in thy grandmother Lois, and thy mother Eunice; and I am persuaded that in thee also."*

      a. Her name means – agreeable, desirable, no standard bearer, no flight
      b. She was Timothy's grandmother.
      c. She had a genuine faith.
      d. She obviously instructed her children and grandchildren in the ways and Word of the Lord.

11. **Phebe** – Romans 16:1-2 – *"I commend unto you Phebe our sister, which is a servant of the church which is at Cenchrea: That ye receive her in the Lord, as becometh saints, and that ye assist her in whatsoever business she hath need of you: for she hath been a succourer of many, and of myself also."*

      a. Her name means – moon, pure or radiant as the moon. The moon is a type of the bride of Christ.
      b. Paul commends her and that she should be received.
      c. She was a servant in the church.
      d. Paul commands the church to help her in any way she needs.
      e. Paul mentions that she had been a helper of many, including himself.
      f. The Greek word for servant is *diakonos* which is translated minister, deacon, servant.

12. **Rhoda**

Acts 12:13-17 – *"¹³And as Peter knocked at the door of the gate, a damsel came to hearken, named Rhoda. ¹⁴And when she knew Peter's voice, she opened not the gate for gladness, but ran in, and told how Peter stood before the gate. ¹⁵And they said unto her, Thou art mad. But she constantly affirmed that it was even so. Then said they, It is his angel. ¹⁶But Peter continued knocking: and when they had opened the door, and saw him, they were astonished.*

[17]But he, beckoning unto them with the hand to hold their peace, declared unto them how the Lord had brought him out of the prison. And he said, Go shew these things unto James, and to the brethren. And he departed, and went into another place."

      a. Her name means – a rose
      b. She was a servant of Mary.
      c. She was also an intercessor.
      d. She immediately recognized Peter's voice.
      e. Even after she was called mad, she continued to hold on.

13. Shiphrah and Puah

Exodus 1:15-21 – *"[15]And the king of Egypt spake to the Hebrew midwives, of which the name of the one was Shiphrah, and the name of the other Puah: [16]And he said, When ye do the office of a midwife to the Hebrew women, and see them upon the stools; if it be a son, then ye shall kill him: but if it be a daughter, then she shall live. [17]But the midwives feared God, and did not as the king of Egypt commanded them, but saved the men children alive. [18]And the king of Egypt called for the midwives, and said unto them, Why have ye done this thing, and have saved the men children alive? [19]And the midwives said unto Pharaoh, Because the Hebrew women are not as the Egyptian women; for they are lively, and are delivered ere the midwives come in unto them. [20]Therefore God dealt well with the midwives: and the people multiplied, and waxed very mighty. [21]And it came to pass, because the midwives feared God, that he made them houses."*

      a. Shiphrah means – He garnished, fairness, beauty, brightness, prolific, to procreate
      b. Puah means – mouth, utterance, a blast, scattered; from a root – to blow away, to scatter into corners
      c. These women feared God more than Pharaoh.
      d. They did not obey his commandment to kill all the men-children.
      e. God blessed these women for their faithfulness.

14. Women at the Temple

Exodus 35:20-22, 25-26 – *"[20]And all the congregation of the children of Israel departed from the presence of Moses. [21]And they came, every one whose heart stirred him up, and every one whom his spirit made willing, and they brought the LORD's offering to the work of the tabernacle of the congregation, and for all his service, and for the holy garments. [22]And they came, both men and women, as many as were willing hearted, and brought bracelets, and earrings, and rings, and tablets, all jewels of gold: and every man that offered offered an offering of gold unto the LORD…[25]And all the women that were wise hearted did spin with their hands, and brought that which they had spun, both of blue, and of purple, and of scarlet, and of fine linen. [26]And all the women whose heart stirred them up in wisdom spun goats' hair."*

      a. These women had willing hearts. Their hearts were stirred up to build God's temple.
      b. They were happy to give offerings to the Lord.
      c. They brought all their jewelry to God.
      d. These were wise-hearted women.
      e. They worked willingly with their hands to make clothes.
      f. These women knew how to stir up their hearts in wisdom.

15. Women were called to sit under the Word just like the men during the Feast of Tabernacles.

Deuteronomy 31:10-13 – *"[10]And Moses commanded them, saying, At the end of every seven years, in the solemnity of the year of release, in the feast of tabernacles, [11]When all Israel is come to appear before the LORD thy God in the place which he shall choose, thou shalt read this law before all Israel in their hearing. [12]Gather the people together, men, and women, and children, and thy stranger that is within thy gates, that they may hear, and that they may learn, and fear the LORD your God, and observe to do all the words of this law: [13]And that their children, which have not known any thing, may hear, and learn to fear the LORD your God, as long as ye live in the land whither ye go over Jordan to possess it."*

16. Women worshipping around the ark, the manifest presence of God

II Samuel 6:15-23 – "15So David and all the house of Israel brought up the ark of the LORD with shouting, and with the sound of the trumpet. 16And as the ark of the LORD came into the city of David, Michal Saul's daughter looked through a window, and saw king David leaping and dancing before the LORD; and she despised him in her heart. 17And they brought in the ark of the LORD, and set it in his place, in the midst of the tabernacle that David had pitched for it: and David offered burnt offerings and peace offerings before the LORD. 18And as soon as David had made an end of offering burnt offerings and peace offerings, he blessed the people in the name of the LORD of hosts. 19And he dealt among all the people, even among the whole multitude of Israel, as well to the women as men, to every one a cake of bread, and a good piece of flesh, and a flagon of wine. So all the people departed every one to his house. 20Then David returned to bless his household. And Michal the daughter of Saul came out to meet David, and said, How glorious was the king of Israel to day, who uncovered himself to day in the eyes of the handmaids of his servants, as one of the vain fellows shamelessly uncovereth himself! 21And David said unto Michal, It was before the LORD, which chose me before thy father, and before all his house, to appoint me ruler over the people of the LORD, over Israel: therefore will I play before the LORD. 22And I will yet be more vile than thus, and will be base in mine own sight: and of the maidservants which thou hast spoken of, of them shall I be had in honour. 23Therefore Michal the daughter of Saul had no child unto the day of her death."

17. The loving caring woman who loved her child and was willing to go without for his salvation!

I Kings 3:16-27 – "16Then came there two women, that were harlots, unto the king, and stood before him. 17And the one woman said, O my lord, I and this woman dwell in one house; and I was delivered of a child with her in the house. 18And it came to pass the third day after that I was delivered, that this woman was delivered also: and we were together; there was no stranger with us in the house, save we two in the house. 19And this woman's child died in the night; because she overlaid it. 20And she arose at midnight, and took my son from beside me, while thine handmaid slept, and laid it in her bosom, and laid her dead child in my bosom. 21And when I rose in the morning to give my child suck, behold, it was dead: but when I had considered it in the morning, behold, it was not my son, which I did bear. 22And the other woman said, Nay; but the living is my son, and the dead is thy son. And this said, No; but the dead is thy son, and the living is my son. Thus they spake before the king. 23Then said the king, The one saith, This is my son that liveth, and thy son is the dead: and the other saith, Nay; but thy son is the dead, and my son is the living. 24And the king said, Bring me a sword. And they brought a sword before the king. 25And the king said, Divide the living child in two, and give half to the one, and half to the other. 26Then spake the woman whose the living child was unto the king, for her bowels yearned upon her son, and she said, O my lord, give her the living child, and in no wise slay it. But the other said, Let it be neither mine nor thine, but divide it. 27Then the king answered and said, Give her the living child, and in no wise slay it: she is the mother thereof."

18. Job's Daughters (the second set)

Job 42:12-15 – "12So the LORD blessed the latter end of Job more than his beginning: for he had fourteen thousand sheep, and six thousand camels, and a thousand yoke of oxen, and a thousand she asses. 13He had also seven sons and three daughters. 14And he called the name of the first, Jemima; and the name of the second, Kezia; and the name of the third, Keren-happuch. 15And in all the land were no women found so fair as the daughters of Job: and their father gave them inheritance among their brethren."

      a. Jemima – Dove, a little dove, daily, He will spoil her
      b. Kezia – Cassia, equally as precious
      c. Keren-happuch – Beautifier or horn of paint, child of beauty
      d. God's blessing of a double portion to Job.

19. Mourning Women, Cunning Women – These women I believe excelled at intercession

Jeremiah 9:17-24 – "*17Thus saith the LORD of hosts, Consider ye, and call for the mourning women, that they may come; and send for cunning women, that they may come: 18And let them make haste, and take up a wailing for us, that our eyes may run down with tears, and our eyelids gush out with waters. 19For a voice of wailing is heard out of Zion, How are we spoiled! we are greatly confounded, because we have forsaken the land, because our dwellings have cast us out. 20Yet hear the word of the LORD, O ye women, and let your ear receive the word of his mouth, and teach your daughters wailing, and every one her neighbour lamentation. 21For death is come up into our windows, and is entered into our palaces, to cut off the children from without, and the young men from the streets. 22Speak, Thus saith the LORD, Even the carcases of men shall fall as dung upon the open field, and as the handful after the harvestman, and none shall gather them. 23Thus saith the LORD, Let not the wise man glory in his wisdom, neither let the mighty man glory in his might, let not the rich man glory in his riches: 24But let him that glorieth glory in this, that he understandeth and knoweth me, that I am the LORD which exercise lovingkindness, judgment, and righteousness, in the earth: for in these things I delight, saith the LORD.*"

20. Women grinding at the mill – type of studying the Word

Matthew 24:37-41 – "*...37But as the days of Noe were, so shall also the coming of the Son of man be. 38For as in the days that were before the flood they were eating and drinking, marrying and giving in marriage, until the day that Noe entered into the ark, 39And knew not until the flood came, and took them all away; so shall also the coming of the Son of man be. 40Then shall two be in the field; the one shall be taken, and the other left. 41Two women shall be grinding at the mill; the one shall be taken, and the other left.*"

21. Women that ministered to Jesus

Matthew 27:55-56 – "*And many women were there beholding afar off, which followed Jesus from Galilee, ministering unto him: Among which was Mary Magdalene, and Mary the mother of James and Joses, and the mother of Zebedee's children.*"
Luke 8:1-3 – "*1And it came to pass afterward, that he went throughout every city and village, preaching and shewing the glad tidings of the kingdom of God: and the twelve were with him, 2And certain women, which had been healed of evil spirits and infirmities, Mary called Magdalene, out of whom went seven devils, 3And Joanna the wife of Chuza Herod's steward, and Susanna* (Susanna means – lily, a white lily), *and many others, which ministered unto him of their substance.*" – Many women gave willingly to minister to Jesus.
Mark 15:40-41 – "*There were also women looking on afar off: among whom was Mary Magdalene, and Mary the mother of James the less and of Joses, and Salome; (Who also, when he was in Galilee, followed him, and ministered unto him;) and many other women which came up with him unto Jerusalem.*"
Luke 23:27-28, 49, 55 – "*27And there followed him a great company of people, and of women, which also bewailed and lamented him. 28But Jesus turning unto them said, Daughters of Jerusalem, weep not for me, but weep for yourselves, and for your children...49And all his acquaintance, and the women that followed him from Galilee, stood afar off, beholding these things...55And the women also, which came with him from Galilee, followed after, and beheld the sepulchre, and how his body was laid.*"

22. Jesus first appeared to women after the resurrection

Luke 24:1-11, 22, 24 – "*1Now upon the first day of the week, very early in the morning, they came unto the sepulchre, bringing the spices which they had prepared, and certain others with them. 2And they found the stone rolled away from the sepulchre. 3And they entered in, and found not the body of the Lord Jesus. 4And it came to pass, as they were much perplexed thereabout, behold, two men stood by them in shining garments: 5And as they were afraid, and bowed down their faces to the earth, they said unto them, Why seek ye the living among the dead? 6He is not here, but is risen: remember how he spake unto you when he was yet in Galilee, 7Saying, The Son of man must be delivered into the hands of sinful men, and be crucified, and the third day rise again. 8And they remembered his words, 9And returned from the sepulchre, and told all these things unto the eleven, and to all the rest. 10It was Mary Magdalene, and Joanna, and Mary the mother of James, and other women that were with them, which told these things unto the apostles. 11And their words seemed to them as idle tales, and they believed them not...22Yea, and certain women also of our company made us astonished, which were early at the sepulchre...24And certain of them which were with us went to the sepulchre, and found it even so as the women had said: but him they saw not."*

23. Women part of the early church

Acts 1:14-15 – *"These all continued with one accord in prayer and supplication, with the women, and Mary the mother of Jesus, and with his brethren. And in those days Peter stood up in the midst of the disciples, and said, (the number of names together were about an hundred and twenty,)"*

24. Women also imprisoned for their faith

Acts 8:3 – *"As for Saul, he made havock of the church, entering into every house, and haling men and women committed them to prison."*
Acts 9:2 – *"And desired of him letters to Damascus to the synagogues, that if he found any of this way, whether they were men or women, he might bring them bound unto Jerusalem."*
Acts 22:4 – *"And I persecuted this way unto the death, binding and delivering into prisons both men and women."*

25. Lydia and her intercessors

Acts 16:14-15, 40 – *"14And a certain woman named Lydia, a seller of purple, of the city of Thyatira, which worshipped God, heard us: whose heart the Lord opened, that she attended unto the things which were spoken of Paul. 15And when she was baptized, and her household, she besought us, saying, If ye have judged me to be faithful to the Lord, come into my house, and abide there. And she constrained us...40And they went out of the prison, and entered into the house of Lydia and when they had seen the brethren, they comforted them, and departed."*

    a.   Lydia means – bending, brought forth, travailing

26. Women believers that sat under the Word of God

Acts 17:1-4, 12 – *"1Now when they had passed through Amphipolis and Apollonia, they came to Thessalonica, where was a synagogue of the Jews: 2And Paul, as his manner was, went in unto them, and three sabbath days reasoned with them out of the scriptures, 3Opening and alleging, that Christ must needs have suffered, and risen again from the dead; and that this Jesus, whom I preach unto you, is Christ. 4And some of them believed, and consorted with Paul and Silas; and of the devout Greeks a great multitude, and of the chief women not a few...12Therefore many of them believed; also of honourable women which were Greeks, and of men, not a few."*

27. Women ministers of the Gospel

Philippians 4:2-3 – *"I beseech Euodias, and beseech Syntyche, that they be of the same mind in the Lord. And I intreat thee also, true yokefellow, help those women which laboured with me in the gospel, with Clement also, and with other my fellowlabourers, whose names are in the book of life."*

    a.   Euodias means – success, prosperous journey
    b.   Syntyche means – fortunate, well-met

28. Women in the Hall of Fame of Faith

Hebrews 11:11 – *"Through faith also Sara herself received strength to conceive seed, and was delivered of a child when she was past age, because she judged him faithful who had promised."*
Hebrews 11:23 – *"By faith Moses, when he was born, was hid three months of his parents, because they saw he was a proper child; and they were not afraid of the king's commandment."*
Hebrews 11:31 – *"By faith the harlot Rahab perished not with them that believed not, when she had received the spies with peace."*

Hebrews 11:35 – *"Women received their dead raised to life again: and others were tortured, not accepting deliverance; that they might obtain a better resurrection:"*
Hebrews 11:38-40 – *"³⁸(Of whom the world was not worthy:) they wandered in deserts, and in mountains, and in dens and caves of the earth. ³⁹And these all, having obtained a good report through faith, received not the promise: ⁴⁰God having provided some better thing for us, that they without us should not be made perfect."*

29. **Women also a part of the last days outpouring**

Joel 2:29 – *"And also upon the servants and upon the handmaids in those days will I pour out my spirit."*
Acts 2:18 – *"And on my servants and on my handmaidens I will pour out in those days of my Spirit; and they shall prophesy:"*

30. **Miriam**

Exodus 15:20-21 – *"And Miriam the prophetess, the sister of Aaron, took a timbrel in her hand; and all the women went out after her with timbrels and with dances. And Miriam answered them, Sing ye to the LORD, for he hath triumphed gloriously; the horse and his rider hath he thrown into the sea."*
Micah 6:4 –*" For I brought thee up out of the land of Egypt, and redeemed thee out of the house of servants; and I sent before thee Moses, Aaron, and Miriam."*

Miriam, Moses and Aaron's sister, was a prophetess with influence in the nation of Israel. The Hebrew word for prophetess, *Nebrah*, means "an inspired woman." She was given inspiration from the Lord to share prophecy to the rest of the people. In this particular passage, we find her leading the men in worship. In other passages she is spoken of in the same context of leadership as Moses and Aaron. She helped lead Israel with her brothers.

31. **Deborah**

Judges 4:4-5 –*"And Deborah, a prophetess, the wife of Lapidoth, she judged Israel at that time. And she dwelt under the palm tree of Deborah between Ramah and Bethel in mount Ephraim: and the children of Israel came up to her for judgment."*
Judges 4:24 – *"And the hand of the children of Israel prospered, and prevailed against Jabin the king of Canaan, until they had destroyed Jabin king of Canaan."* – The children of Israel prospered under her ministry. They prevailed over their foes. Women can be warriors!
Judges 5:1-12 -*" Then sang Deborah and Barak the son of Abinoam on that day, saying, ye the LORD for the avenging of Israel, when the people willingly offered themselves.³Hear, O ye kings; give ear, O ye princes; I, even I, will sing unto the LORD; I will sing praise to the LORD God of Israel.⁴LORD, when thou wentest out of Seir, when thou marchedst out of the field of Edom, the earth trembled, and the heavens dropped, the clouds also dropped water.⁵The mountains melted from before the LORD, even that Sinai from before the LORD God of Israel.⁶In the days of Shamgar the son of Anath, in the days of Jael, the highways were unoccupied, and the travellers walked through byways.⁷The inhabitants of the villages ceased, they ceased in Israel, until that I Deborah arose, that I arose a mother in Israel.⁸They chose new gods; then was war in the gates: was there a shield or spear seen among forty thousand in Israel?⁹My heart is toward the governors of Israel, that offered themselves willingly among the people. Bless ye the LORD.¹⁰Speak, ye that ride on white asses, ye that sit in judgment, and walk by the way.¹¹They that are delivered from the noise of archers in the places of drawing water, there shall they rehearse the righteous acts of the LORD, even the righteous acts toward the inhabitants of his villages in Israel: then shall the people of the LORD go down to the gates.¹²Awake, awake, Deborah: awake, awake, utter a song: arise, Barak, and lead thy captivity captive, thou son of Abinoam."* – Here we see Deborah as a psalmist and song leader. Notice that there was no struggle between Barak and Deborah. He had peace about her place in leadership. In Judges 4:8 we see he refused to go to battle without her!

The Hebrew word for judge, *shapat*, means to pronounce a sentence, or to govern. Deborah was the leader of Israel at this time, as well as a prophetess. The only other judge at that time was Samuel. It was said the children of Israel came to her for judgment. She was their counselor, or close comparison to a pastor.

32. Huldah

II Kings 22:13-20 –"*13Go ye, inquire of the LORD for me, and for the people, and for all Judah, concerning the words of this book that is found: for great is the wrath of the LORD that is kindled against us, because our fathers have not hearkened unto the words of this book, to do according unto all that which is written concerning us.14 So Hilkiah the priest, and Ahikam, and Achbor, and Shaphan, and Asahiah, went unto Huldah the prophetess, the wife of Shallum the son of Tikvah, the son of Harhas, keeper of the wardrobe; (now she dwelt in Jerusalem in the college;) and they communed with her.15And she said unto them, Thus saith the LORD God of Israel, Tell the man that sent you to me,16Thus saith the LORD, Behold, I will bring evil upon this place, and upon the inhabitants thereof, even all the words of the book which the king of Judah hath read:17Because they have forsaken me, and have burned incense unto other gods, that they might provoke me to anger with all the works of their hands; therefore my wrath shall be kindled against this place, and shall not be quenched.18But to the king of Judah which sent you to inquire of the LORD, thus shall ye say to him, Thus saith the LORD God of Israel, As touching the words which thou hast heard;19Because thine heart was tender, and thou hast humbled thyself before the LORD, when thou heardest what I spake against this place, and against the inhabitants thereof, that they should become a desolation and a curse, and hast rent thy clothes, and wept before me; I also have heard thee, saith the LORD.20Behold therefore, I will gather thee unto thy fathers, and thou shalt be gathered into thy grave in peace; and thine eyes shall not see all the evil which I will bring upon this place. And they brought the king word again.*" (Also note II Chronicles 34:22-33)

Huldah was a prophetess who had such influence and authority that the high priest, the king's scribe and his men of stature went to her for inspiration and direction from the Lord. Notice in verse 13, Josiah wants her to inquire of the Lord for all the people and for himself, the king. Her prophecy changed the spiritual life of Israel. Her name means – weasel because of its quickness, endurance, perpetuity.

33. Esther

Esther 4:8 –"*Also he gave him the copy of the writing of the decree that was given at Shushan to destroy them, to shew it unto Esther, and to declare it unto her, and to charge her that she should go in unto the king, to make supplication unto him, and to make request before him for her people.*"
Esther 4:13-16 - "*Then Mordecai commanded to answer Esther, Think not with thyself that thou shalt escape in the king's house, more than all the Jews. For if thou altogether holdest thy peace at this time, then shall there enlargement and deliverance arise to the Jews from another place; but thou and thy father's house shall be destroyed: and who knoweth whether thou art come to the kingdom for such a time as this? Then Esther bade them return Mordecai this answer,Go, gather together all the Jews that are present in Shushan, and fast ye for me, and neither eat nor drink three days, night or day: I also and my maidens will fast likewise; and so will I go in unto the king, which is not according to the law: and if I perish, I perish.*"

God used Esther to deliver ALL OF HIS PEOPLE! She was the one chosen by God for this important ministry.

34. Women who assembled at the door of the Tabernacle of Moses

Exodus 38:8 – "*And he made the laver of brass, and the foot of it of brass, of the looking glasses of the women assembling, which assembled at the door of the tabernacle of the congregation.*" – It seems in this verse of Scripture that women had a place of service in the Tabernacle of Moses. The Hebrew word for assembled is "*tsaba*" meaning "to be in the host, or to serve it." This word is also translated in other places as "wait upon," which would lead us to believe they assembled at the door of the Tabernacle to wait upon or serve people in the outer court.

35. Women taking the vow of a Nazarite

Numbers 6:2 –"*Speak unto the children of Israel, and say unto them, When either man or woman shall separate themselves to vow a vow of a Nazarite, to separate themselves unto the LORD*" – Here we see either a man or a woman may take the vow of a Nazarite, to be consecrated unto the Lord for the purpose of some special service.

36. Wise woman who convinced Joab not to destroy city

II Samuel 20:16-22 – "*Then cried a wise woman out of the city, Hear, hear; say, I pray you, unto Joab, Come near hither, that I may speak with thee.[17]And when he was come near unto her, the woman said, Art thou Joab? And he answered, I am he. Then she said unto him, Hear the words of thine handmaid. And he answered, I do hear.[18]Then she spake, saying, They were wont to speak in old time, saying, They shall surely ask counsel at Abel: and so they ended the matter.[19]I am one of them that are peaceable and faithful in Israel: thou seekest to destroy a city and a mother in Israel: why wilt thou swallow up the inheritance of the LORD? [20]And Joab answered and said, Far be it, far be it from me, that I should swallow up or destroy.[21]The matter is not so: but a man of mount Ephraim, Sheba the son of Bichri by name, hath lifted up his hand against the king, even against David: deliver him only, and I will depart from the city. And the woman said unto Joab, Behold, his head shall be thrown to thee over the wall.[22]Then the woman went unto all the people in her wisdom. And they cut off the head of Sheba the son of Bichri, and cast it out to Joab. And he blew a trumpet, and they retired from the city, every man to his tent. And Joab returned to Jerusalem unto the king.*"

Here we see a man named Sheba had tried to overthrow David, had to flee and was heading to a city called Abel. Joab, the king's commander, had come to destroy the entire city. The city was spared because of this wise woman, who obviously had great influence in the city, for she was their spokesperson and gave counsel that all the people followed.

37. The great company of women who will be all over the earth ministering

Psalms 68:11 – "*The Lord gave the word: great was the company of those that published it.*"

> **Amplified Version** – "*The Lord gives the word [of power]; the women who bear and publish [the news] are a great host*"
> **New American Standard** – "*The Lord gives command, the women who proclaim the good tidings are a great host.*"

The Hebrew word for publish is "*basar*" meaning to announce, messenger, preach and show forth. This verse for Scripture should be enough to release women to minister.

Isaiah 40:9 – "*O Zion, that bringest good tidings, get thee up into the high mountain; O Jerusalem, that bringest good tidings, lift up thy voice with strength; lift it up, be not afraid; say unto the cities of Judah, Behold your God!*" – The literal Hebrew reads: "O woman that publishest good tidings to Zion, get thee up into the high mountain; O woman, that publishest good tidings to Jerusalem, lift up thy voice with strength; lift it up, be not afraid; say unto the cities of Judah, Behold your God."

38. Women leading worship

I Chronicles 25:1, 5-7 –"*Moreover David and the captains of the host separated to the service of the sons of Asaph, and of Heman, and of Jeduthun, who should prophesy with harps, with psalteries, and with cymbals: and the number of the workmen according to their service was."[5]All these were the sons of Heman the king's seer in the words of God, to lift up the horn. And God gave to Heman fourteen sons and three daughters.[6]All these were under the hands of their father for song in the house of the LORD, with cymbals, psalteries, and harps, for the service of the house of God, according to the king's order to Asaph, Jeduthun, and Heman.[7]So the number of them, with their brethren that were instructed in the songs of the LORD, even all that were cunning, was two hundred fourscore and eight.*" – His daughters served under him leading worship in the house of God.

39. Priscilla

Acts 18:2-3, 18, 26 – "*²And found a certain Jew named Aquila, born in Pontus, lately come from Italy, with his wife Priscilla; (because that Claudius had commanded all Jews to depart from Rome:) and came unto them. ³And because he was of the same craft, he abode with them, and wrought: for by their occupation they were tentmakers…¹⁸And Paul after this tarried there yet a good while, and then took his leave of the brethren, and sailed thence into Syria, and with him Priscilla and Aquila; having shorn his head in Cenchrea: for he had a vow…²⁶And he began to speak boldly in the synagogue: whom when Aquila and Priscilla had heard, they took him unto them, and expounded unto him the way of God more perfectly.*"

1 Corinthians 16:19 – "*The churches of Asia salute you. Aquila and Priscilla salute you much in the Lord, with the church that is in their house.*"

        a.   Her names means – ancient, little old woman.
        b.   She laid her life down for Paul.

40. **The Woman Elder**

II John 1-5, 13 – "*¹The elder unto the elect lady and her children, whom I love in the truth; and not I only, but also all they that have known the truth; ²For the truth's sake, which dwelleth in us, and shall be with us for ever. ³Grace be with you, mercy, and peace, from God the Father, and from the Lord Jesus Christ, the Son of the Father, in truth and love. ⁴I rejoiced greatly that I found of thy children walking in truth, as we have received a commandment from the Father. ⁵And now I beseech thee, lady, not as though I wrote a new commandment unto thee, but that which we had from the beginning, that we love one another…¹³The children of thy elect sister greet thee. Amen.*"

41. **Mary who worked hard for those ministering the Gospel**

Romans 16:6 – "*Greet Mary, who bestowed much labour on us.*"

42. **Junia**

Romans 16:7 – "*Salute Andronicus and Junia, my kinsmen, and my fellowprisoners, who are of note among the apostles, who also were in Christ before me.*"

        a.   Junia was a woman apostle.
        b.   Some debate whether this is a man or a woman. Junia was a common Latin female name in the Roman times. The early church fathers considered her a woman. Only the biased translators tried to indicate she might be a man.

43. **Phillip's Daughters**

Acts 21:8-9 – "*And the next day we that were of Paul's company departed, and came unto Caesarea: and we entered into the house of Philip the evangelist, which was one of the seven; and abode with him. And the same man had four daughters, virgins, which did prophesy.*"

        a.   They were virgins.
        b.   They were prophets.

44. **Damaris**

Acts 17:34 – "*Howbeit certain men clave unto him, and believed: among the which was Dionysius the Areopagite, and a woman named Damaris, and others with them.*"

        a.   Her name means – calf, a heifer, a yoke bearing wife.
        b.   She was a believer.

45. **Tryphena, Tryphosa and Persis,** Romans 16:12 – *"Salute Tryphena and Tryphosa, who labour in the Lord. Salute the beloved Persis, which laboured much in the Lord."*

   a.   All these women worked in the ministry greatly.
   b.   Tryphena means – delicate, dainty one.
   c.   Tryphosa means – luxuriating, delicate, dainty one.
   d.   Persis means – one who takes by storm, that which divides.

46. **Rufus' Mother,** Romans 16:13 – *"Salute Rufus chosen in the Lord, and his mother and mine."*

   a.   This woman may have been Paul's spiritual mother.

47. **Julia, Nereus' sister,** Romans 16:15 – *"Salute Philologus, and Julia, Nereus, and his sister, and Olympas, and all the saints which are with them."*

   a.   Julia means – having curly hair, tender shoot, covered with green vegetation.
   b.   These obviously belonged and worked in their local church.

48. **Chloe,** I Corinthians 1:11 – *"For it hath been declared unto me of you, my brethren, by them which are of the house of Chloe, that there are contentions among you."*

   a.   Her name means – green herb
   b.   This could have been another household church, guided by a woman.

49. **Claudia,** II Timothy 4:21 – *"Do thy diligence to come before winter. Eubulus greeteth thee, and Pudens, and Linus, and Claudia, and all the brethren."*

   a.   Her name means – lame

50. **Isaiah's wife**

Isaiah 8:1-3 – *"¹Moreover the LORD said unto me, Take thee a great roll, and write in it with a man's pen concerning Maher-shalal-hash-baz. ²And I took unto me faithful witnesses to record, Uriah the priest, and Zechariah the son of Jeberechiah. ³And I went unto the prophetess; and she conceived, and bare a son. Then said the LORD to me, Call his name Maher-shalal-hash-baz."* – She was a prophetess.

51. **Manoah's wife**

Judges 13:2-7 – *"²And there was a certain man of Zorah, of the family of the Danites, whose name was Manoah; and his wife was barren, and bare not. ³And the angel of the LORD appeared unto the woman, and said unto her, Behold now, thou art barren, and bearest not: but thou shalt conceive, and bear a son. ⁴Now therefore beware, I pray thee, and drink not wine nor strong drink, and eat not any unclean thing: ⁵For, lo, thou shalt conceive, and bear a son; and no rasor shall come on his head: for the child shall be a Nazarite unto God from the womb: and he shall begin to deliver Israel out of the hand of the Philistines. ⁶Then the woman came and told her husband, saying, A man of God came unto me, and his countenance was like the countenance of an angel of God, very terrible: but I asked him not whence he was, neither told he me his name: ⁷But he said unto me, Behold, thou shalt conceive, and bear a son; and now drink no wine nor strong drink, neither eat any unclean thing: for the child shall be a Nazarite to God from the womb to the day of his death."*

   a.   Receives a visitation from God
   b.   Birthed Samson, God's deliverer.

52. **The woman that dropped a piece of a millstone to kill Abimelech**

Judges 9:52-54 – "*52And Abimelech came unto the tower, and fought against it, and went hard unto the door of the tower to burn it with fire. 53And a certain woman cast a piece of a millstone upon Abimelech's head, and all to brake his skull. 54Then he called hastily unto the young man his armourbearer, and said unto him, Draw thy sword, and slay me, that men say not of me, A woman slew him. And his young man thrust him through, and he died.*"

53. **A little maid**

II Kings 5:1-5 – "*1Now Naaman, captain of the host of the king of Syria, was a great man with his master, and honourable, because by him the LORD had given deliverance unto Syria: he was also a mighty man in valour, but he was a leper. 2And the Syrians had gone out by companies, and had brought away captive out of the land of Israel a little maid; and she waited on Naaman's wife. 3And she said unto her mistress, Would God my lord were with the prophet that is in Samaria! for he would recover him of his leprosy. 4And one went in, and told his lord, saying, Thus and thus said the maid that is of the land of Israel. 5And the king of Syria said, Go to, go, and I will send a letter unto the king of Israel. And he departed, and took with him ten talents of silver, and six thousand pieces of gold, and ten changes of raiment.*" – She believed in God's prophet and cared for her master.

54. **Israel was referred to as a woman** (Jeremiah 3:1-20)
56. **The church is spoken of as a bride** (Ephesians 5:23-32)

Lesson 12
Daughters Of Zelophehad

I.   Numbers 27:1-7

"*¹Then came the <u>daughters of Zelophehad</u>, the son of Hepher, the son of Gilead, the son of Machir, the son of Manasseh, of the families of Manasseh the son of Joseph: and these are the names of his daughters; Mahlah, Noah, and Hoglah, and Milcah, and Tirzah. ²And they <u>stood before Moses</u>, and before Eleazar the priest, and <u>before the princes and all the congregation</u>, by the door of the tabernacle of the congregation, <u>saying</u>, ³Our father died in the wilderness, and he was not in the company of them that gathered themselves together against the LORD in the company of Korah; but died in his own sin, and had no sons. ⁴<u>Why</u> should the name of our father be done away from among his family, because he hath no son? <u>Give unto us therefore a possession</u> among the brethren of our father. ⁵And Moses brought their cause before the LORD. ⁶And the LORD spake unto Moses, saying, ⁷<u>The daughters of Zelophehad speak right</u>: thou shalt surely give them a possession of an inheritance among their father's brethren; and thou shalt cause the inheritance of their father to pass unto them.*"

    A.   These daughters background or heritage

        1.   Great 5x grandfather, Joseph – may God add, increasing, he shall add; from a root – to add
        2.   Great 4x grandfather, Manasseh – forgetting, to cause to forget; from a root – to forget, to be forgotten
        3.   Great 3x grandfather, Machir – sold, a seller, to betroth, a daughter
        4.   Great 2x grandfather, Gilead – perpetual fountain, a heap of testimony, a witness, mass of testimony
        5.   Grandfather, Hepher – well, digging
        6.   Father, Zelophehad – first rupture, firstborn, the firstborn

    B.   The daughter's names – they were born during the wanderings of Israel

        1.   Mahlah – disease, sick, ill, in pain, mildness
        2.   Noah – motion, wandering; from a root – to move to and fro, to wander, to shake the head
        3.   Hoglah – partridge, the feast has languished
        4.   Milcah – queen, counsel
        5.   Tirzah – pleasantness, delight, she is willing, liberal; from a root – to delight

II.   What Really Took Place?

    A.   Their heroic story

        1.   These women came from a great heritage passed down from their fathers
        2.   From Joseph - God would increase them and add unto them
        3.   From Manasseh – God would not allow them to be forgotten
        4.   From Machir – they were to be the bride, betrothed, sold, to the Lord
        5.   From Gilead – they had a massive mountain of testimony in God as well as being a perpetual fountain of God's presence
        6.   From Hepher – they had learned how to dig a well; they knew how to dig and bring God's river forth
        7.   And from their father Zelophehad – they knew they were to be a part of that great firstborn company, the firstfruits of God

    B.   Why are their names significant?

        1.   From Mahlah – they knew what it was to be sick; perhaps they were wick of being subjugated to men.

2. From Noah – They knew what it meant to shake their heads at Israel's backslidden wandering from God.
3. From Hoglah – They understood that the blessing of God had been removed off of those that had wandered in the wilderness; they knew God's intent was for them to be a beautiful bird (like the dove – Holy Spirit)
4. From Milcah – They knew their destiny was to rule as a queen and as one who has true godly counsel
5. From Tirzah – They knew how to stay pleasant in the most undesirable circumstances and yet still be willing to go on with God; they also know how to bring delight (joy) to all those around them; they also knew how to give liberally and freely.

C. What the rest of the story brings out?

1. They were not going to be cheated out of their inheritance.
2. They were tired of being treated like second class citizens.
3. They went directly to Moses (their leader) and Eleazar (the high priest) without fear, and they spoke their peace before all the princes and the whole congregation.
4. They made it known that they and their fathers were not among the rebellious ones, like Korah, but that their father had simply died on his own.
5. So why, just because they were women, should their inheritance be taken from them?
6. They boldly declared "give us our inheritance".
7. Therefore, Moses brought their cause to the Lord.
8. God quickly answered Moses and said that these women had spoken correctly.
9. They must "surely" be given their inheritance
10. They also set in motion that other women should not be denied.

D. Other interesting facts

1. There were five daughters; five is the number of grace in Scripture and God's grace was upon them to break old customs of men getting everything, and God's grace caused it to happen.

2. Numbers 36:1-13

"*1And the chief fathers of the families of the children of Gilead, the son of Machir, the son of Manasseh, of the families of the sons of Joseph, came near, and spake before Moses, and before the princes, the chief fathers of the children of Israel: 2And they said, The LORD commanded my lord to give the land for an inheritance by lot to the children of Israel: and my lord was commanded by the LORD to give the inheritance of Zelophehad our brother unto his daughters. 3And if they be married to any of the sons of the other tribes of the children of Israel, then shall their inheritance be taken from the inheritance of our fathers, and shall be put to the inheritance of the tribe whereunto they are received: so shall it be taken from the lot of our inheritance. 4And when the jubile of the children of Israel shall be, then shall their inheritance be put unto the inheritance of the tribe whereunto they are received: so shall their inheritance be taken away from the inheritance of the tribe of our fathers. 5And Moses commanded the children of Israel according to the word of the LORD, saying, The tribe of the sons of Joseph hath said well. 6This is the thing which the LORD doth command concerning the daughters of Zelophehad, saying, Let them marry to whom they think best; only to the family of the tribe of their father shall they marry. 7So shall not the inheritance of the children of Israel remove from tribe to tribe: for every one of the children of Israel shall keep himself to the inheritance of the tribe of his fathers. 8And every daughter, that possesseth an inheritance in any tribe of the children of Israel, shall be wife unto one of the family of the tribe of her father, that the children of Israel may enjoy every man the inheritance of his fathers. 9Neither shall the inheritance remove from one tribe to another tribe; but every one of the tribes of the children of Israel shall keep himself to his own inheritance. 10Even as the LORD commanded Moses, so did the daughters of Zelophehad: 11For Mahlal, Tirzah, and Hoglah, and Milcah, and Noah, the daughters of Zelophehad, were married unto their father's brothers' sons: 12And they were married into the families of the sons of Manasseh the son of Joseph, and their inheritance remained in the tribe of the family of their father. 13These are the commandments and the judgments, which the LORD commanded by the hand of Moses unto the children of Israel in the plains of Moab by Jordan near Jericho."*

   a. The leaders of the tribe of Manasseh petitioned to Moses that if any of the daughters of Zelophehad married someone from another tribe, the first tribe would lose the inheritance. The solution became that the daughters could marry who they wanted to but only keep it within their tribe. For us that would simply mean not marrying outside the kingdom of God.

3. These women showed great faith, patience, wisdom, and courage.
4. These women had their eyes on the prize and nothing or no one could deter them.
5. They certainly were not silent in the house of God. Remember they were at the door of the Tabernacle.
6. These women made sure to point out that they weren't rebellious like Korah.
7. They also spoke freely to Moses the leader, and to Eleazar the high priest, as well as to all the princes of the tribes, the elders, and the whole congregation.

8. God always takes care of the fatherless

   a. Psalms 82:3 – "*Defend the poor and fatherless: do justice to the afflicted and needy.*"
   b. Psalms 27:10 – "*When my father and my mother forsake me, then the LORD will take me up.*"
   c. Exodus 22:22-24 – "*22Ye shall not afflict any widow, or fatherless child. 23If thou afflict them in any wise, and they cry at all unto me, I will surely hear their cry; 24And my wrath shall wax hot, and I will kill you with the sword; and your wives shall be widows, and your children fatherless.*"
   d. Psalms 10:14, 18 – "*Thou hast seen it; for thou beholdest mischief and spite, to requite it with thy hand: the poor committeth himself unto thee; thou art the helper of the fatherless…To judge the fatherless and the oppressed, that the man of the earth may no more oppress.*"
   e. Psalms 68:5 – "*A father of the fatherless, and a judge of the widows, is God in his holy habitation.*"

9. These were five wise virgins like those in Matthew 25:1-10. These later became the bride of Christ.
10. God says in Psalms 60:7, "*Gilead is mine, and Manasseh is mine…*" – These women belonged to the Lord.
11. No man judged this but God. I hope that by this, we can see God's heart towards women.
12. These women weren't just thinking of themselves, but for future generations.
13. Not only were they unafraid to speak, but God said, "They have spoken right"
14. These women were of the seventh generation – Seven is the number for perfection.

Lesson 13
The Story Of Anna

Luke 2:36-38 – "*36And there was one Anna, a prophetess, the daughter of Phanuel, of the tribe of Aser: she was of a great age, and had lived with an husband seven years from her virginity; 37And she was a widow of about fourscore and four years, which departed not from the temple, but served God with fastings and prayers night and day. 38And she coming in that instant gave thanks likewise unto the Lord, and spake of him to all them that looked for redemption in Jerusalem.*"

This is another woman in Scripture who has quite an honorable place. Even though she is spoken of only once, her story is central to the birth of our Lord Jesus. She witnessed the coming of Jesus along with Simeon. Simeon was a just and devout man, who was led by the Holy Spirit into the temple just as Jesus' parents brought the Messiah to Jerusalem to present him to the Lord and to offer the sacrifice God required for newborn males. Simeon had been told by the Holy Spirit that he would not see death before he had seen God's true anointed one. His prophetic pronouncement that Jesus was God's salvation, not only to Israel but also to the Gentiles, was one of the two witnesses that day that confirmed Jesus as the Messiah. Anna was the other witness that confirmed Jesus as the Messiah. Remember the Scripture has said, "*that in the mouth of two or three witnesses every word may be established*" (Matthew 18:16, II Corinthians 13:1, Deuteronomy 17:6, Deuteronomy 19:15, I Timothy 5:19, Hebrews 10:28). As we consider this, note that of the two witnesses, one was a man, and the other a woman. Both sexes are represented here proclaiming to each other's genders that Jesus was God's true anointed one.

I.   Facts About Anna

    A.   Definitions of Anna (Greek), Hannah (Hebrew)

        1.   Greek, *ahyah* – strength, <u>the stout part</u>, the fat tail of the oriental sheep; from a root, *alah* – to swear, to adjure; her name also means grace
        2.   Hebrew – gratuitous gift, grace, mercy, favor; from a root word, *chanan* – one who gives, gracious, bestowed, she was gracious, graciousness, <u>to bend or stoop in kindness to an inferior</u>; this root word is also translated – pray, make supplication, to show mercy, have pity upon, intreated, to be merciful

    B.   Important principles concerning Anna

        1.   She is a sign and a fulfillment of Joel's prophecy, which proclaimed, "*And it shall come to pass afterward, that I will pour out my spirit upon all flesh; and your sons and your daughters shall prophesy, your old men shall dream dreams, your young men shall see visions: And also upon the servants and upon the handmaids in those days will I pour out my spirit*" (Joel 2:28-29). The Word declares that Anna was a prophetess.
        2.   She represents all women, married and unmarried, young and old, virgin and widow.
        3.   She is a type of women proclaiming the Gospel. (Luke 2:38 – "*And she coming in that instant gave thanks likewise unto the Lord, and spake of him to all them that looked for redemption in Jerusalem.*")
        4.   She confirms that women are called to be prophets.
        5.   She made a public confession of her faith. (Luke 2:38)
        6.   She is a type of how faithful and diligent women are to God's house. (Luke 2:37 – "*And she was a widow of about fourscore and four years, which departed not from the temple, but served God with fastings and prayers night and day.*")
        7.   She is a type of women "seeing the real Jesus".
        8.   She is a type of women that wait and look for God's redemption.
        9.   She is a type of women that believe God's promises by faith.
        10.   She is a type of women intensely longing for Jesus.
        11.   She is one of the 43 references to women in the book of Luke.

12. She lived alone and separated to God for a long time.
13. Her husband's name is not given. It also appears that he died young.
14. She is a type of women unto whom God becomes their Husband.
15. She never married again. The life of the flesh didn't have any rule over her. "She loved not the world".
16. It appears she really didn't start serving the Lord until after the death of her husband.
17. She must have been married in her teens (Jewish women normally married in their teens).
18. She lived with her husband 7 years. Considering she was 84 years old, when you add her teenage years, it puts her at over 100 years old. 100 in Scripture is the number that represents – fruitfulness or full measure.
19. She met Jesus when He was 40 days old. 40 is the number of trial and testing, probation, and chastening. She must have understood all that He would go through and suffer.
20. She was also married to her husband 7 years. It must have been a perfect marriage.
21. She is the only person of note mentioned in Scripture of the tribe of Asher.
22. Jewish tradition says the tribe of Asher was noted for the beauty and talent of its women and because of their gifting, they were qualified for royal and high priestly marriage.

23. Anna was 84 years old when she met Jesus

    a. 2 x 42 – 2 is the number for witness, 42 is the number of antichrist; this symbolizes women's ability to witness and discern the spirit of antichrist. She was just like Eve in the garden exposing satan (Genesis 2:13).
    b. 4 x 21 – 4 is the number in the word that means – creation, that which is created, and the new creation man. 21 is the number of divine perfection. As part of God's creation, she may have reached divine perfection and was allowed not only to see Jesus, but to testify of Him being God's anointed.
    c. 7 x 12 – 7 once again means perfection, 12 is the number of Divine order, Divine government. She must have been walking in perfect order and was rightly aligned to God's government.
    d. 6 x 14 – 6 is the number for man and Satan, 14 is the number for doubling of perfection. She is a type of all the overcomers and God's perfect ones walking in true perfection.
    e. 3 x 28 – 3 is the number for the Godhead and resurrection, 28 is the number for eternal life. She is a type of those who will have a full revelation of the Godhead and resurrection, granting her eternal life. It means to me she was saved, especially considering her public confession of her faith.
    f. 1 x 84 – 1 is the number for God and unity. 80 is the number for fulfilled life.

25. She is a type of women who desire the Lord. (Psalms 27:4 – *"One thing have I desired of the LORD, that will I seek after; that I may dwell in the house of the LORD all the days of my life, to behold the beauty of the LORD, and to inquire in his temple."*)

26. She is a type of women who don't get weary in well doing.

    a. Galatians 6:9 – *"let us not be weary in well doing: for in due season we shall reap, if we faint not"*
    b. II Thessalonians 3:13 – *"But ye, brethren, be not weary in well doing."*

27. She is a type of women who through faith and patience inherit the promise.

    a. Hebrews 11:11 – *"Through faith also Sara herself received strength to conceive seed, and was delivered of a child when she was past age, because she judged him faithful who had promised."*
    b. Hebrews 10:35-36 – *"Cast not away therefore your confidence, which hath great recompence of reward. For ye have need of patience, that, after ye have done the will of God, ye might receive the promise."*
    c. Hebrews 6:12 – *"That ye be not slothful, but followers of them who through faith and patience inherit the promises."*

d. I Thessalonians 1:3 – "*Remembering without ceasing your work of faith, and labour of love, and patience of hope in our Lord Jesus Christ, in the sight of God and our Father.*"

28. She is a type of all women, everywhere, and in all churches, that seem to serve and worship God faithfully, fasting and praying often. They who outnumber men in most churches. They do most of the work, and attend meetings most frequently. They are the most spiritual among those in the local church.

II. Revelation of Anna's Story in Luke 2:36-38

Luke 2:36-38 – "*³⁶And there was one Anna, a prophetess, the daughter of Phanuel, of the tribe of Aser: she was of a great age, and had lived with an husband seven years from her virginity; ³⁷And she was a widow of about fourscore and four years, which departed not from the temple, but served God with fastings and prayers night and day. ³⁸And she coming in that instant gave thanks likewise unto the Lord, and spake of him to all them that looked for redemption in Jerusalem.*"

A. Verse 36

1. "*And there was <u>one</u> Anna…*" – Anna is chosen by God as a special example, one whose life is meaningful, significant, and prophetic.

2. "*…a prophetess…*" – This blows away the theory of women being silent in churches, for in this very story she testifies out loud of the Messiah. It later says that she, in verse 38, "*…spake of him to all them that looked for redemption in Jersusalem.*"

   a. Prophetess in Greek, *proorao* – to behold in advance, to pre-determine; from a root, *pronoeo* – to look out beforehand.
   b. Others of note in Scripture – Exodus 15:20, Judges 4:4, II Kings 22:14, Acts 21:9
   c. I Corinthians 14:3-5 – "*³But he that prophesieth speaketh unto men to edification, and exhortation, and comfort. ⁴He that speaketh in an unknown tongue edifieth himself; but he that prophesieth edifieth the church. ⁵I would that ye all spake with tongues, but rather that ye prophesied: for greater is he that prophesieth than he that speaketh with tongues, except he interpret, that the church may receive edifying.*"

3. "*… the daughter of Phanuel…*"

   a. Phanuel in Greek – the face or appearance of God, God's face, vision of God, to behold God
   b. This is the same word as the Hebrew word Peniel which means – the face of God, God's face, turn ye to God. The Hebrew word is also the Hebrew word translated "presence".
   c. Her heritage was one of being able to behold the face of God. She is a type of all women who are true disciples and they can see God, who know and enter into God's manifest presence. What an anointing she must have had.

4. "*…of the tribe of Aser…*" (Asher in Hebrew)

   a. Greek for Aser – fortunate, happy; it is the same word as Asher
   b. Hebrew for Asher – fortunate, happy, fortress
   c. Here Anna is a type of all women that are fortunate, happy, and a strong fortress

5. "*…she was of a great age…*"

   a. Principle found herein – Most of the time, women live longer than men. She was old, but not senile. She had gained great wisdom from God in her years of service to Him! Age can either be a blessing or a detriment. In her case it was a blessing. Her age brought her the wisdom of God and out of her lifetime of service, she gained the gift of discernment.

b. What does this term "of a great age" mean Scripturally?

1) Maturity

a) Hebrews 5:14 – "*But strong meat belongeth to them that are of full age, even those who by reason of use have their senses exercised to discern both good and evil.*"

b) Titus 2:2-3 – "*That the aged men be sober, grave, temperate, sound in faith, in charity, in patience. The aged women likewise, that they be in behaviour as becometh holiness, not false accusers, not given to much wine, teachers of good things;*"

c) Leviticus 19:32 – "*Thou shalt rise up before the hoary head, and honour the face of the old man, and fear thy God: I am the LORD.*"

d) Proverbs 16:31 – "*The hoary head is a crown of glory, if it be found in the way of righteousness.*"

e) I Kings 12:6-8 – "*⁶And king Rehoboam consulted with the old men, that stood before Solomon his father while he yet lived, and said, How do ye advise that I may answer this people? ⁷And they spake unto him, saying, If thou wilt be a servant unto this people this day, and wilt serve them, and answer them, and speak good words to them, then they will be thy servants for ever. ⁸But he forsook the counsel of the old men, which they had given him, and consulted with the young men that were grown up with him, and which stood before him.*"

f) Proverbs 20:29 – "*The glory of young men is their strength: and the beauty of old men is the gray head.*"

g) I Timothy 5:1-2 – "*Rebuke not an elder, but intreat him as a father; and the younger men as brethren; The elder women as mothers; the younger as sisters, with all purity.*"

2) One who has lived a full life

a) Genesis 15:15 – "*And thou shalt go to thy fathers in peace; thou shalt be buried in a good old age.*"

b) Genesis 25:8 – "*Then Abraham gave up the ghost, and died in a good old age, an old man, and full of years; and was gathered to his people.*"

c) Judges 8:32 – "*And Gideon the son of Joash died in a good old age, and was buried in the sepulchre of Joash his father, in Ophrah of the Abi-ezrites.*"

d) I Chronicles 29:28 – "*And he died in a good old age, full of days, riches, and honour: and Solomon his son reigned in his stead.*" – speaking of David here.

e) Job 42:17 – "*So Job died, being old and full of days.*"

3) One who has seen the faithfulness of God throughout their lives

a) Isaiah 46:4 – "*And even to your old age I am he; and even to hoar hairs will I carry you: I have made, and I will bear; even I will carry, and will deliver you.*"

b) Psalms 71:9 – "*Cast me not off in the time of old age; forsake me not when my strength faileth.*"

c) I Samuel 12:2 – "*And now, behold, the king walketh before you: and I am old and grayheaded; and, behold, my sons are with you: and I have walked before you from my childhood unto this day.*"

d) Psalms 37:25 – "*I have been young, and now am old; yet have I not seen the righteous forsaken, nor his seed begging bread.*"

e) I Peter 5:1 – "*The elders which are among you I exhort, who am also an elder, and a witness of the sufferings of Christ, and also a partaker of the glory that shall be revealed.*"

4) Those who have endured God's chastening

    a) Job 5:17-26

"*17Behold, happy is the man whom God correcteth: therefore despise not thou the chastening of the Almighty: 18For he maketh sore, and bindeth up: he woundeth, and his hands make whole. 19He shall deliver thee in six troubles: yea, in seven there shall no evil touch thee. 20In famine he shall redeem thee from death: and in war from the power of the sword. 21Thou shalt be hid from the scourge of the tongue: neither shalt thou be afraid of destruction when it cometh. 22At destruction and famine thou shalt laugh: neither shalt thou be afraid of the beasts of the earth. 23For thou shalt be in league with the stones of the field: and the beasts of the field shall be at peace with thee. 24And thou shalt know that thy tabernacle shall be in peace; and thou shalt visit thy habitation, and shalt not sin. 25Thou shalt know also that thy seed shall be great, and thine offspring as the grass of the earth. 26Thou shalt come to <u>thy grave in a full age</u>, like as a shock of corn cometh in in his season.*"

    b) John 21:18 – "*Verily, verily, I say unto thee, When thou wast young, thou girdedst thyself, and walkedst whither thou wouldest: but <u>when thou shalt be old</u>, thou shalt stretch forth thy hands, and another shall gird thee, and carry thee whither thou wouldest not.*"

    c) Philemon 9 – "*Yet for love's sake I rather beseech thee, being such an one as <u>Paul the aged</u>, and now also <u>a prisoner</u> of Jesus Christ.*"

5) Still able to bear fruit

    a) Proverbs 17:6 – "*Children's <u>children are the crown of old men</u>; and the glory of children are their fathers.*"

    b) Hebrews 11:11 – "*Through faith also Sara <u>herself received strength to conceive seed</u>, and was delivered of a child when <u>she was past age</u>, because she judged him faithful who had promised.*"

    c) Luke 1:36 – "*And, behold, thy cousin Elisabeth, she hath <u>also conceived a son in her old age</u>: and this is the sixth month with her, who was called barren.*"

    d) II Samuel 19:32-33 – "*32Now Barzillai was a very aged man, <u>even fourscore years old</u>: and he had provided the <u>king of sustenance</u> while he lay at Mahanaim; for he was a very great man. 33And the king said unto Barzillai, Come thou over with me, and I will feed thee with me in Jerusalem.*"

    e) Leviticus 25:22 – "*And ye shall sow the eighth year, and eat yet of old fruit until the ninth year; until her fruits come in ye shall eat of the old store.*"

    f) Joshua 13:1, 7 – "*1Now Joshua was <u>old and stricken in years</u>; and the LORD said unto him, Thou <u>art old and stricken in years, and there remaineth yet very much land to be possessed</u>...7Now therefore divide this land for an inheritance unto the nine tribes, and the half tribe of Manasseh,*"

    g) Psalms 71:18 – "*Now also <u>when I am old and grayheaded</u>, O God, forsake me not; until <u>I have shewed thy strength</u> unto this generation, and thy power to every one that is to come.*"

    h) Joel 2:28 – "*And it shall come to pass afterward, that I will pour out my spirit upon all flesh; and your sons and your daughters shall prophesy, <u>your old men shall dream dreams</u>, your young men shall see visions:*"

    i) Romans 4:19-21 – "*19And being not weak in faith, he considered not <u>his own body now dead</u>, when he was about <u>an hundred years old</u>, neither yet the <u>deadness of Sara's womb</u>: 20He staggered not at the promise of God through unbelief; <u>but was strong in faith</u>, giving glory to God; 21And being fully persuaded that, what he had promised, he was able also to perform.*"

    j) Deuteronomy 34:7 – "*And Moses was <u>an hundred and twenty years old</u> when he died: <u>his eye was not dim, nor his natural force abated</u>.*"

        k)   Joshua 14:10-14 – Caleb

"¹⁰And now, behold, the LORD hath kept me alive, as he said, <u>these forty and five years</u>, even since the LORD spake this word unto Moses, while the children of Israel wandered in the wilderness: and now, lo, I am this day <u>fourscore and five years old</u>. ¹¹<u>As yet I am as strong this day as I was in the day that Moses</u> sent me: as my strength was then, even so is my strength now, <u>for war, both to go out, and to come in</u>. ¹²Now therefore <u>give me this mountain</u>, whereof the LORD spake in that day; for thou heardest in that day how the Anakims were there, and that the cities were great and fenced: if so be the LORD will be with me, then I shall be able to drive them out, as the LORD said. ¹³And Joshua blessed him, and gave unto <u>Caleb</u> the son of Jephunneh Hebron for an inheritance. ¹⁴Hebron therefore became the inheritance of Caleb the son of Jephunneh the Kenezite unto this day, because that he wholly followed the LORD God of Israel."

        6)   One who has walked with God many years

            a)   Psalms 92:13 – *"Those that be planted in the house of the LORD shall flourish in the courts of our God."*

            b)   Job 11:13-19 – *"¹³If thou prepare thine heart, and stretch out thine hands toward him; ¹⁴If iniquity be in thine hand, put it far away, and let not wickedness dwell in thy tabernacles. ¹⁵For then shalt thou lift up thy face without spot; yea, thou shalt be stedfast, and shalt not fear: ¹⁶Because thou shalt forget thy misery, and remember it as waters that pass away: ¹⁷<u>And thine age shall be clearer than the noonday</u>; thou shalt shine forth, thou shalt be as the morning. ¹⁸And thou shalt be secure, because there is hope; yea, thou shalt dig about thee, and thou shalt take thy rest in safety. ¹⁹Also thou shalt lie down, and none shall make thee afraid; yea, many shall make suit unto thee."*

    5.   *"...and had lived with an husband seven years from her virginity."*

She, like the virtuous woman in Proverbs 31, was a good wife and obviously loved her husband and was truly submitted to him. She was also a virgin when she married him. This speaks of her keeping herself and remaining pure for her one, true husband, similar to the bride of Christ. Anna was a special woman, a godly, faithful, worshipping, praying, fasting, and wonderful woman. She is an example to all women of what they should be like. She shows the way to true Brideship as well as how to deal with the loss of your loved one and how to find the peace of God in your life after tragedy strikes. She also shows us how to give ourselves completely to the Lord and the service of His house. Also, she shows how a true prophet should live their life. Anna also shows that if we are faithful, in the end, we will see Jesus!

    B.   Verse 37 – *"And she was a widow of about fourscore and four years, which departed not from the temple, but served God with fastings and prayers night and day."*

        1.   Other translations:

            "A widow even for or up to 84 years..."
            "...she did not go out from the temple enclosures, but was worshiping..."
            "...who did not depart from the temple..."
            "...she never left the temple courtyard, but worshipped day and night..."
            "...she was never absent from the temple..."
            "...she did not leave the temple, rendering sacred service to God..."
            "...she spent her whole life..."

        2.   *"...A widow..."*

            a.   I Timothy 5:3-6 – *"³Honour widows that are widows indeed. ⁴But if any widow have children or nephews, let them learn first to shew piety at home, and to requite their parents: for that is good and acceptable before God. ⁵Now she that is a widow indeed, and desolate, trusteth in God, and continueth in supplications and prayers night and day. ⁶But she that liveth in pleasure is dead while she liveth."*

    b.   Matthew 23:14 – *"Woe unto you, scribes and Pharisees, hypocrites! for ye devour widows' houses, and for a pretence make long prayer: therefore ye shall receive the greater damnation."*

    c.   Psalms 68:5 – *"A father of the fatherless, and a judge of the widows, is God in his holy habitation."*

    d.   Psalms 146:9 – *"The LORD preserveth the strangers; he relieveth the fatherless and widow: but the way of the wicked he turneth upside down."*

    e.   Isaiah 54:1-5 – *"¹Sing, O barren, thou that didst not bear; break forth into singing, and cry aloud, thou that didst not travail with child: for more are the children of the desolate than the children of the married wife, saith the LORD. ²Enlarge the place of thy tent, and let them stretch forth the curtains of thine habitations: spare not, lengthen thy cords, and strengthen thy stakes; ³For thou shalt break forth on the right hand and on the left; and thy seed shall inherit the Gentiles, and make the desolate cities to be inhabited. ⁴Fear not; for thou shalt not be ashamed: neither be thou confounded; for thou shalt not be put to shame: for thou shalt forget the shame of thy youth, and shalt not remember the reproach of thy widowhood any more. ⁵For thy Maker is thine husband; the LORD of hosts is his name; and thy Redeemer the Holy One of Israel; The God of the whole earth shall he be called."*

3.   *"...which departed not from the temple..."* – So much the more she is a picture of true devotion and faithfulness to God. God and His house were her life. She was consumed by a passion to serve others above herself.

4.   *"...served God with fastings and prayers..."* – She fasted righteously

    a.   Luke 18:10-14 – unlike the Pharisee
    b.   Isaiah 58:6-14 – all these blessings of fasting were hers

5.   *"...night and day..."*

    a.   Being in His Word night and day – Principle of the daily sacrifice

        1)   Joshua 1:8 – *"This book of the law shall not depart out of thy mouth; but thou shalt meditate therein day and night, that thou mayest observe to do according to all that is written therein: for then thou shalt make thy way prosperous, and then thou shalt have good success."*

        2)   Psalms 1:2 – *"But his delight is in the law of the LORD; and in his law doth he meditate day and night."*

C.   Verse 38 – *"And she coming in that instant gave thanks likewise unto the Lord, and spake of him to all them that looked for redemption in Jerusalem."*

    1.   Other translations:

    "And she came up at that same hour, and she returned thanks to God, and talked to all who were looking for redemption."
    "At the very time Simeon was praying, she showed up, and broke into an anthem of praise."
    "And she coming up the same hour, gave praise to the Lord, and spake of Him to all."
    "...she coming in, confessed to the Lord..."
    "From the moment she came in, and began to praise God..."
    "...she kept on talking about Him..."
    "...she spoke about Jesus long afterwards..."
    "...and publically proclaiming the Messiah's arrival to everyone in Jerusalem."

2. The term "*coming in*" in Greek really means "*bursting in*"
3. Upon seeing Jesus, her spirit rejoices and witnesses to who He is immediately

4. This shows these things:

   a. She had great discernment.
   b. She had an anointing.
   c. She was a worshipper.
   d. She truly was a prophet.
   e. She was bold.
   f. She did not fear to preach the Gospel, even to men.

Elisabeth – Mother Of A Prophetic Company

In our ongoing study of women in Scripture, we come to another story of an outstanding woman who, even though she is one of many barren women in Scripture, is given a child supernaturally by God. She gave birth to "John the Baptist", who was the forerunner of the Lord and was to "prepare the way of the Lord." She had an awesome responsibility. We will look at Elisabeth's life in the natural, and we will see that she will birth a child that was important to God and His people, just as all the other barren women in Scripture did. Elisabeth represents the mother of a last day's "John the Baptist ministry" that will prepare the way of the Lord the second and last time. Elisabeth is a type of the last day church that will bring forth a remnant, a manchild (Revelation 12:5). She represents the last great move of God upon His people and the remnant of prophetic sons that will come out of her womb.

I.   Elisabeth's Story – Luke 1:5-7, 13-17, 24-25, 36-37, 39-45, 57-66

    A.   Her background – Verses 5-7 – "*⁵There was in the days of Herod, the king of Judaea, a certain priest named Zacharias, of the course of Abia: and his wife was of the daughters of Aaron, and her name was Elisabeth. ⁶And they were both righteous before God, walking in all the commandments and ordinances of the Lord blameless. ⁷And they had no child, because that Elisabeth was barren, and they both were now well stricken in years.*"

        1.   Elisabeth's name means – God is my oath, a worshipper of God, God of the covenant, my God has sworn, God of the seven – The revelation of her name is that her life, her all, and her supreme reason for being is God Himself (God is my oath). She has sworn an oath to serve God. She was a worshipper. She reveals that our God will keep His covenant and bring to pass what He has sworn. Also, seven is the number for perfection which means that what God would do through her would be perfect and complete.

        2.   She was a daughter of Aaron – She came from the lineage of priests. This means her heritage was one of serving and worshipping the Lord, and ministering to God's people. She came out of a holy and separated line of ancestors.

        3.   She was righteous

        4.   She walked in all God's commandments (obedient to the Word of God).

        5.   She was blameless – She is part of the church that is holy and pure in heart; she was a true worshipper and lover of God.

        6.   She was barren – Barren in Greek, *steiros* – stiff, unnatural, sterile; from a root, *steros* – stiff, solid, stable, strong, steadfast, sure – She is one of many outstanding women in Scripture who were barren. All of these women birthed sons that represented a powerful revelation of a supernatural child. While some might consider barrenness a curse, for Elisabeth and the other women, it showed the faithfulness and the miraculous power of God. It also showed that their barrenness was for a holy reason that would be fulfilled later. We will consider these barren women and who, why, and what they represent in another lesson. Below are other barren women found in Scripture.

            a.   Sarai – Genesis 11:30 – Isaac
            b.   Rebekah – Genesis 25:25 – The 12 patriarchs, but specifically Jacob
            c.   Rachel – Genesis 29:31 – Benjamin
            d.   Manoah's wife – Judges 13:2 – Samson
            e.   Hannah – I Samuel 1:3 – Samuel

She and these others were allowed to be barren on purpose, for the Word says no women shall be barren among His people (Exodus 23:26, Deuteronomy 7:14), because God had a special plan for their children. These women had to go through the dealings of God (travail) to bring forth God's purpose.

7. She was an old woman, "well stricken in years" – This speaks to us of maturity, wisdom, experience, and substance. Also God wanted to show Himself miraculous in Elisabeth.

B. Verse 13-19 – "*13But the angel said unto him, Fear not, Zacharias: for thy prayer is heard; and thy wife Elisabeth shall bear thee a son, and thou shalt call his name John. 14And thou shalt have joy and gladness; and many shall rejoice at his birth. 15For he shall be great in the sight of the Lord, and shall drink neither wine nor strong drink; and he shall be filled with the Holy Ghost, even from his mother's womb. 16And many of the children of Israel shall he turn to the Lord their God. 17And he shall go before him in the spirit and power of Elias, to turn the hearts of the fathers to the children, and the disobedient to the wisdom of the just; to make ready a people prepared for the Lord. 18And Zacharias said unto the angel, Whereby shall I know this? for I am an old man, and my wife well stricken in years. 19And the angel answering said unto him, I am Gabriel, that stand in the presence of God; and am sent to speak unto thee, and to shew thee these glad tidings.*"

1. Obviously Zacharias and Elisabeth had been praying to have a child.
2. God answered their prayer by giving them the forerunner of the Lord.
3. Zacharias, for whatever reason, could not believe the angel Gabriel's message whom God had sent to him directly from His presence.
4. He was made speechless by the Lord because of His unbelief.
5. We find that Elisabeth must have believed instantly because she later demanded that the child's name was to be John. John's name means – God has been gracious, Jehovah has graciously given, the mercy or favor of God, God is a gracious giver. This shows she had believed the Word from the Lord (verse 60).

C. Verse 24-25 – "*24And after those days his wife Elisabeth conceived, and hid herself five months, saying, 25Thus hath the Lord dealt with me in the days wherein he looked on me, to take away my reproach among men.*"

1. She conceives miraculously.
2. She hides herself five months – Five is the number for grace and spiritual ministry. In the last days, God will have "hidden ones" in His church. Who will know the grace of God and truly be prepared for true spiritual ministry on the earth.
3. She had endured reproach, but God eventually showed Himself strong on her behalf. Bearing His reproach means bearing His disgrace. The church will and must also bear the "reproach of the Lord" if they are going to be true disciples. Reproach in the Greek, *oneidizo* – to defame, to fail at, to chide, to upbraid, to cast in teeth.

   a. Hebrews 13:13 – "*Let us go forth therefore unto him without the camp, bearing his reproach.*"
   b. Hebrews 11:26 – "*Esteeming the reproach of Christ greater riches than the treasures in Egypt: for he had respect unto the recompence of the reward.*" – Speaking of Moses.
   c. I Timothy 4:10 – "*For therefore we both labour and suffer reproach, because we trust in the living God, who is the Saviour of all men, specially of those that believe.*"
   d. Romans 15:3 – "*For even Christ pleased not himself; but, as it is written, The reproaches of them that reproached thee fell on me.*"
   e. II Corinthians 12:10 – "*Therefore I take pleasure in infirmities, in reproaches, in necessities, in persecutions, in distresses for Christ's sake: for when I am weak, then am I strong.*"
   f. I Peter 4:14 – "*If ye be reproached for the name of Christ, happy are ye; for the spirit of glory and of God resteth upon you: on their part he is evil spoken of, but on your part he is glorified.*"

D. Verses 36-37 – "*36And, behold, thy cousin Elisabeth, she hath also conceived a son in her old age: and this is the sixth month with her, who was called barren. 37For with God nothing shall be impossible.*"

1. Gabriel has now been sent to the Virgin Mary who would bring forth the Messiah! And he speaks to her of Elisabeth.

2. Elisabeth was the cousin of Mary. This woman who represents the church is close to the Lord and in the family of God. In other words, she is not of this world. She is in God's kingdom.

3. Old age – speaks of maturity

   a. Hebrews 5:14 – "*But strong meat belongeth <u>to them that are of full age</u>, even those who by reason of use have their senses exercised to discern both good and evil.*"
   b. Luke 2:36 – "*And there was one Anna, a prophetess, the daughter of Phanuel, of the tribe of Aser: <u>she was of a great age</u>, and had lived with an husband seven years from her virginity;*"
   c. Titus 2:3-5 – "*³The <u>aged women</u> likewise, that they <u>be in behaviour as becometh holiness</u>, not false accusers, not given to much wine, teachers of good things; ⁴That they may teach the young women to be sober, to love their husbands, to love their children, ⁵To be discreet, chaste, keepers at home, good, obedient to their own husbands, that the word of God be not blasphemed.*"
   d. Job 32:7 – "*I said, <u>Days should speak</u>, and <u>multitude of years should teach wisdom</u>.*"
   e. Job 5:26 – "*Thou shalt come to thy grave in a full age, like as a shock of corn cometh in in his season.*" – This is God's promise to those who allow God's correction.
   f. Job 11:17 – "*And thine age shall be clearer than the noonday; thou shalt shine forth, thou shalt be as the morning.*" – This is God's promise to those who prepare their hearts toward Him.
   g. Psalms 92:13-14 – "*Those that be planted in the house of the LORD shall flourish in the courts of our God. They shall still bring forth fruit in old age; they shall be fat and flourishing;*" – This is God's promise to those planted in a local church.
   h. Isaiah 46:4 – "*And even to your old age I am he; and even to hoar hairs will I carry you: I have made, and I will bear; even I will carry, and will deliver you.*" – Even in this season of life, God will carries, makes, bears, and delivers you.

4. Elisabeth was in the sixth month of her pregnancy – Six is the number for man. Jesus came for man's salvation. Elisabeth carried in her womb the "man sent from God" to prepare for the coming of our Saviour.
5. She once was barren but no more. God has blessed her. Only those who have been barren can really know the joy of bringing forth what God intends.
6. With God nothing shall be impossible – Elisabeth had received just like Mary, albeit differently, a miraculous intervention of God. The church in the last days will be and experience the miracles of the Lord.

E. Verse 39-45 – "*³⁹And Mary arose in those days, and went into the hill country with haste, into a city of Juda; ⁴⁰And entered into the house of Zacharias, and saluted Elisabeth. ⁴¹And it came to pass, that, when Elisabeth heard the salutation of Mary, the babe leaped in her womb; and Elisabeth was filled with the Holy Ghost: ⁴²And she spake out with a loud voice, and said, Blessed art thou among women, and blessed is the fruit of thy womb. ⁴³And whence is this to me, that the mother of my Lord should come to me? ⁴⁴For, lo, as soon as the voice of thy salutation sounded in mine ears, the babe leaped in my womb for joy. ⁴⁵And blessed is she that believed: for there shall be a performance of those things which were told her from the Lord.*"

1. Elisabeth lived in the hill country – This speaks of the mountains and valley experiences of our lives, which are the dealings of God. This speaks of the fact that Elisabeth had endured the dealings of God.
2. Elisabeth lived in a city of Judah – Judah means praise. The place where this woman abides and dwells is in praise and worship.
3. Elisabeth immediately responded to the sound of Mary's voice, which had Jesus inside it. She knew the Lord's voice. She had a discerning, prophetic nature and witnessed to His holy voice.
4. The babe (manchild) leaped in her womb. That remnant inside of Elisabeth couldn't wait to get out and do the work of the Lord.
5. Elisabeth was filled with the Holy Ghost – This obviously speaks of the Spirit-filled church in the last days, that part of the church that has received the "baptism of the Holy Ghost". The manchild,

remnant, bride, overcomers, or whatever one would choose to call this company must come out of a Spirit-filled environment.

6. She, by speaking out with a loud voice, is prophesying. This prophesying church will be the one the forerunner comes out of. She had a prophetic nature and spoke spontaneously (Psalms 110:3, *"Thy people shall be willing [spontaneous] in the day of thy power [army]"*).

7. Elisabeth blessed Mary and witnessed to the Messiah she was carrying.

8. Mother of my Lord – Elisabeth is the very first person to recognize Jesus as Lord.

9. She then encourages Mary for her faith. She also proclaims there will be a "performance of those things which were told her from the Lord". She is an affirming witness that the Messiah was coming and that God's Word always comes to pass.

F. Verse 57-58 – *"⁵⁷Now Elisabeth's full time came that she should be delivered; and she brought forth a son. ⁵⁸And her neighbours and her cousins heard how the Lord had shewed great mercy upon her; and they rejoiced with her."*

1. Elisabeth carried this baby to the full time and she birthed a son. This woman knew that God does everything in His timing. Also, she knew that there would be a particular time when it would be accomplished. Below are Scriptures speaking of God's fullness of time.

   a. Psalms 105:19 – *"Until the time that his word came: the word of the LORD tried him."*
   b. Acts 2:1 – *"And when the day of Pentecost was fully come, they were all with one accord in one place."* – Outpouring of the Holy Ghost
   c. Galatians 4:4 – *"But when the fulness of the time was come, God sent forth his Son, made of a woman, made under the law,"*
   d. Ephesians 1:10 – *"That in the dispensation of the fulness of times he might gather together in one all things in Christ, both which are in heaven, and which are on earth; even in him:"*

2. She brought forth a son – Revelation 12:1, 5 – *"And there appeared a great wonder in heaven; a woman clothed with the sun, and the moon under her feet, and upon her head a crown of twelve stars...And she brought forth a man child, who was to rule all nations with a rod of iron: and her child was caught up unto God, and to his throne."* – Elisabeth is a type of the woman, the church, whom out of, will come forth the manchild, the company of overcomers.

3. All of her neighbors and her family saw how God had showed her <u>great</u> <u>mercy</u>. This is a woman who has known the great mercy of God. This must be a characteristic of the last days church. They have to know and understand God's great mercy for His people. They must know this side of God's character.

4. They rejoiced with her – All those that love God will rejoice with this last days church.

G. Verse 59-62 – *"⁵⁹And it came to pass, that on the eighth day they came to circumcise the child; and they called him Zacharias, after the name of his father. ⁶⁰And his mother answered and said, Not so; but he shall be called John. ⁶¹And they said unto her, There is none of thy kindred that is called by this name. ⁶²And they made signs to his father, how he would have him called."*

1. She was obedient to the law of Moses (Word of God and came on the eighth day to present him to the Lord and have him circumcised).

2. When others tried to interfere and call him after his father's name, she adamantly refused. She knew he had to have a prophetic name. God rewarded her for her obedience.

Lesson 15
Abishag

There are women in the Scriptures that had distinct callings upon their lives that are never thought of or mentioned and many of them are very important as far as the move of God is concerned. As we saw in a previous chapter, the five daughters of Zelophehad had everything to do with releasing forever out of God's mouth the command for women to receive their inheritance. At that time, women were not allowed to speak, yet they stood right at the door of the Tabernacle and spoke very clearly. God said to Moses that they spoke rightly.

In this section, we want to look at a woman by the name of Abishag in the book of I Kings 1. In this story, David is about to die and Solomon is about to come forth to be the new king. All scholars agree that Solomon's reign was a peaceful reign and is a type of the millennial reign of Christ. David's reign was filled with warfare, fighting, and the gathering up of money to build the temple of Solomon. David is a type of the old move of God, or the move of God that precedes that last great move of God. David was one of the greatest overcomers and worshippers of the Bible. David was told by God that he couldn't build His house because there was too much blood on his hands. The last house of God is going to be a house of peace and we find at the dedication of the temple of Solomon in II Chronicles 5 that the glory of God descends upon it. The temple of Solomon being built is symbolic to the last great move of God that is coming. You and I have been part of the old move, as we prepare to see the last great move of God come.

As such, it is so vital to see women released into their ministry. We hope to get a better understanding of this importance as revealed by this story in I Kings. I remember Arthur Burt saying years ago that the prior wave, as it comes in and is finished rolling in, begins to then recede back and pushes and resists the new wave coming in. The old wave always tries to resist the new wave. We don't want to be a partaker of that. As seen in this story, there will be a people that come out of that former move who will bridge the gap into the final move of God and be the very ones who will become the bride of Christ. It is not very often that people can say they were part of two moves of God. So let's read:

I Kings 1:1 says, "*Now king David was old and stricken in years...*" At this part of his life, David was about 70 years old. Why was David so old and stricken in years at only 70? Because David was the greatest overcomer (apart from Jesus) that the world has ever known. He fought battle after battle after battle for the Kingdom of God and literally brought forth the kingdom of Israel to a place of peace and left billions of dollars to finance the temple of Solomon (a type of the last great move of God). The word "stricken" in Hebrew simply means the comings and goings of one's life. He had so many comings and goings in his life and so much warfare, that at 70 years of age he was done. I personally would rather be 70 and have been used up by God than to be 120 and never been used of God. If God uses you, trust me, it will take a toll, and it will also bring joy and great substance in your life.

So here we find him old and stricken in years, "*...and they covered him with clothes, but he gat no heat. ²Wherefore his servants said unto him, Let there be sought for my lord the king a young virgin: and let her stand before the king, and let her cherish him, and let her lie in thy bosom, that my lord the king may get heat. ³So they sought for a fair damsel throughout all the coasts of Israel, and found Abishag a Shunammite, and brought her to the king. ⁴And the damsel was very fair, and cherished the king, and ministered to him: but the king knew her not.*" Now, at this point David is about to pass on and so there is a great battle to take the throne. David had many wives and concubines. One may ask the question, because he had all those wives and concubines, why didn't one of them lay down with him and give him heat? Because they were part of the old move of God as well, and there needed to be somebody fresh. Somebody who may have been a part of the old move, but who were not so engrossed in it that they were unable to be fresh, and flow with the new move of God that was coming.

David had many sons, and Adonijah was one of them. Adonijah knew that his father was about to die, so he tried to orchestrate being king. There are other things happening in this story that we need to understand as well. The old priesthood is dying and even the captain of the Lord's host, the head of the army is about to pass away as well. So you have King David dying, you have Abiathar the priest who came down the line of Eli, and you have Joab who had been with David, shed much blood and killed Absalom. Joab had never sided with Absalom against David, but when Adonijah said, "I will be king", Joab had sided with him and went and proclaimed later on in this chapter that Adonijah was the new king. So Bathsheba, knowing that Solomon was going to be the rightful heir, went into the king and King David said we're going to anoint Solomon as king. But David had to use another priest and that brings us to this point. As the old move passes away, the old priesthood has to go with it. You see Eli in I Samuel 3, where God had spoken a word to Eli that his line was going to be cursed even though at the time he was the high priest of Israel. At the point when Solomon takes the throne, Zadok (Hebrew – righteousness) becomes the high priest. This means that in the last great move of God, the sons of Zadok (the sons of righteousness) become the priests of God. The last great priest was Zadok. So in this story we have a lot going on, a lot of things going away and new things coming and it is vital that we see what Abishag had to do with this important transition, and how she represents to us all of the women in the last days.

As the story continues in I Kings, Adonijah tries to take the throne, but David anoints Solomon as king. Adonijah then pleads for his life and Solomon says he can live and then something else happens in I Kings 2 starting in verse 12, "*12Then sat Solomon upon the throne of David his father; and his kingdom was established greatly. 13And Adonijah the son of Haggith came to Bath-sheba the mother of Solomon. And she said, Comest thou peaceably? And he said, Peaceably.*" Normally, Adonijah would have been killed but Solomon spared him. Adonijah is lucky to be alive and has the audacity to go to the mother of the king. "*14He said moreover, I have somewhat to say unto thee. And she said, Say on. 15And he said, Thou knowest that the kingdom was mine, and that all Israel set their faces on me, that I should reign: howbeit the kingdom is turned about, and is become my brother's: for it was his from the LORD. 16And now I ask one petition of thee, deny me not. And she said unto him, Say on. 17And he said, Speak, I pray thee, unto Solomon the king, (for he will not say thee nay,) that he give me Abishag the Shunammite to wife. 18And Bath-sheba said, Well; I will speak for thee unto the king. 19Bath-sheba therefore went unto king Solomon, to speak unto him for Adonijah. And the king rose up to meet her, and bowed himself unto her, and sat down on his throne, and caused a seat to be set for the king's mother; and she sat on his right hand. 20Then she said, I desire one small petition of thee; I pray thee, say me not nay. And the king said unto her, Ask on, my mother: for I will not say thee nay. 21And she said, Let Abishag the Shunammite be given to Adonijah thy brother to wife." 22And king Solomon answered and said unto his mother, And why dost thou ask Abishag the Shunammite for Adonijah? ask for him the kingdom also; for he is mine elder brother; even for him, and for Abiathar the priest, and for Joab the son of Zeruiah.*" Adonijah was one of the elder brothers. Does this remind you of something in the Bible? He is like the elder brother in the story of the prodigal in Luke 15. Remember, Abiathar and Joab had gone against Solomon in trying to anoint Adonijah king. So Solomon recognized that Adonijah was trying to go through the back door and sneak his way back into the kingdom by marrying Abishag. Adonijah tries to use Bathsheba to influence Solomon. One of the greatest assets a woman has is her intelligence and sensitivity. But also, she has to watch out for one other thing. This one thing is always out there if women want to reach out and grab it and that is one word called manipulation. Sisters and wives know that they can cry at the drop of a hat in order to change things. A man could be furious with a woman, but she can begin to cry and the whole situation changes. Women's wiles are very well established. But Solomon figures this out quickly.

"*23Then king Solomon sware by the LORD, saying, God do so to me, and more also, if Adonijah have not spoken this word against his own life. 24Now therefore, as the LORD liveth, which hath established me, and set me on the throne of David my father, and who hath made me an house, as he promised, Adonijah shall be put to death this day. 25And king Solomon sent by the hand of Benaiah the son of Jehoiada; and he fell upon him that he died.*" Before I get back to Abishag, who is Benaiah? Turn to II Samuel 23. Benaiah was one of David's mighty men. He wasn't in the first three, but he was in the second three. David had 37 mighty men in all. Within the 37, he had the first three and then the second three which never attained to the first. In verses 20-23 of II Samuel it reads, "*20And Benaiah the son of Jehoiada, the son of a valiant man, of Kabzeel, who had done many acts, he slew two lionlike men of Moab: he went down also and slew a lion in the midst of a pit in time of snow: 21And he slew an Egyptian, a goodly man: and the Egyptian had a spear in his hand; but he went down to him with a staff, and plucked the spear out of the Egyptian's hand, and slew him with his own spear. 22These things did Benaiah the son of Jehoiada, and had the name among three mighty men. 23He was more honourable than the thirty, but he attained not to the first three. And David set him over his guard.*" Here is another man who transcends two moves. He comes out of the overcomers, the mighty men of David and he is appointed captain of the army in Joab's place. This is my hope for my life, that those of us that have been part of God's last move will also want to be one of those who bridge the gap and make it into the next move. In Benaiah's case, it was a promotion.

There is a people then who will be able to see beyond where they have been. Where we've been is not all that God has. All we've seen is not all that God could show us. No matter how great it is or was, how wonderful the worship and words were we experienced, there is always more. There's always a greater place and the temptation in men is to build a nest, and build a tabernacle. Hosea 8:14 says, "*For Israel hath forgotten his Maker, and buildeth temples*". On the mount of transfiguration in Matthew 17, Peter, upon seeing the vision, said let us build three tabernacles. Our tendency, even in a supernatural experience, is to build an altar to the experience. All that many Christians talk about is the great experiences that happened to them in the past, but nothing has happened to them since then. Every day, you and I want to see and experience God doing great things. I can point back to many, many great, glorious, and miraculous experiences during my walk with God over the last 38 years. Nevertheless, I will never forget something Bill Briton said years ago, "Never let the glory of past triumphs hinder you from future triumphs". It is so easy to settle on your lees after you win a battle. This is exactly what happened to David earlier in his life. He fought, he fought, and he fought, but one day, when it was time for him to go back to battle, you find him on a roof top falling into sin. The problem with most of us, is that when God moves, we form camps. There are so many camps in the body of Christ. There is the river camp, the prophetic camp, the worship camp, the word of faith camp, the deep teacher camp, this evangelical quasi-charismatic camp, etc. Paul in the later part of his life, while writing from prison, even after going up to heaven and coming back earlier in his life, said in Philippians 3:13-14, "*13Brethren, I count not myself to have apprehended: but this one thing I do, forgetting those things which are behind, and reaching forth unto those things which are before, 14I press toward the mark for the prize of the high calling of God in Christ Jesus.*"

In this day we live, God wants to move again, and we want to bridge the gap as John the Baptist did from the old to the new. So much depends on the people that bridge this gap. They are so essential for the coming move of God and the enemy wants to wipe them out. Adonijah is a type of this enemy. He wants to usurp Solomon's throne and now he is trying to steal this virgin, this young damsel that was given to David to encourage and help him. Solomon sees through all of this and in I Kings 2:25-28, "*25And king Solomon sent by the hand of Benaiah the son of Jehoiada; and he fell upon him that he died. 26And unto Abiathar the priest said the king, Get thee to Anathoth, unto thine own fields; for thou art worthy of death: but I will not at this time put thee to death, because thou barest the ark of the Lord GOD before David my father, and because thou hast been afflicted in all wherein my father was afflicted. 27So Solomon thrust out Abiathar from being priest unto the LORD; that he might fulfil the word of the LORD, which he spake concerning the house of Eli in Shiloh. 28Then tidings came to Joab: for Joab had turned after Adonijah, though he turned not after Absalom. And Joab fled unto the tabernacle of the LORD, and caught hold on the horns of the altar.*" Grabbing the horns of the altar is akin to begging for mercy, thinking nobody will kill me in the tabernacle. "*29And it was told king Solomon that Joab was fled unto the tabernacle of the LORD; and, behold, he is by the altar. Then Solomon sent Benaiah the son of Jehoiada, saying, Go, fall upon him. 30And Benaiah came to the tabernacle of the LORD, and said unto him, Thus saith the king, Come forth. And he said, Nay; but I will die here. And Benaiah brought the king word again, saying, Thus said Joab, and thus he answered me. 31And the king said unto him, Do as he hath said, and fall upon him, and bury him; that thou mayest take away the innocent blood, which Joab shed, from me, and from the house of my father. 32And the LORD shall return his blood upon his own head, who fell upon two men more righteous and better than he, and slew them with the sword, my father David not knowing thereof, to wit, Abner the son of Ner, captain of the host of Israel, and Amasa the son of Jether, captain of the host of Judah. 33Their blood shall therefore return upon the head of Joab, and upon the head of his seed for ever: but upon David, and upon his seed, and upon his house, and upon his throne, shall there be peace for ever from the LORD. 34So Benaiah the son of Jehoiada went up, and fell upon him, and slew him: and he was buried in his own house in the wilderness. 35And the king put Benaiah the son of Jehoiada in his room over the host: and Zadok the priest did the king put in the room of Abiathar.*" This is the story.

Now, I want to go back and look at Abishag and her part in the story. First of all, Abishag's name in Hebrew means "ignorance of the father, or father of error, or my father causes wandering". What does this have to do with the story? Abishag is part of a former move that has fallen into error, that has wandered from God's original intent. She was a Shunammite which means "two resting places, or their sleep". Many people think she might be the Shulamite in Song of Solomon, but there is no evidence for that. We do know that she did live on and never married. What does this mean? Do you remember the parable of the ten virgins (five foolish and five wise) in Matthew 25:1-13? The word "sleeping" is involved in the story. There are two types of "sleeping" in Scripture, two resting places. One is resting in God, the other is slothfulness. So Abishag is coming from a company of people who have fallen into error and have wandered from God's original purpose. They have even progressed from a place of slothfulness into a place of a nest. Abishag was of the tribe of Issachar which means in the Hebrew "he is wages, he is hired" and comes from a root word meaning "to hire or to be rewarded". Remember in the book of Revelation, what is the last church? The last church is Laodicea and they say in Revelation 3:17, "*I am rich, and increased with goods, and have need of nothing*". This is the same move in this story. David is the church of Laodicea in this story. David at the end of his life was very prosperous. Laodicea in the Greek means "opinion of the people". God warns the church of Laodicea as we read revelation 3:17 in its entirety, "*Because thou sayest, I am rich, and increased with goods, and have need of nothing; and knowest not that thou art wretched, and miserable, and poor, and blind, and naked:*" Abishag's background was Issachar. The only word for Issachar in Revelation is hireling. She has now come out of a move that has erred and has wandered, sleeping, and has become a hireling. Can anyone of us disagree that when we turn on Christian television any day of the week, we see men begging for money? The earth is full of this type of ministry. This is what it has become. So this is our move right now, just like when Jesus went into the temple and began to cast out all them that sold and bought in the temple. He said, "*My house shall be called the house of prayer; but ye have made it a den of thieves.*" Jesus was signifying that a new move has come. Jesus wants to remove the hirelings that are asleep and wandering. This is what Abishag was a part of.

All of the men that were part of David's army were great men. They fought many battles and brought great victory. But it is just like in the beginning of Joshua when God had to charge him by saying, "*Moses my servant is dead; now therefore arise, go over this Jordan, thou, and all this people, unto the land which I do give to them, even to the children of Israel.*" Isn't it amazing how only two men out of all of the first generation children of Israel made it through the wilderness into the Promise land? Only Joshua and Caleb were part of the old move (coming out of Egypt) and made it into the new move (going into the promise land). A remnant is going to make it. Only a remnant will make it to the last great move of God. While so many are settling on their lees and building nests, big buildings, edifices to men, a remnant won't settle for what God's past works. It doesn't mean the people who were only part of what God did in an old move aren't good and sincere people, they have simply fallen into error. There are many like David that have done much good for the Kingdom of God, but it is dying out and is stricken in years, but God has a provision and her name is Abishag. In the last days, the bridge between the move we are in and the move that is coming is going to be women! Women will carry us into the next great move of God! Glory to God!

For many, the church is old and well stricken in years. They are cold and need a covering. They shouldn't be dying at 70. David couldn't get warm. The church has lost its power, having no heat, no fire! Where is the church going to get some fire? **Bring Abishag the woman**! What's coming is greater than anything we've ever known, exceedingly abundantly above all we could ever ask or think! Our minds cannot contain the power that will be released upon the earth through a people. And when this people arise, forged through the fire of adversity, chosen in the furnace of affliction, having survived the horror and also the glories of the previous move, they will be open and ready. In Israel, only two came out of the wilderness. They did not consider themselves grasshoppers like everyone else. They believed they were well able to go in and possess the land. What kind of spirit do we have? Do you think you are a grasshopper?

David is cold. Therefore they go in search for a young fair damsel. David had a many wives and concubines, but they must have knew it wasn't enough. Something fresh had to be brought, something new, something that was not of the old. It was part of the old, but not stuck with the old. It was open and ready to receive that which was new and they found Abishag. She was beautiful. All she was asked to do was stand before David, to cherish him, and minister to him. We are to cherish every man or woman of God that came before us that was part of the previous move of God. We give them the honor for what they did. I wonder what it was like for Joshua stepping in the shoes of Moses. That is why five times God said to Joshua, be strong and of good courage, because Joshua had seen all that Moses had done: the sea parting, the ten plagues, water coming out of a rock, etc. It is too easy to be comfortable in what we have. Our loins need to be girded about and our fire burning. Stay stoked, stirred, on fire for Jesus. Don't build a nest. Be open to what God wants to do. God has saved the best wine for last! The old wineskins were good, but not good enough. It's not about us being rich, increased with goods, and having need of nothing. We need to have intimacy with God.

So they brought this fair damsel to David and the Bible says she cherished him and ministered to him, and the king knew her not. Abishag was a virgin when she came in and was a virgin when David died. Adonijah even tries to come on the scene and steal this woman and corrupt the next move of God. But Solomon sees through it. His own mother was deceived. He had to tell his mother no and realized Abiathar could not be the priest in the new order. It is time for the Zadok priesthood to come forth. The old priesthood was finished. Abiathar was a faithful man. That is why Solomon wouldn't kill him. He told him to just go home and finish out his life. Thank God for Abiathar. Thank God for the men and women that have gone before us, but if we are honest about the body of Christ, it is obvious that there is something still lacking. We're still waiting for the fulfillment of what Jesus wants to do. No one person is going to be part of the last great move of God. It is going to be a many membered, male and female, priesthood that is coming forth. Scripture explains to us that the only ones who can bring the ark of God are the priests of God. Zadok means righteousness. The calling upon the last days priesthood is holiness, true and pure, unadulterated holiness and it will cost everything in your life to be a part of this company. Abishag, this dear little woman, cared for the old church, the old man, until the new one was birthed in Solomon. And then after Solomon, the new move comes, and Satan doesn't stop trying to resist God by moving upon Adonijah, another one of David's sons. Just because you are part of the household, doesn't mean God's hand is upon you. How many times have sons of famous ministries tried to come forth, yet there is no anointing?

Why did Adonijah want Abishag? Her name again means "my father is in error, wanderer". There has to be a people inside who recognize where we are, what time it is, and what is going on. But David dies and Abishag is free to be taken by another, but this glorious woman is not taken by another man. Why? Because she is supposed to be married to Jesus and nobody by the name of Adonijah is going to destroy or spoil this holy virgin. Abishag represents every woman across the earth in the body of Christ that have been a part of what God has done. God has called her to cherish the body of Christ, minister to it, and bring heat to it. David could not generate any fire. So Abishag comes and generates heat for him.

Right now in the body of Christ, there are Abishag's all over the world and God is preparing them to be the bridge in the next move. Rise up ye women that are at ease in Zion. Shake off the shackles of religion and traditions of men and get ready. It is so beyond us, we can't even conceive what God is getting ready to do. What God is going to do is the former and latter rain combined in one move. There is going to be an explosion, but we need women to bring the fire. Abishag remained a virgin, waiting for the coming of the Lord. Sisters, it is time to arise. You need as Isaiah 32 says, to get up, because if you women do not, the harvest will not come. Rise up, stop waiting for a man to do everything. Stop looking to a man to be everything. Look to Jesus. Paul said it is time to act like you are not even married, if you can receive it. Our focus should be on the King of kings and Lord of lords. Natural things should be receding in our lives as spiritual things begin to overwhelm us as we see the dawn of a new day approaching. Elijah is about to be carried away and Elisha is coming forth! Where is the God of Elijah?! Well, where are the Elijahs who can handle the mantle of power that falls to them?

The glory of the Lord wants so desperately to fall on the earth. God so wants His name vindicated. He so wants His Son to have the bride He's waited so long for. He wants it so much more than we want it. But God has a little problem. He has a people with little faith, a people comfortable with success, being rich, increased with goods, and having need of nothing. The Bible says "*Love not the world, neither the things that are in the world. If any man love the world, the love of the Father is not in him.*" (I John 2:15). If you love the world and the soulish carnal realm, which is the "*lust of the flesh, and the lust of the eyes, and the pride of life*" (I John 2:16), in this life you will lose it. But if you hate it, you will gain eternal life. How often have you not prophesied when the Lord quickened you? How many times have you wanted to abandon yourself in worship and dance, but you stood still? How many times have you been somewhere and God has prompted you to do something and you didn't move? No condemnation, but it is time to repent and start doing the work. It is not who says it, but who does it. It is not who talks it, but who walks it. It is not who dreams it, but who lives it.

This is a day where God is saying the last move is coming. The old move is dying out and as it dies out the temptation will be to keep the old move together. But you see, Abishag is not just meant for the old move, but she is destined for the new move as well. She will minister to David stricken in years, but she is not stopping there. She will be there when the temple of Solomon is built and the glory of the Lord falls. Every time an old move was dying and a new move was coming there was a fight. The Lord spoke to Samuel in I Samuel 16:1, *"And the LORD said unto Samuel, How long wilt thou mourn for Saul, seeing I have rejected him from reigning over Israel? fill thine horn with oil, and go, I will send thee to Jesse the Bethlehemite: for I have provided me a king among his sons."* Joshua faithfully served Moses for 40 years. He watched what Moses had to go through and witnessed his pettiness and anger towards the people of God that prevented him from entering into the Promise Land. As Deuteronomy closes, Moses put some of his spirit on Joshua, and as the book of Joshua begins, Joshua needs to be encouraged and strengthened because of his insecurities. The only reason why Moses was great was because of the Lord. Why do we attribute the acts of God to a man? That is the problem. We have to get delivered from hero worship, idolizing men and women of God. We've heard the same messages time and time again. We've been told how to give a billion times. We are tired of hearing that God is a healer and we want to begin to see Him actually doing it and healing people. I'm tired of meetings. I want to see God move! God is finished with the old move and wants to use you now to bridge the gap. The same God that was with Moses, was with Joshua, and will be with you. The last move is about to happen. We need new wineskins! There is something better coming. The old is not good enough anymore. We have to let go of Moses, Elijah, and Eli and his filthy sons. We have to say goodbye to uncleanness and unrighteousness. We have to say goodbye to the success syndrome, because Jesus' report is we are miserable, poor, blind, and naked.

No more excuses. Sisters, I don't want to hear anymore that you can't do it. I want to see true women of God come forth: teaching, preaching, prophesying, leading worship, pastoring churches, being the Abishag of our generation. Only you can decide. Brothers, are you going to let the women come forth? What if your wife has a better ministry, can you live with that? I envy you sisters. I want to be Abishag. It is your hour. No more excuses. No more hiding behind tradition and hiding behind your husband. Come forth, in Jesus name!

Lesson 16
Abigail

I. Abigail – I Samuel 25:2-42

A. Principle characters in her story

1. Abigail – her name in Hebrew means – Father of joy, cause of joy, the joy of my father, my father is joy, gladness; Abigail is a type of the bride of Christ, God's holy remnant within His church. Verse 3 describes her as, "*a woman of good understanding, and of a beautiful countenance*".

2. Nabal her husband – his name in Hebrew means – a fool, impious, foolish, prominence; comes from a root – to be withered, to faint, to act foolishly, to despise; Nabal is a type of foolish men leaders in the body of Christ, leaders who don't recognize God's anointed, leaders who don't think about the rest of the house (body), and men used by Satan; Nabal was extremely wealthy.

   a. Verse 3 – "*the man was churlish and evil in his doings; and he was of the house of Caleb.*"
   b. Verse 10 – here he meets God's anointed and basically calls him nothing more than a runaway slave, "*And Nabal answered David's servants, and said, Who is David? and who is the son of Jesse? there be many servants now a days that break away every man from his master.*"
   c. Verse 11 – refuses David (type of Jesus and overcomers) provision, "*Shall I then take my bread, and my water, and my flesh that I have killed for my shearers, and give it unto men, whom I know not whence they be?*"
   d. Verse 14 – "*But one of the young men told Abigail, Nabal's wife, saying, Behold, David sent messengers out of the wilderness to salute our master; and he railed on them.*"
   e. Verse 17 – The men of Nabal's household tell Abigail what he's done and what evil will come upon the whole household because of his actions. They also declare that Nabal is a "son of Belial", or a "worthless moon", and that he won't listen to anyone.
   f. Verse 25 – Abigail is interceding for her household to David and calls Nabal a man of Belial, and a fool.
   g. Verses 36-38 – Nabal threw a feast like a king and got very drunk. Abigail then tells him what had happened, his heart gives out, and he becomes paralyzed and dies.
   h. Verse 39 – David rejoices that God had kept him from attacking Nabal's household. He says God was the author of his death. David then asks Abigail to marry him.

3. The names and conditions of Abigail's story

   a. David in the wilderness of Paran, which means in Hebrew – abounding in foliage, fruitful cavernous, their beautifying. This is a type of what God brought David to. Fruit is to come out of our wildernesses. We are made beautiful by them.
   b. Nabal of Malon, which means in Hebrew – place of habitations. This is a type of God's house, God's dwelling place, God's presence. Nabal is in God's house, Nabal being again a type of foolish leadership over God's house.
   c. Nabal's possessions were in Carmel, which means in Hebrew – fruitful field, park, fertile. Your inheritance is in the fruitful field.
   d. Nabal's household and family's lives were at stake because of his foolishness.
   e. David's mighty, overcoming army would have had to destroy them; His army is a type of overcomers.

4. David – His name in Hebrew means – beloved; comes from a root – to boil in love towards. He is a type of Jesus. David was only seeking some provision for his army. He had protected Nabal and his men in times past. It is never wise to make the Lord angry, mock Him, or refuse to offer our help when He calls on us. As we see here God uses these things to determine and choose His bride. David was overwhelmed by Abigail's kindness and courtesy. He was taken back by her

repenting for her husband's foolishness. He was also glad and blessed by the provision that she brought to him , her great humility and recognition of who he was, who was chasing and attacking him, ultimately who he was to become, and her willingness to save her own household. He was duly impressed by her wisdom. He was also pleased by her physical beauty, but most importantly her inward beauty. He later asks her to marry him.

B.   Abigail's story as revealed in this passage (I Samuel 25) - Abigail

1.   Verses 14-17 – The young men of the household seek out Abigail's help. They obviously recognize her leadership. This is a type of women leaders coming forth in the last days to help the household where foolish leadership brought harm and did not do their job. Abigail is the reasonable one in the house. She acts like a true elder.

3.   Verses 18-20 – She brings a bountiful offering to David and his army, she let her servants go before her, had the wisdom not to tell Nabal, and she herself then goes to meet with God's anointed.

4.   Verse 23 – Abigail humbles herself and worships David. Notice the difference between her and her husband's response to God's anointed. She comes bowing and worshipping. Nabal comes with arrogance, pride, and rebellion.

5.   Verses 24-25 – She takes the blame for the situation, asks humbly to talk to him, tells him to not even regard this foolish Nabal, and tells him she had not heard of the request from the young men.

6.   Verses 26-27 – Tells him the Lord has stopped him from acting in retribution. She prays that David's enemies will be like Nabal (foolish), and asks him to receiver her offering.

7.   Verse 28 – Once again she asks for forgiveness and recognizes that God will build David a sure house because he fights the Lord's battles (not like one with a fool like Nabal). She recognizes there is no evil in him.

8.   Verses 29-31 – This speaks of David's greatest enemy (Saul). She prophesies to David that his soul is bound up in the bundle of life with the Lord and that God will destroy David's enemies. Remember Nabal took Saul's side. She takes David's side and speaks of his ultimate appointment as ruler over all Israel and that this instance and experience with Nabal will not be a grief to him or an offense to his heart. She praises him for not acting foolishly and shedding blood without a true cause and asks him to remember "thine handmaid" when it is all over.

9.   Verses 36-38 – Abigail attends Nabal's feast and tells him nothing until the morning. She watches as God judges him and sees Nabal die.

10. Verses 39-40 – David rejoices over Nabal's death. He sent for Abigail so he could commune with her and the servants of David come and tell her David wants her to be his wife.

11. Verses 41-42 – Once again she bows humbly and worships, and asks to wash his servant's feet (what a servant). She then hastens to go to David and become his wife.

Lesson 17
Rahab

In the story involving Rahab, we will see how God used a woman to help God's people enter into the promise land. We will see her in the natural setting but also we will consider the spiritual implications of her and the story as it would relate to us as New Testament children of God.

I.   Rahab's Story

    A.   Defining Rahab – spacious, broad, a wide place; from a root – to expand in every direction, proud; also known as Rachab in the Greek

        1.   Matthew 1:4-6 – "*4And Aram begat Aminadab; and Aminadab begat Naasson; and Naasson begat Salmon; 5And Salmon begat Booz of Rachab; and Booz begat Obed of Ruth; and Obed begat Jesse; 6And Jesse begat David the king; and David the king begat Solomon of her that had been the wife of Urias;*"

        2.   Hebrews 11:31 – "*By faith the harlot Rahab perished not with them that believed not, when she had received the spies with peace.*"

        3.   James 2:25 – "*Likewise also was not Rahab the harlot justified by works, when she had received the messengers, and had sent them out another way?*"

    B.   The story in Joshua

        1.   Joshua 2:1-22

"*1And Joshua the son of Nun sent out of Shittim two men to spy secretly, saying, Go view the land, even Jericho. And they went, and came into an harlot's house, named Rahab, and lodged there. 2And it was told the king of Jericho, saying, Behold, there came men in hither to night of the children of Israel to search out the country. 3And the king of Jericho sent unto Rahab, saying, Bring forth the men that are come to thee, which are entered into thine house: for they be come to search out all the country. 4And the woman took the two men, and hid them, and said thus, There came men unto me, but I wist not whence they were: 5And it came to pass about the time of shutting of the gate, when it was dark, that the men went out: whither the men went I wot not: pursue after them quickly; for ye shall overtake them. 6But she had brought them up to the roof of the house, and hid them with the stalks of flax, which she had laid in order upon the roof. 7And the men pursued after them the way to Jordan unto the fords: and as soon as they which pursued after them were gone out, they shut the gate. 8And before they were laid down, she came up unto them upon the roof; 9And she said unto the men, I know that the LORD hath given you the land, and that your terror is fallen upon us, and that all the inhabitants of the land faint because of you. 10For we have heard how the LORD dried up the water of the Red sea for you, when ye came out of Egypt; and what ye did unto the two kings of the Amorites, that were on the other side Jordan, Sihon and Og, whom ye utterly destroyed. 11And as soon as we had heard these things, our hearts did melt, neither did there remain any more courage in any man, because of you: for the LORD your God, he is God in heaven above, and in earth beneath. 12Now therefore, I pray you, swear unto me by the LORD, since I have shewed you kindness, that ye will also shew kindness unto my father's house, and give me a true token: 13And that ye will save alive my father, and my mother, and my brethren, and my sisters, and all that they have, and deliver our lives from death. 14And the men answered her, Our life for yours, if ye utter not this our business. And it shall be, when the LORD hath given us the land, that we will deal kindly and truly with thee. 15Then she let them down by a cord through the window: for her house was upon the town wall, and she dwelt upon the wall. 16And she said unto them, Get you to the mountain, lest the pursuers meet you; and hide yourselves there three days, until the pursuers be returned: and afterward may ye go your way. 17And the men said unto her, We will be blameless of this thine oath which thou hast made us swear. 18Behold, when we come into the land, thou shalt bind this line of scarlet thread in the window which thou didst let us down by: and thou shalt bring thy father, and thy mother, and thy brethren, and all thy father's household, home unto thee. 19And it shall be, that whosoever shall go out of the doors of thy house into the street, his blood shall be upon his head, and we will be guiltless: and whosoever shall be with thee in the house, his blood shall be on our head, if any hand be upon him. 20And if thou utter this our business, then we will be quit of thine oath which thou hast made us to swear. 21And she said,*

According unto your words, so be it. And she sent them away, and they departed: and she bound the scarlet line in the window. ²²And they went, and came unto the mountain, and abode there three days, until the pursuers were returned: and the pursuers sought them throughout all the way, but found them not."

    2.   Joshua 6:17, 22-25

"*¹⁷And the city shall be accursed, even it, and all that are therein, to the LORD: only Rahab the harlot shall live, she and all that are with her in the house, because she hid the messengers that we sent...²²But Joshua had said unto the two men that had spied out the country, Go into the harlot's house, and bring out thence the woman, and all that she hath, as ye sware unto her. ²³And the young men that were spies went in, and brought Rahab, and her father, and her mother, and her brethren, and all that she had; and they brought out all her kindred, and left them without the camp of Israel. ²⁴And they burnt the city with fire, and all that was therein: only the silver, and the gold, and the vessels of brass and of iron, they put into the treasury of the house of the LORD. ²⁵And Joshua saved Rahab the harlot alive, and her father's household, and all that she had; and she dwelleth in Israel even unto this day; because she hid the messengers, which Joshua sent to spy out Jericho.*"

C.   She was called a harlot

    1.   Harlot in Hebrew, *zanah* – highly red and therefore wanton, to commit adultery, to commit fornication, to go a whoring.
    2.   Harlot in Gree, *porne* – a strumpet, idolater, whore, fornicator, a female prostitute

She represents all of the unsaved women in the last days, coming to the Lord and assisting in helping God's overcomers enter into their inheritance or promise land. The scarlet thread in her window represents salvation or the Passover because the army did not destroy her or her family but passed over it.

D.   After her deliverance, Rahab married Salmon

    1.   Salmon's name means – His peace, peaceable, clothing.
    2.   He was the son of Nashan which means – an enchanter, oracle, one that foretells
    3.   He was a prince of the tribe of Judah
    4.   King David descended out of his line
    5.   He was David's great, great, grandfather
    6.   Some believe he was one of the two spies
    7.   He may have been the son of Caleb (I Chronicles 2:51)
    8.   Out of his and Rahab's union would come Jesus the Savior

E.   Rahab lived in Jericho

    1.   Jericho means – fragrant place, moon city
    2.   Jericho was strongly fortified
    3.   It was a walled city, no one could go in or out because of the children of Israel

F.   The king of Jericho ruled over her

    1.   This king is a type of Satan and his kingdom
    2.   He knew about the two spies
    3.   He ordered his gates to be shut, to keep out God's followers
    4.   He controlled who went out and who came in
    5.   He and his men (demons) were said to be mighty
    6.   Ultimately it was to be destroyed by Joshua (type of Jesus), and by the anointing
    7.   He had pursuers follow after the two spies; pursuers in Hebrew – to run or follow after in order to overtake, to persecute, to stick to, to accompany wherever one goes, to pursue with words; these pursuers were types of demons

8. Rahab was in bondage to this king of Jericho.

G. Though a harlot, she was said to be beautiful; Rabbinic tradition says Rahab was one of the four most beautiful women in the world.

H. Her name reveals her character (Rahab – spacious, broad, a wide place; from a root – to expand in every direction, proud)

1. She was open minded
2. She was free to expand her soul to embrace the God of Israel

I. She hides the two spies (two is the number for witness and separation; two witnesses) from the king (Satan) of Jericho.
J. She lies to protect God's witnesses.
K. She hid them amongst stalks of flax (linen, which represents the righteousness of the saints). These two spies were covered in righteousness (Revelation 19:7-9)
L. She hid them on the roof (under an open heaven)
M. She acknowledges the Lord had given the land to Israel, also that they were a mighty people, that the Lord had done great miracles for them, and that they had already destroyed the land of the giants (Sihon and Og), types of powerful demons.
N. She then confesses her faith in the God of Israel
O. She cares not only for herself, but her family
P. She makes an oath not to betray them to the king of Jericho (Satan)
Q. She helps them to escape
R. She had let them down by a scarlet cord (thread); scarlet in Scripture is a type of the blood (a revelation of the blood of Jesus)

II. A Look At The Other Characters In This Study And Who They Represent

A. Joshua – type of the Lord Jesus
B. King of Jericho – type of Satan; tried to kill the two witnesses, pressured Rahab to give him information on the two spies, kept everyone in bondage, and He has mighty men under his control which are types of demons; He will ultimately be destroyed, both him and his kingdom.
C. The Pursuers – type of demons

D. The two spies – two in Scripture is the number meaning witness and separation; they are a type of the two witnesses (Zechariah 4, Revelation 11)

1. They were sent out of Shittim

a. Wood – type of humanity
b. Wood used to make the Tabernacle and Noah's ark
c. They submitted to Rahab's counsel and wisdom

E. The Wall of Jericho – type of Satan's bondage

1. The king controlled all the lives within this city
2. He wouldn't let them go out or come in
3. The wall is a type of barrier of sin and demonic stronghold, keeping out God and His truth and people.
4. It will fall under God's Word and anointing. Also, the shout of Israel speaks of praise defeating the enemy.

III. So Who Does Rahab Really Represent And What Does She Really Do?

A. Who she represents

1. The women on earth before the last great move of God, before God's people enter into their inheritance. She represents unsaved women living in sin (harlot).
2. Upon being witnessed to, she becomes saved (her confession and the scarlet thread).
3. And then helps the sons of God destroy Satan and his kingdom.
4. Helps God's people enter into the promise land (their inheritance)
5. Typifies the grace of God upon women and how they and then their households can be saved.
6. Typifies God's great love to all people, Jew and Gentile
7. Shows how even with a terrible past, one can change completely and ultimately become one who is identified in the ancestry of Jesus.
8. All of the Rahab's (women) of the world are waiting for the two witnesses and though they have heard about God's great exploits and miracles, now see them for themselves and participate in them.
9. Shows how women are unafraid of defying Satan because that has been their call since the fall.
10. Shows women's willingness to help in the defeat of Satan and his kingdom.
11. Women can have great faith (Hebrews 11:31)
12. Shows how women will be involved in the works of the Lord (James 2:25)
13. Shows how women know how afraid Satan really is of God and His people.
14. Shows how women do not just care about themselves but their family.
15. Illustrates how women hold on to the promise of God (the promise made to her by the two spies; also the promise of the scarlet thread).
16. She also shows how women love worship, by marrying a prince of the tribe of Judah (Matthew 1:5-6, Ruth 4:21), and becoming an ancestor to the mighty David.
17. She also represents how most of the time it is a woman who brings salvation to her household.
18. She also shows how that in the last days women are going to be used mightily by God in the entering into our inheritance.
19. Also that women are willing to go outside the camp (Joshua 6:22-25) to go to Jesus; they will bear this reproach willingly.
20. And last but not least, how once they make a decision to join God's army they will be faithful and stay within the camp of God's people (Joshua 6:25).

Lesson 18
Leah

I. Leah's Profound Story

Ruth 4:11 – *"And all the people that were in the gate, and the elders, said, We are witnesses. The LORD make the woman that is come into thine house like Rachel and like Leah, which two did build the house of Israel: and do thou worthily in Ephratah, and be famous in Bethlehem:"* – She helped build the house of Israel

This wonderful woman, whose story begins in an uncomely way and then ends up in such a marvellous way, should be and is a true Word from God to all women everywhere. She begins her life treated shamefully. She is used, despised, and then tries desperately to make her husband love her, only in the end to realize it is the Lord we must revere and worship, not a man, position, etc. Because of this she won over her husband and even earns the respect of a whole nation and is honoured in love at her death.

  A. Facts about Leah

   1. Her name means – weary, exhausted, tired, dull, faint, sluggish, wearied; from a root – to be exhausted, to labour, to be wearied, faint from sickness
   2. Her father was Laban – white, glorious; from a root – to be white, to be clean.
   3. She was the elder daughter

   4. She gave Jacob six sons and one daughter (7 children – perfection)

       a. Reuben – behold a son, vision of the son
       b. Simeon – he who hears, hearkening, hearing with acceptance
       c. Levi – joined; from a root – to be joined to
       d. Judah – praise, the Lord be praise, He shall be praised
       e. Issachar – reward (understanding of the times), to be rewarded
       f. Zebulon – habitation, wished for; from a root – to dwell with
       g. Dinah – judgment, vindicated, justice

   5. She was used by God to repay Jacob for his deception
   6. Even though she was in the beginning the despised wife, Jacob buried her with him and his parents and grandparents. It was quite an honor (Genesis 49:28-33). Rachel was buried elsewhere.
   7. Leah was the one chosen by God to bear Judah, through whose line Jesus our Messiah would eventually be born.
   8. She had to endure her father's deception. He must have thought no one else would marry her.
   9. She was buried in the cave of Machpelah which means – double, a doubling; from a root – to fold together, to double, one above another. This means in the end she received a double portion for her life, while Rachel died "in the way".
   10. She also was the mother of the priesthood Levi
   11. She was *"tender eyed"* – Other translations: *"Her eyes were weak and dull looking"*, *"Leah had weak eyes"*, *"there was no sparkle in Leah's eyes"*, *"Leah had nice eyes"*, *"Leah's eyes were delicate"*, *"Leah's eyes were tender"*, *"Leah had lovely eyes"*, *"Leah had attractive eyes"*, *"Leah's eyes were clouded"*, *"Leah was bleary eyed"*
   12. Leah was hated and because of that God opened her womb, but Rachel was barren.
   13. Jacob initially loved Rachel more than Leah (Genesis 29:30).
   14. Rachel envied Leah (Genesis 30:1)
   15. Leah gave Jacob her handmaid Zilphah who bore Jacob 2 sons, Gad and Asher. Gad means – a good fortune, luck, a troop; from a root – a seer. Asher means – fortunate, happy, fortress.
   16. She accused Rachel of taking her husband (Genesis 30:15)
   17. Tricked Rachel into letting Jacob sleep with her (Genesis 30:14-18)

18. Accused Laban of selling her out (Genesis 31:14-16)
19. Her Daughter Dinah was raped (Genesis 34:1-5), but saw justice in the end (Genesis 34:25-29).
20. When Rachel dies, Jacob doesn't seem to care for her anymore and ignores the name she gave for his last son and changes from Benoni (which means – my suffering) to Benjamin (which means – son of the right hand).

Someone wrote me a letter who I had ministered to and shared some things about her life and mentioned Leah who is in the Scriptures. When I read the letter something pricked in my spirit and knew there was something from God for me there. I began to look at Leah in a new light.

B. Genesis 29:16-17 – *"And Laban had two daughters: the name of the elder was Leah, and the name of the younger was Rachel. Leah was tender eyed; but Rachel was beautiful and well favoured."*

1. The name Leah means *"wearied, to be exhausted, to labour"*
2. Rachel means *"a lamb"* – The Scriptures go on to declare about Rachel that she was beautiful and well favoured.

Proverbs 31:30 says, *"Favour is deceitful, and beauty is vain: but a woman that feareth the LORD, she shall be praised."* Leah was tender eyed. One Hebrew scholar says this means *"the only beauty she had was in her eyes."* Another one says she was *"bleary eyed."* It means she was crying all the time. Leah was the oldest. We all know that those who are born first in any family, there is a lot of responsibility placed on them. From the start they are expected to perform and pressure is put on them from a child. Leah was not a beautiful woman naturally. Beauty is of the heart. Physical beauty as great as it may be is only temporal; it's only for this life. Those who will be beautiful for the ages to come will be those who shine with the glory of God.

So we see that the Scriptures say that Leah was tender eyed. The only beauty she had was in her eyes. Isn't that something! It's amazing how we're so moved by the outward appearance that seems to be successful and beautiful and we miss so much. There is so much beauty in the lives of people around us that lies waste because no one will tap it and bring it forth.

I remember the time when a friend and I were driving to Georgia and we stopped to get a bite to eat at a restaurant. When we sat down, the waitress comes walking towards us and my goodness all I can say there has never been a more naturally ugly woman that I have seen, in my life. In the natural she was like a monster. It was the kind of person that when you look at her you would wince. You didn't want to make eye contact with her because if you did you feared expressing something. I believe that there is something beautiful about everyone but for this woman it was a challenge. So I looked and studied this woman and I found that it wasn't so hard to look at her anymore. I noticed something about her eyes. This woman had the most beautiful eyes that I had ever seen, and I told her so. All of her beauty was in her eyes. I'm so glad that Jesus doesn't judge us by our outward appearance.

Rachel was so beautiful on the outside, so well favoured, everyone wanted to be next to Rachel. No one wanted to be near Leah. But all her beauty was in her eyes. Leah had beauty on the inside. The eyes are the window to the inward man. Beauty is vain and is deceitful. I don't know why we naturally think that just because someone is naturally attractive that means they're a nice person.

Think for a moment if you were Leah, remember her name means wearied, exhausted or to labour. Imagine spending your whole life trying to please everybody else, trying to prove your own self-worth, that you are somebody. Trying to find someone, somewhere who will confirm to you your worth. We are all God's children and He loves every one of us. He is no respecter of persons.

Leah grew up like this, having a sister more highly favoured than her by her own parents. Maybe you were like Leah, despised in your family, while your sisters or brothers were favoured highly. Or maybe you were the Rachel and your brothers and sisters were despised. There is nothing worse than a spoiled child who the parents dote on and never speak the word of truth to. I imagine Rachel had a problem. The little lamb Rachel, while Leah, like Cinderella, is always doing the dishes. For those of you who are like Leah, listen: God used every bit of it because all of her beauty was in her eyes. What she saw, endured and went through did something in Leah. It did something for her, it made her a woman of God.

C. Genesis 29:20-21 *"And Jacob served seven years for Rachel; and they seemed unto him but a few days, for the love he had to her. And Jacob said unto Laban, Give me my wife, for my days are fulfilled, that I may go in unto her."* Jacob was going to serve seven years for Rachel and at the end of the seven years he demanded his wife because he wanted to go in unto her. This means he was burning in lust.

D. Genesis 29:23 *"And it came to pass in the evening, that he took Leah his daughter, and brought her to him; and he went in unto her."* Laban slips Leah into the bedroom chamber instead of Rachel. How would you like to be Leah? Disguised and knowing your husband is speaking tender words of love to you and finding out you're not the one he wanted.

E. Genesis 29:25 *"And it came to pass, that in the morning, behold, it was Leah: and he said to Laban, What is this thou hast done unto me? did not I serve with thee for Rachel? wherefore then hast thou beguiled me?"* Jacob deceived his father and God the Father made Jacob to be deceived. He was just getting paid back. A man sows what he reaps. He tried to steal the first born blessing. Now it was all in the hands of God but still principles work themselves out. Can you imagine Leah, her husband going into her and then to be rejected.

F. Genesis 29:27 *"Fulfil her week, and we will give thee this also for the service which thou shalt serve with me yet seven other years."* Laban says Jacob has to stay with her for a week and fulfil this week of the marriage vow and then he will give him Rachel and work another seven years. Can you imagine what Leah is thinking, "yeah great, he has to, he has to stay with me."

G. Genesis 29:30-31 *"And he went in also unto Rachel, and he loved also Rachel more than Leah, and served with him yet seven other years. And when the LORD saw that Leah was hated, he opened her womb: but Rachel was barren."*

God sees when someone is despised. God sees when someone is hated and not treated right. Rachel's womb was barren for a reason. The Lord saw that Leah was despised and hated even by her own husband. We find out that she loved Jacob. Here she is bleary eyed Leah. Crying all her life, labouring, working, trying to get someone to tell her she's worth something. Her own father slipped her into the bedroom chamber. What a life this poor woman lived. Her own husband loving Rachel more than her. God opened Leah's womb and she bore a son and called his name Reuben.

H. Genesis 29:32 *"And Leah conceived, and bare a son, and she called his name Reuben: for she said, Surely the LORD hath looked upon my affliction; now therefore my husband will love me."* Reuben means *"behold a son."* Look I've given you a son, now you will love me! How many women have tried to do things to get their husband to love them. We need to stop labouring under the idea that we need to please anyone other than God himself. If you're looking for your fulfilment in a man, woman, or a people you will always be unsatisfied. People will fail you. Only Jesus will fill that satisfaction.

I. Genesis 29:33 *"And she conceived again, and bare a son; and said, Because the LORD hath heard that I was hated, he hath therefore given me this son also: and she called his name Simeon."*

Simeon means: *"hearing with acceptance."* In other words, when my husband hears this he will accept me now! I have ministered to people who have tried all their life to win the favour of their natural father. They would do anything to get it but yet it didn't happen. They felt for their whole life that there was something wrong with them because their relationship with their earthly father was out of whack. It's so important for earthly fathers to be men of God. Fathers set the standard in the image in the minds of our children of who God is.

Leah believed that if Jacob hears about this son, he will accept her now and be received. That didn't happen. Then she conceived again.

J.   Genesis 29:34 *"And she conceived again, and bare a son; and said, Now this time will my husband be joined unto me, because I have born him three sons: therefore was his name called Levi."*

Levi means: *"joined"* Leah wanted not only for her husband to be joined to her physically; she wanted her husband to be joined to her heart. You can never make someone be joined to you. Try as you might to please and to serve. Leah laboured until she was exhausted and bleary eyed. Who are you trying to bless, trying to serve, to please and looking to find your acceptance from? Your answer is the word of God. It will make you free! My earthly father left ravages on my family and in my own soul. I remember one day while reading the Scriptures and being instantly delivered when I read what God the Father thought of me.

You cannot please someone and find your worth as a human being through some other human being. It may help you and bless you a little bit but it will be temporary.

So Leah conceived again and this is the fourth time. Four means *"creation"* in the Scriptures. All of Leah's beauty was in her eyes. God was dealing with her, ministering to her and working things in her. Leah was storing up a great fountain of revelation and understanding. Still she kept trying and labouring. God was about to create in Leah a deliverance that she needed.

K.   Genesis 29:35 *"And she conceived again, and bare a son: and she said, Now will I praise the LORD: therefore she called his name Judah; and left bearing."*

She didn't say "now will my husband love me, now my husband will be joined to me, now will people accept me because I've done something good." You reach a place where you get tired of all of that and don't care what someone may think about you anymore. Now Leah says she will praise the Lord! She got a revelation! It doesn't matter anymore about the rest of them. It doesn't even matter about her husband. *"Now will I praise the Lord."* Leah realized that her confidence as a human being, her self-worth came out of a relationship with God and not anyone else. God has to create that in us. We're born in this world with some serious difficulties. We need help. God needs to recreate in us that ability to see that it's only what He thinks is what matters.

Leah named her last child, Judah. Jesus came out of the tribe of Judah. Jesus will come out of that revelation. Jesus will come forth out of that revelation in our lives as well.

The thing that Leah wanted the most was the love of her husband. When she let it go and began to praise the Lord, she was free. In the end, her doubly-loved sister, Rachel, died in the way and was not buried with Jacob. When Jacob died he was buried with Abraham and Sarah, Isaac and Rebekah, and Leah. Leah was buried with Jacob. What do you think happened? I believe Jacob got a revelation, that the woman whose only beauty was in her eyes was the most beautiful one. At the end of her life she had the honourable place of being buried with her husband and with his parents and his grandparents. But only because she honoured the Lord! . *"Now will I praise the Lord"* Leah decided she wasn't going to find her self-worth in anything else but the Word of God and the Spirit of God.

The woman who was bleary eyed, laboured and exhausted ended up getting the desire of her heart. The honourable place that Rachel did not get.

1.   Psalms 36:9 *"For with thee is the fountain of life: in thy light shall we see light."*

It just may be we will get the desire of our heart in the end if we stay sweet and low. Leah became a mighty woman of God because she stuck with it and learned a great principle of worship and honouring Jesus. Leah found her worth in Him.

Lesson 19
The Story Of Naomi – *Ruth 1*

I believe that the story of Naomi in the book of Ruth has great significance beyond the fact that it was a story about a woman named Ruth and Naomi. Most scholars agree that Naomi represents the church. Ruth represents the bride of Christ who was to be married to Boaz, the kinsman redeemer, a type of the Lord Jesus. All of this took place at the beginning of barley harvest or harvest time. This is about to happen spiritually speaking in the earth, where Jesus is going to find his bride and bring redemption to His people.

In our study of women in ministry, I would like to devote this chapter to the story of Naomi as found in Ruth 1. Naomi returns to Bethlehem-Judah from living in Moab, where she suffered the loss of her husband and two sons. She then says to not call her Naomi anymore (which means "pleasant"), but to call her Mara (which means "bitter"). When she told the people to call her Mara, it signified what she wanted them to know and think about her life. Being bitter was what she wanted them to know who she was now. She wasn't willing to be referred to as pleasant anymore.

In relating the story of Naomi to our lives, I want to talk to you about the bitter experiences that all of us have had. Not one of us has escaped experiencing what Naomi experienced. Naomi is the church. What she went through, we will have gone through. Naomi at this point in her life did not have a revelation of the sovereignty of God. She did not understand all of what God was doing. As the Scriptures say, we know in part and we prophesy in part and we see through a glass darkly (I Corinthians 13:12). We do not see and understand everything that we are going through. However, God sees the end from the beginning! He knows everything and He is working all things together for good to them who love God, and who are the called! God has a purpose in everything He is doing. God's sovereignty and His working all things according to His purpose and glory is the whole principle of this story. There is not one of us who hasn't been affected by people, circumstances, family, life and mistakes that we have made. It has left many of us bitter. If someone were to look at us they may not see that we are bitter (our name is still Naomi). We may put on a good pleasant face most of the time. However, deep inside the secret chambers of our hearts, there are areas that are bitter and despairing and that has given up because of the loss we have experienced.

What Naomi did not see at this point was the sovereign hand of God. God even uses our mistakes and the mistakes of others to bring forth His glory. Even when you and I utterly and completely fall, God's sovereign hand is there to lead us out of our mistakes. Moreover, Psalms 76:10 says, "*Surely the wrath of man shall praise thee.*" God causes the foolishness and wrath of man to even be turned to the glory of God.

When Naomi said to call her name Mara, she was confessing that she believed the Almighty had dealt bitterly with her. One translation says "*He's cruelly marred me.*" The word Almighty here is *El Shaddai* which means "the breasty one, the God who is more than enough, the provider, the giver of life." This very word *El Shaddai* causes us to know that God does not cruelly mar us like she was confessing here. God gets blamed for a lot of things that He has never done. God may not do it but He uses all things for His glory's sake. There is no place you and I can go that God cannot find us. There is no mistake we can make that God cannot turn and redeem for His glory.

We see here Naomi is saying the Almighty has cruelly marred her. Most of us would be a little hesitant to do that in fear of lightning striking. But inside of us, there is a little thought occasionally that says, "Why did God do this? Why did God do that? Why did He have to allow this? Why am I like the way I am? It all could have been so different, so better..." There can reside in all of us a subtle bitterness. When I say bitterness please understand that there are different levels and shades of bitterness. I do not mean someone who is necessarily angry or yelling. I am talking about the kind of bitter that Naomi was saying. It is the kind of bitterness where we are blaming the Almighty. Humans always think that we have to blame someone for our situations we go through.

When the famine comes in the beginning of Ruth 1, Naomi's husband, Elimelech (whose name means, "my God is King") decides to take his family and leave his place in Bethlehem-Judah. He did not have much faith.

How many people have you heard stand up and tell you how much great faith they have? Then, when trouble hits, they are the first ones out the door. Where is their faith then? Our faith is proven by not just what we say, but what we do.

So Elimelech takes his family to sojourn in the country of Moab. A famine will not destroy the people of God. If we wait long enough, bread will eventually come forth, even if God has to multiply it supernaturally. Provision will come and we do not need to hastily leave our place because of trouble and affliction. God is our source. Our provision is sure because of Him. If there happens to be no bread, then we must keep our peace and wait on Him. We do not go to Moab. The city of Moab originated when Lot had sex with his daughter and he named the son Moab. Moab was wicked from the start. You do not go that place! Is it any wonder that Elimelech's sons died, as Ecclesiastes 10:8 *"...and whoso breaketh an hedge, a serpent shall bite him."* When you come out from behind that protective hedge, you make yourself susceptible to the enemy. God watched his son Elimelech to see if he really believed that God is king. So Elimilech, Naomi and his two sons went to Moab. His sons married women of Moab which was prohibited by the law.

Ruth 1:4-5 *"And they took them wives of the women of Moab; the name of the one was Orpah, and the name of the other Ruth: and they dwelled there about ten years. ⁵And Mahlon and Chilion died also both of them; and the woman was left of her two sons and her husband."*

While in Moab, Elimilech and his sons; Mahlon and Chilion died. I can understand Naomi's bitterness. I would be upset if both my spouse and two children died. When we are upset, we want to blame somebody. Naomi is like so many of us who allow circumstances dictate what we believe, allowing past experiences to stay ever vibrant in our life when they should be long gone from our lives. Even past triumphs can hinder future glory. How much more will past failures hold on and hinder you from future successes? We have people all over the world who are burdened down with terrible bitterness, despair and emptiness because of things that have happened to them that they did not understand.

Naomi was unwilling to be called by her name because she was not pleasant anymore. For some people, walking with the Lord has become unpleasant and bitter for them. Many have lost their hope and vision, have given up and have remained disappointed. I love the poem written my C.S. Lewis, "Disappointment is His Appointment." We do not see God's appointment; we see only what has happened to us. According to Naomi, she got nothing out of her experience in Moab. She didn't even want to acknowledge her two daughter-in-laws. However, God sent Naomi into Moab and brought back the bride of Christ. Naomi had no revelation of this fact. She just returned to Bethlehem-Judah feeling bitter at God. However, Ruth went with her. There is purpose in what God is doing. We don't see the hand of God bringing forth the bride within us!

I remember the night in my own life when I was desperately pleading with God. I had reached the end of my rope and was despairing even of life. I didn't understand how God could have allowed these circumstances in my life. I wanted to even end my life. Everything in me could not understand why such a horrible thing could happen. Ultimately all I could do was look at Him and say, "You allowed it! You could've prevented it? Why didn't you do something, God?" Some people do not utter those words but they think them, being angry, bitter and broken. In my despair, I remember the Lord quoting me Job 33:13, which says, *"for he giveth not account of any of his matters."* It was almost like God was offended that I was demanding an answer. I could not see beyond the end of my nose. I did not see a sovereign hand bringing forth the bride within me. You can never be truly used by God until you have lost everything; until everything that can bind you and hold you back is gone. You get to the place where nothing can keep you from the will of God! Jeremiah 18:4 says, *"And the vessel that he made of clay was marred in the hand of the potter: so he made it again another vessel."* Even in marring, God is making another vessel in us that is beautiful in His eyes.

The next thing Naomi says is in Ruth 1:21, *"I went out full, and the LORD hath brought me home again empty..."* Did Naomi really come back empty? She came back with the answer; she came back with everything and did not even know she had it. She was sitting there complaining, upset, and angry and did not even know the hand of God had brought her home with the bride. I want you to know that this is God's purpose. He is going to empty us until there is nothing left. But then he is going to fill us.

Naomi might have been bitter at the end of Ruth 1. But by the end of the story, the bitterness had left her. Ruth had met Boaz, the kinsman redeemer, in whose field she gleaned barley. During the course of events, Naomi suddenly got a revelation. All of a sudden she understood. Maybe she lost her husband and sons, but she ends up gaining what she was born to get, the kinsmen redeemer!

In Ruth 1, it says that when Naomi and Ruth returned from Moab, it was the beginning of barley harvest. For you and I, harvest is coming. This is about to happen spiritually in a people. Brought out of Moab, is there any one of us that has not been brought out of great wickedness, loss, despair and bitterness? We must thank Naomi, a type of the church, who has brought us out of Moab.

I will tell you that we can though some hard times with people hurting us and damaging us. However, we must not remain bitter. Many people never deal with their past experiences, which can keep them from their destiny in God. There are so many casualties littered along the side roads of the narrow way than you can ever imagine. Ministries have been aborted because of past experiences. They could not get over what had happened to them and could not get free to make it through into their calling. We must understand that God even uses the terrible things to bring forth His glory in us. Spiritually speaking, it is harvest time. What do you want people to call you? Are you willing to stay bitter, to continue to be upset at people around you? Every one of us has a story. I've lost children in life! I know what it means to have sorrow and to hurt, but I am still walking with Jesus! And Ruth is living within me. The experiences were not wasted. I could have allowed the bitterness to eat away my calling in God.

Even to this day there are things that have happened in my life that I don't completely understand. However, Hosea 6:3 says, "*Then shall we know, if we follow on to know the LORD: his going forth is prepared as the morning.*" We might not know everything now, because we see only in part. But if we follow on to know the Lord, we will understand that in everything, He had purpose in what He was doing. He did not just throw us down here. From the moment we took our first breath He was watching us and overseeing our lives. God says in Isaiah 63:9, "*In all their affliction he was afflicted.*"

Someday we have to grow up and place our trust into the sovereign hands of our God. On the darkest night of my life I made that commitment in a hotel room, when God quoted the passage in Genesis 18:25 to me, which says, "*Shall not the Judge of all the earth do right?*" That was it for me; that was the end of the discussion. I decided not to ask anymore questions. I decided not to be bitter against God. I saw His hand. Every now and then I see little glimmers of Ruth shining through in my life.

People have hurt us and believe me, I know it hurts. I know it was a wrong and terrible thing that has happened. But we must be bigger than that. The God who lives within us is bigger than that. The devil wants to get us down and cause what has happened to us to still live in us in order to keep us from pressing on into anything else in God. We have all messed up and have all been hurt. We live in a victim society where we are taught to feel sorry for ourselves. What are we going to do about it? Harvest time is coming. We must get a revelation of the purpose of God and see beyond the end of our nose and our circumstances to see that God may have been using that thing to change us and bring forth His bride in us. Jesus' blood can wash all our sins, hurts, bitterness and disappointments away.

I would like to share one final story about my life. There was a time when my wife had a miscarriage. I held the little baby in my hands. I carried it to the doctor and stood there in the hallway believing God was going to raise that baby from the dead. For years I kept that loss inside of me. I never allowed myself to cry because I thought that was a lack of faith from what I was taught. I never allowed myself to grieve. However, one day I sat in a glorious meeting after leading the worship. As I was listening to the brother standing up there talking the Spirit of God fell upon me. God began talking to me about my little child that was in heaven. I began to weep and I cried so much my shirt was stained. When I finished crying I realized Jesus was on the throne. I also realized that He never left His throne. He is on the throne today. There is a holy purpose being worked out in our lives. Like this story in Ruth 1, we must realize our name is Naomi and not Mara. We were born to be pleasant, to have the joy of the Lord in my life.

I. Names are Important in this Story

    A. Names and their definitions

        1. Bethlehem Judah – house of bread and praise
        2. Moab – waste, nothingness, seed, prodigy, water of a father
        3. Elimelech – God is king, God of the king
        4. Naomi – pleasant, agreeable, attractive, my joy, my bliss
        5. Mahlon – great infirmity, a sick person, painful, weak, sickly
        6. Chilion – pining, consuming, wasting away
        7. Ephrathas – fruitful, double fruitfulness
        8. Orpah – neck of an animal, hardened, double minded, turning the back
        9. Ruth – beauty, something worth seeing, delightful, pleasing, mate, to tend of flock
        10. Mara – bitterness, sad, he was arrogant, grief, great depression, chafe
        11. Almighty (*El Shaddai*) – the all sufficient one, the breasty one, nourishes, supplies, satisfies
        12. Boaz – the Lord is strength, in Him is strength, fleetness

II. Naomi's story has some interesting truths

    A. Facts to consider

        1. The book of Ruth is one of only two books that use the name of a woman as the title; the other being the book of Esther.
        2. Both of these women had marriages that affected the body of Christ.
        3. Esther, a Jew, marries a Gentile king and Ruth, a Gentile, marries a Jew kinsman redeemer.
        4. Both ladies represent the bride of Christ and both men represent Jesus.

        5. Naomi, Orpah, and Ruth represent the ranks within the body of Christ.

            a. Ruth – the bride, 100-fold, most holy place
            b. Naomi – the church, 60-fold, holy place
            c. Orpah – backslidden church, 30-fold, outer court

III. Naomi's story itself

    A. Ruth 1:1-22

        1. During the time the judges ruled, it was a time of rebellion and lawlessness.
        2. A famine in the land. This is simply a time of testing.
        3. You don't leave the "house of bread and praise" (word of worship)
        4. Moab is a type of all that is sinful and unholy. Moab came from Lot's unholy incestuous line (Genesis 19:30-38).
        5. This was Elimelech and Naomi's choice to leave and backslide.
        6. They didn't go there just for a little while, but 10 years (verse 4).
        7. When you are out of the will of God, you open the door to Satan and bad things happen.
        8. Her husband dies (verse 3) and she was left. She could have moved then but chooses not to.
        9. Her son's disobeyed God taking heathen wives and they both died as well (Deuteronomy 23:3). Romans 6:23 – "*For the wages of sin is death...*"
        10. She is left again and now all she has are the Gentile daughter-in-laws.
        11. Verse 6 says, "Then she arose". She finally came to herself akin to the prodigal son returning home (Luke 15:18-20).
        12. It seems her motivation was hearing that the famine was over in her old country.
        13. The Lord was visiting His people.

14. All three actually left together (Matthew 25:1). This is so like the body of Christ, always running after visitations of the Lord. The three women represent the threefold church (the bride, the church, and the backsliders).

15. She then tells Ruth and Orpah to leave her and go back. Naomi does not see the hand of the Sovereign God at work here to bring Ruth, a type of all Gentiles, into the lineage of Christ.

16. She told them to go back to their own families (verse 8).

17. In verse 13, she says the hand of the Lord is gone out against her. One translations reads *"for the Eternal is against me"*, and another reads *"it is bitter to me exceedingly"*. Naomi is bitter against God and blames Him (as so many do) for her own mistakes. Remember a man reaps what he sows (Galatians 6:7).

18. Orpah, as her name defines "turning the back", departs. In verse 15 she is gone back unto her own people and unto her gods". Her god (as a Moabite) was Chemosh which means – to subdue (Numbers 21:29, Judges 11:24, I Kings 11:7, 33, Jeremiah 48:7, 13, 16). Chemosh demanded the sacrifice of children as burnt offerings.

19. In verse 16-17, you hear in Ruth the heart of the bride of Christ.

    a. Don't ask me to leave you
    b. Or to turn back (or backslide) from following Jesus.
    c. Wherever you go, I will go.
    d. Where you lodge, I will lodge.
    e. Your people shall be my people.
    f. You God, my God – this is a confession of faith in the Lord. This Gentile woman represents all Gentiles coming to a true revelation of Jesus.
    g. Where you die, I will die, and I will be buried there.
    h. Only death could part us (Revelation 12:11) and she swears in an oath to the Lord.

20. Eight principles Ruth emphasizes here. This is a time of new beginnings for her and the Gentile people.

21. She represents those who are saved, water baptized, and sanctified. The old Ruth had died and was now born again.

22. Ruth was steadfast minded (I Corinthians 15:58).

23. So they journeyed to the house of "bread and praise". Notice, a Jew and a Gentile, representing the two witnesses.

24. As they came, the whole city is moved.

25. They said, *"Is this Naomi ("pleasant")?"* One translation reads *"all the gossips were saying..."*

26. Naomi says "don't call me pleasant, call me bitter" (Exodus 15:23-26, Hebrews 12:15).

B. A look at bitterness (verse 20 – *"And she said unto them, Call me not Naomi, call me Mara: for the Almighty hath dealt very bitterly with me."*)

    1. Naomi again means – pleasant, agreeable, attractive, my joy, my bliss; Mara again means – bitterness, sad, he was arrogant, grief, great depression, chafe.

    2. Exodus 15:23-26 – *"23And when they came to Marah, they could not drink of the waters of Marah, for they were bitter: therefore the name of it was called Marah. 24And the people murmured against Moses, saying, What shall we drink? 25And he cried unto the LORD; and the LORD shewed him a tree, which when he had cast into the waters, the waters were made sweet: there he made for them a statute and an ordinance, and there he proved them, 26And said, If thou wilt diligently hearken to the voice of the LORD thy God, and wilt do that which is right in his sight, and wilt give ear to his commandments, and keep all his statutes, I will put none of these diseases upon thee, which I have brought upon the Egyptians: for I am the LORD that healeth thee."* (we are either bitter (Job 6:1-4, 7:11) or better (I Samuel 1:10-20).

    3. Proverbs 27:7 – *"The full soul loatheth an honeycomb; but to the hungry soul every bitter thing is sweet."*

4. Colossians 3:19 – "*Husbands, love your wives, and be not bitter against them.*"
5. James 3:11-16 – "*[11]Doth a fountain send forth at the same place sweet water and bitter? [12]Can the fig tree, my brethren, bear olive berries? either a vine, figs? so can no fountain both yield salt water and fresh. [13]Who is a wise man and endued with knowledge among you? let him shew out of a good conversation his works with meekness of wisdom. [14]But if ye have bitter envying and strife in your hearts, glory not, and lie not against the truth. [15]This wisdom descendeth not from above, but is earthly, sensual, devilish. [16]For where envying and strife is, there is confusion and every evil work.*"
6. Job 21:25 – "*And another dieth in the bitterness of his soul, and never eateth with pleasure.*"
7. Proverbs 14:10 – "*The heart knoweth his own bitterness; and a stranger doth not intermeddle with his joy.*"
8. Isaiah 38:17-18 – "*[17]Behold, for peace I had great bitterness: but thou hast in love to my soul delivered it from the pit of corruption: for thou hast cast all my sins behind thy back. [18]For the grave cannot praise thee, death can not celebrate thee: they that go down into the pit cannot hope for thy truth.*"
9. Hebrews 12:15 – "*Looking diligently lest any man fail of the grace of God; lest any root of bitterness springing up trouble you, and thereby many be defiled;*"
10. Ephesians 4:31-32 – "*[31]Let all bitterness, and wrath, and anger, and clamour, and evil peaking, be put away from you, with all malice: [32]And be ye kind one to another, tenderhearted, forgiving one another, even as God for Christ's sake hath forgiven you.*"

C. A look at what God Almighty is really like (verse 20 – "*And she said unto them, Call me not Naomi, call me Mara: for <u>the Almighty</u> hath dealt very bitterly with me.*")

1. The Almighty in Hebrew is *El Shaddai* and it means – all sufficient one, breasty one, nourisher, supplies, satisfies. This is God's female, nurturing, mothering nature.
2. Genesis 28:3 – "*And God Almighty bless thee, and make thee fruitful, and multiply thee, that thou mayest be a multitude of people;*"
3. Genesis 48:3 – "*And Jacob said unto Joseph, God Almighty appeared unto me at Luz in the land of Canaan, and blessed me,*"
4. Genesis 49:25 – "*Even by the God of thy father, who shall help thee; and by the Almighty, who shall bless thee with blessings of heaven above, blessings of the deep that lieth under, blessings of the breasts, and of the womb:*"
5. Job 5:17-24 – "*[17]Behold, happy is the man whom God correcteth: therefore despise not thou the chastening of the Almighty: [18]For he maketh sore, and bindeth up: he woundeth, and his hands make whole. [19]He shall deliver thee in six troubles: yea, in seven there shall no evil touch thee. [20]In famine he shall redeem thee from death: and in war from the power of the sword. [21]Thou shalt be hid from the scourge of the tongue: neither shalt thou be afraid of destruction when it cometh. [22]At destruction and famine thou shalt laugh: neither shalt thou be afraid of the beasts of the earth. [23]For thou shalt be in league with the stones of the field: and the beasts of the field shall be at peace with thee. [24]And thou shalt know that thy tabernacle shall be in peace; and thou shalt visit thy habitation, and shalt not sin.*" – The blessings of His chastening.
6. Job 33:4 – "*The Spirit of God hath made me, and the breath of the Almighty hath given me life.*"
7. Job 34:12 – "*Yea, surely God will not do wickedly, neither will the Almighty pervert judgment.*"
8. Job 22:23-30
9. Job 37:23 – "*Touching the Almighty, we cannot find him out: he is excellent in power, and in judgment, and in plenty of justice: he will not afflict.*"
10. Psalms 91:1 – "*He that dwelleth in the secret place of the most High shall abide under the shadow of the Almighty.*"
11. Revelation 15:3 – "*And they sing the song of Moses the servant of God, and the song of the Lamb, saying, Great and marvellous are thy works, Lord God Almighty; just and true are thy ways, thou King of saints.*"
12. Revelation 16:7 – "*And I heard another out of the altar say, Even so, Lord God Almighty, true and righteous are thy judgments.*"

D. Verse 21 – *"I went out full, and the LORD hath brought me home again empty: why then call ye me Naomi, seeing the LORD hath testified against me, and the Almighty hath afflicted me?"*

   1.   "I went out full" – full in Hebrew here means abundance.
   2.   She could have stayed that way if she had stayed home. God did not bring her home empty, she did. Empty in Hebrew means – vain, void, worthless.
   3.   Naomi is saying she is not pleasant anymore.
   4.   Once again she insults *El Shaddai*.
   5.   Afflicted in Hebrew means – to break in pieces, to do ill towards.
   6.   She had reaped what she had sown (Galatians 6:7).

E. Verse 22 – *"So Naomi returned, and Ruth the Moabitess, her daughter in law, with her, which returned out of the country of Moab: and they came to Bethlehem in the beginning of barley harvest."*

   1.   So the two witness, a Jew and a Gentile returns home.
   2.   Right at harvest time.
   3.   Typically this is speaking of the last days "two witnesses" in the earth.
   4.   Notice that Ruth had been silent during Naomi's cursing of the Almighty.

Delilah – Stealer Of The Anointing

I.   The Story in Judges 16:4-21

"*4And it came to pass afterward, that he loved a woman in the valley of Sorek, whose name was Delilah. 5And the lords of the Philistines came up unto her, and said unto her, Entice him, and see wherein his great strength lieth, and by what means we may prevail against him, that we may bind him to afflict him: and we will give thee every one of us eleven hundred pieces of silver. 6And Delilah said to Samson, Tell me, I pray thee, wherein thy great strength lieth, and wherewith thou mightest be bound to afflict thee. 7And Samson said unto her, If they bind me with seven green withs that were never dried, then shall I be weak, and be as another man. 8Then the lords of the Philistines brought up to her seven green withs which had not been dried, and she bound him with them. 9Now there were men lying in wait, abiding with her in the chamber. And she said unto him, The Philistines be upon thee, Samson. And he brake the withs, as a thread of tow is broken when it toucheth the fire. So his strength was not known. 10And Delilah said unto Samson, Behold, thou hast mocked me, and told me lies: now tell me, I pray thee, wherewith thou mightest be bound. 11And he said unto her, If they bind me fast with new ropes that never were occupied, then shall I be weak, and be as another man. 12Delilah therefore took new ropes, and bound him therewith, and said unto him, The Philistines be upon thee, Samson. And there were liers in wait abiding in the chamber. And he brake them from off his arms like a thread. 13And Delilah said unto Samson, Hitherto thou hast mocked me, and told me lies: tell me wherewith thou mightest be bound. And he said unto her, If thou weavest the seven locks of my head with the web. 14And she fastened it with the pin, and said unto him, The Philistines be upon thee, Samson. And he awaked out of his sleep, and went away with the pin of the beam, and with the web. 15And she said unto him, How canst thou say, I love thee, when thine heart is not with me? thou hast mocked me these three times, and hast not told me wherein thy great strength lieth. 16And it came to pass, when she pressed him daily with her words, and urged him, so that his soul was vexed unto death; 17That he told her all his heart, and said unto her, There hath not come a rasor upon mine head; for I have been a Nazarite unto God from my mother's womb: if I be shaven, then my strength will go from me, and I shall become weak, and be like any other man. 18And when Delilah saw that he had told her all his heart, she sent and called for the lords of the Philistines, saying, Come up this once, for he hath shewed me all his heart. Then the lords of the Philistines came up unto her, and brought money in their hand. 19And she made him sleep upon her knees; and she called for a man, and she caused him to shave off the seven locks of his head; and she began to afflict him, and his strength went from him. 20And she said, The Philistines be upon thee, Samson. And he awoke out of his sleep, and said, I will go out as at other times before, and shake myself. And he wist not that the LORD was departed from him. 21But the Philistines took him, and put out his eyes, and brought him down to Gaza, and bound him with fetters of brass; and he did grind in the prison house.*"

As we continue our study of women in Scripture, we find that many women in the Word are spoken of specifically and can be used as a type to us to speak of our own lives. Many of these women mentioned speak of something larger than their own personal and natural story. For as the Bible makes them prominent, I believe they can speak spiritually of a certain type of woman that all of us must deal with at some point in our lives. In this particular story of Delilah, all ministers should take heed to the how, what, when, why, and the ending result of what happens when this type of woman comes into our lives (Delilah).

We cannot speak of Delilah without mentioning Samson and how this mighty man of God ended up because of her. We would do well to look closely to this story and all that it represents and try to learn from it, consider the potentiality of it happening in our own lives, and try then by the grace of God to keep it from happening to us. The truth is Scripture would not mention this tragic story of how Samson, once a mighty man of God with a powerful anointing, could fall so low if there wasn't a chance of it happening to us (Proverbs 24:30-34). We certainly learn from this story that "anointing without character" costs you in the end. It is not enough just to have an anointing. We need to seek for an abiding anointing that remains on our lives all the time. We should also note that all of us have unresolved issues buried deep in our soulish man, that if they go undealt with will wind up costing us in the end by not only destroying ourselves, but all the lives of the people who look to us, trust us, and depend on us. We must remember <u>our lives are not our own</u>, especially in ministry. The devil "*as a roaring lion, walketh about, seeking whom he may devour*" (I Peter 5:8) and "*The thief cometh not, but for to steal, and to kill, and to destroy ...*" (John 10:10). He watches and waits to attack us when we are the most vulnerable as he did with Jesus in the wilderness (Matthew 4). We must allow God to remove from us all ambition and the drive for success in ministry while dealing with the deep, personal issues many of us have. If there is a crack somewhere in your foundation, believe me, devils will use it to try to exploit it and he will also use people to do this. This in no way should be used to blame someone else for our sin, but simply use this powerful Biblical story to speak to us personally. Please know and remember, any one of us are capable of anything apart from the grace and mercy of God, *"By whom also we have access by faith into this grace wherein we stand"* (Romans 5:2). This story also shows us the need for accountability in all of our lives, especially in ministry. Secret sins will destroy us if left unchecked, for it is *"the little foxes, that spoil the vines"* (Song of Solomon 2:15). We must never think that just because someone is anointed that this means all is right in their lives. Jesus said, *"Ye shall know them by their fruits"* (Matthew 7:16). Especially in this day of the many charismatic T.V. ministries who have great followings, who have great amounts of anointing, money, power, recognition, and influence. We see them falling like leaves in the autumn. Perhaps if they had studied "Delilah's story", it may have prevented them from falling from grace. The rise to the top in ministry is slow and arduous, but the descent is like a skier coming down a mountain. When a minister falls it doesn't just affect him, but all those whom he has influence over. So let's learn from this and not give Satan anything to exploit in our lives. Job 4:11 says, *"The old lion perisheth for lack of prey..."* Jesus said, *"the prince of this world cometh, and hath nothing in me"* (John 14:30). Let this be true for us as well.

II. The Story Of Delilah, The Woman Who Robbed The Anointing – Judges 16:4-21

    A. Personal facts about Delilah

        1. Delilah in Hebrew, *Deliylah*, means – delicate or dainty one, languishing with lustful desire, poor, small, head of hair, weak, pining one; it comes from a root, *Dalal* – to be brought low, to hang down, to be languid, a drawer of water, to slacken or be feeble, to be oppressed, to bring low, dry up, be emptied, be not equal, fail, be impoverished, to be made thin. Below is the revelation of her name:

            a. She appears as a delicate or dainty women.
            b. However, she is really languishing with lust.
            c. She is poor and small minded, thinking of herself only.
            d. She must have had beautiful hair; this also means a type of covering that was Satanic.
            e. Her desire is to bring a man of God low.
            f. Her desire is to make men languish (David on the rooftop), to not stay alert or watching.
            g. Her hope is to make a man of God feeble.
            h. Her hope is to make him slacken from his steadfastness.
            i. She brings oppression (unnecessarily) into his life.
            j. She hopes with the help of Satan to "dry him up" and to empty him of his anointing
            k. She is not balanced (Proverbs 11:1 – *"A false balance is abomination to the LORD: but a just weight is his delight."*). We must beware of the doctrines we hear.
            l. Her desire is to "make him fail" to make him "impoverished" to "make him thin" so that he can't hurt the enemy by his anointing anymore.
            m. She wants to draw away his water (type of the Holy Ghost and anointing)
            n. She wants him emptied out of all his anointing, all his God given gifts, power and strength.

        2. She was of the valley of Sorek, which means in Hebrew – choice vine, noble vine, a kind of vine, to intertwine, hissing, a color inclining to yellow. This valley of Sorek, scholars say, was in the neighborhood of Samson's birth place and where his family dwelt (Judges 13:1). Below is the revelation of the valley of Sorek

            a. Though she may be a choice woman (noble vine), she is a whore. The dictionary definition of the word whore means – a woman who engages in promiscuous sexual activity for money or gifts.
            b. She is used of the devil to "hiss" at Samson. A hiss is expressing contempt for.

c. Her color is not true yellow or gold which is a type of the divine nature. She simply inclines towards it. What this means is if she can't have it, she's jealous of those who do and will do or try anything to rob them of God's nature. Yellow can also mean sickly.

d. There is really nothing noble about Delilah. She was a deceiver, betrayer, and a liar.

e. Her goal is to get Samson enticed with her thereby causing him to be later deceived by her.

3. She was a courtesan of the higher class (a rich whore or expensive call girl)

4. She was used as a political agent of the "Lords of the Philistines"

5. She was obviously not an Israelite, but a Philistine; Philistine in Hebrew means – land of wanderers, strangers, rolled in dust, wallowing. Here we clearly see by revelation she is the "strange woman" of Scripture, wallowing in the flesh, with no purpose. God had already commanded His people not to marry or have dealings with the world. She wanted to entwine him in bondage. She used and exploited his inner weakness and lusts to bind him.

6. Delilah kept on pressing him until she wore down his resistance

a. Don't you think he would have wondered why she was doing this?

b. Her questions gave her away.

c. After every time he lied to her, he was attacked according to what he had told her.

d. Ecclesiastes 7:26 – "And I find more bitter than death the woman, whose heart is snares (Hebrew – luring) and nets (Hebrew – enticing), and her hands as bands (Hebrew – chains): whoso pleaseth God shall escape from her; but the sinner shall be taken by her."

e. Proverbs 21:9 – "It is better to dwell in a corner of the housetop, than with a brawling woman in a wide house."

f. The word seduction means – the deliberate enticement or persuasion of someone into the abandonment of Godly principles, both naturally and spiritually.

g. She made four attempts to deceive Samson. She succeeded in the forth try. Four is the number of creation and the world. She simply appealed to his Adamic nature and finally caused him to fall and his carnal nature came through.

7. Satan wants to wear us down

a. Daniel 7:25 – "And he shall speak great words against the most High, and shall wear out the saints of the most High..."

b. Psalms 56:1-2 – "Be merciful unto me, O God: for man would swallow me up; he fighting daily oppresseth me. Mine enemies would daily swallow me up: for they be many that fight against me, O thou most High."

c. Psalms 42:9-10 – "I will say unto God my rock, Why hast thou forgotten me? why go I mourning because of the oppression of the enemy? As with a sword in my bones, mine enemies reproach me; while they say daily unto me, Where is thy God?"

d. I Samuel 1:6 – "And her adversary also provoked her sore, for to make her fret, because the LORD had shut up her womb."

e. Luke 22:31 – "And the Lord said, Simon, Simon, behold, Satan hath desired to have you, that he may sift you as wheat:"

8. Her name in Scripture is mentioned six times. Six is the number for man and Satan, or man and Satan combined, which is antichrist (666). This is an evil spirit.

9. Delilah was nothing but a harlot, being paid for her services. She is the strange woman in Proverbs 7 and the harlot found in Revelation. She is Babylon, the great whore. She was the strange woman who used her words (false doctrine) to deceive him.

10. She was probably destroyed beneath the temple of Dagon when Samson regained his anointing. It just goes to show you that everyone reaps what they sow. Our enemies and seducers can laugh all they want, but there will be a day of judgment!

11. Other places in Scripture where the root of Delilah's name, *Dalal*, is found (underlined)

    a. Judges 6:6 – "*And Israel was <u>greatly impoverished</u> because of the Midianites; and the children of Israel cried unto the LORD.*"

    b. Job 28:4 – "*The flood breaketh out from the inhabitant; even the waters forgotten of the foot: <u>they are dried up</u>, they are gone away from men.*"

    c. Psalms 79:8 – "*O remember not against us former iniquities: let thy tender mercies speedily prevent us: for <u>we are brought very low</u>.*"

    d. Psalms 116:6 – "*The LORD preserveth the simple: <u>I was brought low</u>, and he helped me.*"

    e. Psalms 142:6 – "*Attend unto my cry; for <u>I am brought very low</u>: deliver me from my persecutors; for they are stronger than I.*"

    f. Proverbs 26:7 – "*The legs of the lame <u>are not equal</u>: so is a parable in the mouth of fools.*"

    g. Isaiah 17:4 – "*And in that day it shall come to pass, that the glory of Jacob <u>shall be made thin</u>, and the fatness of his flesh shall wax lean.*"

    h. Isaiah 19:6 – "*And they shall turn the rivers far away; and the brooks of defence <u>shall be emptied</u> and dried up: the reeds and flags shall wither.*"

    i. Isaiah 38:14 – "*Like a crane or a swallow, so did I chatter: I did mourn as a dove: mine eyes <u>fail</u> with looking upward: O LORD, I am oppressed; undertake for me.*"

B. Warnings from Scripture about this kind of woman that relate to this story

1. Proverbs 6:23-29 – "*...26For by means of a whorish woman a man is brought to a piece of bread: and the adulteress will hunt for the precious life...*"
2. Ezekiel 6:9 – "*And they that escape of you shall remember me among the nations whither they shall be carried captives, because I am broken with their whorish heart, which hath departed from me, and with their eyes, which go a whoring after their idols: and they shall lothe themselves for the evils which they have committed in all their abominations.*"
3. Ezekiel 16:23-39
4. Deuteronomy 23:17-18 – "*There shall be no whore of the daughters of Israel, nor a sodomite of the sons of Israel. Thou shalt not bring the hire of a whore, or the price of a dog, into the house of the LORD thy God for any vow: for even both these are abomination unto the LORD thy God.*"
5. Proverbs 23:26-28 – "*26My son, give me thine heart, and let thine eyes observe my ways. 27For a whore is a deep ditch; and a strange woman is a narrow pit. 28She also lieth in wait as for a prey, and increaseth the transgressors among men.*"
6. Proverbs 6:32-33 – "*But whoso committeth adultery with a woman lacketh understanding: he that doeth it destroyeth his own soul. A wound and dishonour shall he get; and his reproach shall not be wiped away.*"
7. Job 31:9-10 – "*If mine heart have been deceived by a woman, or if I have laid wait at my neighbour's door; Then let my wife grind unto another, and let others bow down upon her.*"
8. Ecclesiastes 7:26 – "*And I find more bitter than death the woman, whose heart is snares and nets, and her hands as bands: whoso pleaseth God shall escape from her; but the sinner shall be taken by her.*"
9. Hosea 4:9-17
10. Psalms 106:39 – "*Thus were they defiled with their own works, and went a whoring with their own inventions.*"
11. Proverbs 2:16-20
12. Proverbs 5:3-23
13. Proverbs 6:24-29
14. Proverbs 7:5-27
15. Psalms 73:26 – "*My flesh and my heart faileth: but God is the strength of my heart, and my portion for ever.*"
16. Ezekiel 44:6-14
17. Mark 14:38 – "*Watch ye and pray, lest ye enter into temptation. The spirit truly is ready, but the flesh is weak.*"

18. John 3:6 – *"That which is born of the flesh is flesh; and that which is born of the Spirit is spirit."*
19. Romans 8:1-9, 12-13
20. Romans 13:14 – *"But put ye on the Lord Jesus Christ, and make not provision for the flesh, to fulfil the lusts thereof."*
21. II Corinthians 7:1 – *"Having therefore these promises, dearly beloved, let us cleanse ourselves from all filthiness of the flesh and spirit, perfecting holiness in the fear of God."*
22. Galatians 5:16-21, 24
23. Galatians 6:8 – *"For he that soweth to his flesh shall of the flesh reap corruption; but he that soweth to the Spirit shall of the Spirit reap life everlasting."*
24. Ephesians 6:12 – *"For we wrestle not against flesh and blood, but against principalities, against powers, against the rulers of the darkness of this world, against spiritual wickedness in high places."*
25. Philippians 3:3-15
26. II Peter 2:10 – *"But chiefly them that walk after the flesh in the lust of uncleanness, and despise government. Presumptuous are they, selfwilled, they are not afraid to speak evil of dignities."*
27. I John 2:15-17 – *"¹⁵Love not the world, neither the things that are in the world. If any man love the world, the love of the Father is not in him. ¹⁶For all that is in the world, the lust of the flesh, and the lust of the eyes, and the pride of life, is not of the Father, but is of the world. ¹⁷And the world passeth away, and the lust thereof: but he that doeth the will of God abideth for ever."*
28. James 1:13-14 – *"Let no man say when he is tempted, I am tempted of God: for God cannot be tempted with evil, neither tempteth he any man: But every man is tempted, when he is drawn away of his own lust, and enticed."*

C. God has provision for us even as He allows us to be dealt with

1. I Corinthians 10:13 – *"There hath no temptation taken you but such as is common to man: but God is faithful, who will not suffer you to be tempted above that ye are able; but will with the temptation also make <u>a way to escape</u>, that ye may be able to bear it."*
2. James 1:12 – *"Blessed is the man that <u>endureth temptation</u>: for when he is tried, he shall receive the crown of life, which the Lord hath promised to them that love him."*
3. Luke 22:28 – *"Ye are they which have continued with me in <u>my temptations</u>."*
4. James 1:2-4 – *"²My brethren, count it all joy when ye fall into divers temptations; ³Knowing this, that the trying of your faith worketh patience. ⁴But let patience have her perfect work, that ye may be perfect and entire, wanting nothing."*
5. I Peter 1:6-7 – *"Wherein ye greatly rejoice, though now for a season, if need be, ye are in heaviness through manifold temptations: That the trial of your faith, being much more precious than of gold that perisheth, though it be tried with fire, might be found unto praise and honour and glory at the appearing of Jesus Christ:"*
6. II Peter 2:9-22
7. I John 5:18 – *"We know that whosoever is born of God sinneth not; but he that is begotten of God <u>keepeth himself, and that wicked one toucheth him not</u>."*
8. Mark 4:18-19 – *"And these are they which are sown among thorns; such as hear the word, And the cares of this world, and the deceitfulness of riches, and the lusts of other things entering in, choke the word, and <u>it becometh unfruitful</u>."*
9. Romans 6:12 – *"<u>Let not sin</u> therefore reign in your mortal body, that ye should obey it in the lusts thereof."*
10. Galatians 5:24 – *"And they that are Christ's <u>have crucified the flesh with the affections and lusts</u>."*
11. II Timothy 2:22 – *"<u>Flee also youthful lusts</u>: but follow righteousness, faith, charity, peace, with them that call on the Lord out of a pure heart."*
12. I Peter 2:11 – *"Dearly beloved, I beseech you as strangers and pilgrims, <u>abstain</u> from fleshly lusts, which war against the soul;"*
13. Numbers 11:4 – *"And the <u>mixt multitude</u> that was among them fell a lusting: and the children of Israel also wept again, and said, Who shall give us flesh to eat?"*

D. Some other facts about this story

1. Samson lied three times – you cannot fool around with God's anointing. It must be guarded, honored, cherished, and protected.
2. Samson deceived her three times but each one he toyed with or allowed, and it finally brought him down.

3. Those with God's anointing who play with the harlot (Babylon) will ultimately be captured by devils.

    a. Revelation 18:2 – *"And he cried mightily with a strong voice, saying, Babylon the great is fallen, is fallen, and is become the habitation of devils, and the hold of every foul spirit, and a cage of every unclean and hateful bird."*
    b. Proverbs 7:7-27 – the foolish young man going the way to her house – *"...21With her much fair speech she caused him to yield, with the flattering of her lips she forced him...26For she hath cast down many wounded: yea, many strong men have been slain by her."*

4. The five lords of the Philistines

    a. The first thing these five lords represent are the five senses of the natural man, the man of the earth that Satan will use to entice and deceive – 5 levels: hearing, seeing, smelling, tasting, touching
    b. These Philistine lords also represent the five levels of leadership in the demonic kingdom (general demons, principalities, power, rulers of the darkness of this world, and spiritual wickedness in high places).
    c. These five lords were hidden in Delilah's chamber – Demons are in the Babylonish, harlot system (Revelation 18:2). Samson was not watching or he would have discerned them. Demons are always close to the anointing.

5. The Philistines thought that Samson's supernatural strength arose from something external, some kind of charm or amulet, or something natural. They had no conception of God's anointing or holy power.

6. The anointing always draws the special attention of Satan and his cohorts because the anointing spells Satan's doom, of his plans, authority, tricks, and power over God's people.

    a. I Samuel 2:10 – *"The adversaries of the LORD shall be broken to pieces; out of heaven shall he thunder upon them: the LORD shall judge the ends of the earth; and he shall give strength unto his king, and exalt the horn of his anointed."*

    b. I Samuel 15:17-29 – Saul here falls prey to one of Satan's attempts to tempt him, and like Samson loses his anointing because of rebellion, disobedience, presumption, pride, as well as rejecting God's Word. Once again this didn't happen over night but came after an accumulation of Saul's sins. God never exposes anyone publicly that He hasn't dealt with for quite some time. (I Samuel 9:16, I Samuel 15:1, I Samuel 16:1, I Samuel 16:14).

        1) Places in Scripture where we see God dealing with sin in His people

            a) I Corinthians 5:1-5

"1It is reported commonly that there is fornication among you, and such fornication as is not so much as named among the Gentiles, that one should have his father's wife. 2And ye are puffed up, and have not rather mourned, that he that hath done this deed might be taken away from among you. 3For I verily, as absent in body, but present in spirit, have judged already, as though I were present, concerning him that hath so done this deed, 4In the name of our Lord Jesus Christ, when ye are gathered together, and my spirit, with the power of our Lord Jesus

Christ, *5To deliver such an one unto Satan for the destruction of the flesh, that the spirit may be saved in the day of the Lord Jesus."*

b)   Hosea 5:12-15

"12Therefore will I be unto Ephraim <u>as a moth</u>, and to the house of Judah <u>as rottenness</u>. 13When Ephraim saw his sickness, and Judah saw his wound, then went Ephraim to the Assyrian, and sent to king Jareb: yet could he not heal you, nor cure you of your wound. 14For I will be unto Ephraim <u>as a lion</u>, and <u>as a young lion</u> to the house of Judah: I, even I, will tear and go away; I will take away, and none shall rescue him. 15I will go and return to my place, till they acknowledge their offence, and seek my face: in their affliction they will seek me early."

c)   Deuteronomy 32:1-9 – *"1Give ear, O ye heavens, and I will speak; and hear, O earth, the words of my mouth. 2My doctrine shall <u>drop as the rain</u>, my speech shall <u>distil as the dew</u>, as the <u>small rain</u> upon the tender herb, and as the <u>showers</u> upon the grass..."*
d)   Hosea 13:2-16
e)   Hosea 14
f)   II Samuel 11, II Samuel 12:1-24

c.   Exodus 30:25, 31-33, 36-38
d.   Leviticus 8:30-36
e.   Leviticus 10:7-11
f.   Leviticus 21:10-15
g.   Leviticus 21:16-24

h.   Isaiah 10:27 – *"And it shall come to pass in that day, that his burden shall be taken away from off thy shoulder, and his yoke from off thy neck, and the yoke shall be destroyed because of the anointing."* – This is why Satan is so against the anointing. It breaks the bondages he puts upon people.

1)   James 1:14-15 – *"But every man is tempted, when he is drawn away of his own lust, and enticed. Then when lust hath conceived, it bringeth forth sin: and sin, when it is finished, bringeth forth death."*
2)   Isaiah 61:1-4 – *"1The Spirit of the Lord GOD is upon me; because the LORD hath anointed me to preach good tidings unto the meek; he hath sent me to bind up the brokenhearted, to proclaim liberty to the captives, and the opening of the prison to them that are bound; 2To proclaim the acceptable year of the LORD, and the day of vengeance of our God; to comfort all that mourn; 3To appoint unto them that mourn in Zion, to give unto them beauty for ashes, the oil of joy for mourning, the garment of praise for the spirit of heaviness; that they might be called trees of righteousness, the planting of the LORD, that he might be glorified. 4And they shall build the old wastes, they shall raise up the former desolations, and they shall repair the waste cities, the desolations of many generations."*
3)   Isaiah 45:1-7
4)   Psalms 20:6-9
5)   Psalms 132:17-18 – *"There will I make the horn of David to bud: I have ordained a lamp for mine anointed. His enemies will I clothe with shame: but upon himself shall his crown flourish."*
6)   Acts 10:38 – *"How God anointed Jesus of Nazareth with the Holy Ghost and with power: who went about doing good, and healing all that were oppressed of the devil; for God was with him."*
7)   Psalms 23:5 – *"Thou preparest a table before me in the presence of mine enemies: thou anointest my head with oil; my cup runneth over."*
8)   Revelation 11:5-7 (Zechariah 4:11-14)

i. II Samuel 5:17-20
j. Psalms 2:1-6
k. Psalms 45:7-17 – Because the bride has God's anointing, Satan hates her and will try anything to rob her.

   1) Satan himself lost the anointing

      a) Ezekiel 28:12-19
      b) Isaiah 14:4-17
      c) Luke 10:18 – *"And he said unto them, I beheld Satan as lightning fall from heaven"*
      d) Revelation 12:9 – *"And the great dragon was cast out, that old serpent, called the Devil, and Satan, which deceiveth the whole world: he was cast out into the earth, and his angels were cast out with him."*
      e) Revelation 20:2, 7-10

l. Luke 4:1-13 – This is the story of Satan tempting Jesus in the wilderness. In verse 13 it reads, *"And when the devil had ended all the temptation, he departed from him <u>for a season</u>."* – *"for a season"* in the Greek means, *"for a more opportune time"*.

m. Matthew 16:21-23 – *"²¹From that time forth began Jesus to shew unto his disciples, how that he must go unto Jerusalem, and suffer many things of the elders and chief priests and scribes, and be killed, and be raised again the third day. ²²Then Peter took him, and began to rebuke him, saying, Be it far from thee, Lord: this shall not be unto thee. ²³But he turned, and said unto Peter, Get thee behind me, Satan: thou art an offence unto me: for thou savourest not the things that be of God, but those that be of men."*

   1) John 12:24-29
   2) Luke 22:28 – *"Ye are they which have continued with me in my temptations."*
   3) Hebrews 4:15 – *"For we have not an high priest which cannot be touched with the feeling of our infirmities; but was in all points tempted like as we are, yet without sin."*

n. Luke 22:31 – *"And the Lord said, Simon, Simon, behold, Satan hath desired to have you, that he may sift you as wheat:"*
o. Acts 5:1-15
p. II Corinthians 2:11 – *"Lest Satan should get an advantage of us: for we are not ignorant of his devices."*
q. II Corinthians 11:12-13 – *"But what I do, that I will do, that I may cut off occasion from them which desire occasion; that wherein they glory, they may be found even as we. For such are false apostles, deceitful workers, transforming themselves into the apostles of Christ."*
r. II Corinthians 12:7-12 – *"⁷And lest I should be exalted above measure through the abundance of the revelations, there was given to me a thorn in the flesh, the messenger of Satan to buffet me, lest I should be exalted above measure..."*
s. Ephesians 6:11-18
t. Ezekiel 44:6-23

7. Keeping God's anointing means guarding the secret of the anointing. The enemy has women always ready to steal the anointing from men of God. We must ever be watching, keeping our hearts pure.

   a. Acts 24:16 – *"And herein do I exercise myself, to have always a conscience void of offence toward God, and toward men."*
   b. Matthew 5:8 – *"Blessed are the pure in heart: for they shall see God."*
   c. Proverbs 4:23 – *"Keep thy heart with all diligence; for out of it are the issues of life."*

    d.   II Corinthians 7:1 – *"Having therefore these promises, dearly beloved, let us cleanse ourselves from all filthiness of the flesh and spirit, perfecting holiness in the fear of God."*

    e.   Hebrews 13:18 – *"Pray for us: for we trust we have a good conscience, in all things willing to live honestly."*

    f.   I Timothy 5:22 – *"...keep thyself pure."*

    g.   I Corinthians 6:18 – *"Flee fornication..."*

    h.   I John 5:18 – *"We know that whosoever is born of God sinneth not; but he that is begotten of God keepeth himself, and that wicked one toucheth him not."*

    i.   Mark 14:38 – *"Watch ye and pray, lest ye enter into temptation. The spirit truly is ready, but the flesh is weak."*

8.   We cannot allow petty sins to remain in our lives. We will eventually be worn down.

9.   The enemy will oppress us daily

10.   Samson made sport of his anointing and ended up in disaster. We should always revere and honor God's holy anointing. We should never, ever make light of it. The only answer here is that Samson must have thought this his great strength was due to him and not God.

    a.   Jeremiah 9:23-24 – *"Thus saith the LORD, Let not the wise man glory in his wisdom, neither let the mighty man glory in his might, let not the rich man glory in his riches: But let him that glorieth glory in this, that he understandeth and knoweth me...."*

    b.   I Corinthians 4:7 – *"For who maketh thee to differ from another? and what hast thou that thou didst not receive? now if thou didst receive it, why dost thou glory, as if thou hadst not received it?"*

    c.   Daniel 4:30 – *"The king spake, and said, Is not this great Babylon, that I have built for the house of the kingdom by the might of my power, and for the honour of my majesty?"*

11.   It is possible to lose out on God's anointing and not know it until it is gone. Samson was ignorant of his loss of the anointing. He thought everything would be as usual, but alas, *"And she said, The Philistines be upon thee, Samson. And he awoke out of his sleep, and said, I will go out as at other times before, and shake myself. And he wist not that the LORD was departed from him."* (Judges 16:20) It is a terrible thing not know if God has departed from you. You really have to be deceived or in bondage if you can't discern or recognize the truth about yourself. Everybody else can clearly see it, but we are oblivious to it. Samson had sold out his Nazarite vow.

    a.   Genesis 28:16-17 – *"And Jacob awaked out of his sleep, and he said, Surely the LORD is in this place; and I knew it not. And he was afraid, and said, How dreadful is this place! this is none other but the house of God, and this is the gate of heaven."*

    b.   John 12:28-30 – *"²⁸Father, glorify thy name. Then came there a voice from heaven, saying, I have both glorified it, and will glorify it again. ²⁹The people therefore, that stood by, and heard it, said that it thundered: others said, An angel spake to him..."*

    c.   Revelation 3:14-18

    d.   Luke 24:13-32

12.   Obviously this didn't happen to Samson overnight. He had been sinning a long time.

13.   Never, ever, tell your whole heart to anyone but Jesus (Micah 7:5 – *"Trust ye not in a friend, put ye not confidence in a guide: keep the doors of thy mouth from her that lieth in thy bosom"*). The secret things belong unto the Lord.

14.   Men must know their weakness and stay accountable to someone.

15.   After Samson's great miraculous feat in Judges 16:1-3, he gives in to his lustful nature again.

16.   Samson could do many powerful acts:

    a.   He could slay a lion, but not his lusts

b. He could lift an entire city gate, but not humble himself to lose his pride.
c. He could kill 300 foxes, but not his own little foxes. (Judges 15:4-5)
d. He could break his bonds, but not his sinful habits

17. Delilah made him fall asleep – speaks of slothfulness

   a. Ecclesiastes 10:18 – *"By much slothfulness the building decayeth; and through idleness of the hands the house droppeth through."*
   b. Proverbs 24:30-34 – *"30I went by the field of the slothful, and by the vineyard of the man void of understanding; 31And, lo, it was all grown over with thorns, and nettles had covered the face thereof, and the stone wall thereof was broken down. 32Then I saw, and considered it well: I looked upon it, and received instruction. 33Yet a little sleep, a little slumber, a little folding of the hands to sleep: 34So shall thy poverty come as one that travelleth; and thy want as an armed man."*
   c. Proverbs 26:13-15 – *"13The slothful man saith, There is a lion in the way; a lion is in the streets. 14As the door turneth upon his hinges, so doth the slothful upon his bed. 15The slothful hideth his hand in his bosom; it grieveth him to bring it again to his mouth."*
   d. Proverbs 19:15 – *"Slothfulness casteth into a deep sleep; and an idle soul shall suffer hunger."*

18. On her knees Samson fell asleep – How arrogant he must have been to think he could dwell so close to evil and remain untouched. This is obviously a position of weakness for him. He was completely vulnerable to her. How she must have laughed. He allowed the enemy to put him to sleep, when he should have been watching. Below are Scriptures talking about sleeping out of the will of God.

   a. Mark 14:37 – *"And he cometh, and findeth them sleeping, and saith unto Peter, Simon, sleepest thou? couldest not thou watch one hour?"*
   b. Luke 22:45-46 – *"And when he rose up from prayer, and was come to his disciples, he found them sleeping for sorrow, And said unto them, Why sleep ye? rise and pray, lest ye enter into temptation."*
   c. Mark 13:35-37 – *"35Watch ye therefore: for ye know not when the master of the house cometh, at even, or at midnight, or at the cockcrowing, or in the morning: 36Lest coming suddenly he find you sleeping. 37And what I say unto you I say unto all, Watch."*

Remember, there are two kinds of sleeping typified in Scripture. One is resting comfortably and peaceably in the will of God. The other is a sleep of slothfulness, laziness, or just having been deceived into a state of idleness and doing nothing.

   d. Romans 11:8 – *"(According as it is written, God hath given them the spirit of slumber, eyes that they should not see, and ears that they should not hear;) unto this day."*
   e. Proverbs 6:4-11
   f. Matthew 25:5 – *"While the bridegroom tarried, they all slumbered and slept."* – This is the parable of the ten virgins, five being wise and five being foolish. The five wise were resting in the will of God and the five foolish were slumbering and being slothful, not preparing themselves for the coming of the Lord.
   g. Proverbs 20:13 – *"Love not sleep, lest thou come to poverty; open thine eyes, and thou shalt be satisfied with bread."*
   h. Song of Solomon 5:2 – *"I sleep, but my heart waketh: it is the voice of my beloved that knocketh, saying, Open to me, my sister, my love, my dove, my undefiled: for my head is filled with dew, and my locks with the drops of the night."*
   i. Isaiah 29:10-14
   j. Romans 13:11 – *"And that, knowing the time, that now it is high time to awake out of sleep: for now is our salvation nearer than when we believed."*
   k. I Thessalonians 5:6-10

    l.   I Kings 19:4-8
    m.   Psalms 76:5-8
    n.   Matthew 13:24-25

19. We see in this story how Samson fell into a threefold deception. The threefold principle is Scripture is well established. We see it in so many things, such as the Tabernacle, the Feasts, the Godhead, mankind, baptisms, and levels of fruit in the body of Christ (some 30-fold, 60-fold, and 100-fold). Below shows are Scriptures showing Samson and others falling backwards in a three-fold way:

Example	30-fold	60-fold	100-fold
Samson	Woman of Timnath (Judges 14)	Harlot of Gaza (Judges 16:1)	Delilah (Judges 16:4-20)
Proverbs 7:9	*"twilight"*	*"evening"*	*"black and dark night"*
Proverbs 7:21-23	*"much fair speech she cause him to yield"*	*"he goeth after her straightway"*	*"till a dart strike through his liver"*
II Timothy 3:13	*"wax worse and worse"*	*"deceiving"*	*"being deceived"*
Proverbs 6:10-11	*"a little sleep, a little slumber, a little folding of the hands to sleep"*	*"so shall thy poverty come as one that travelleth"*	*"thy want as an armed man"*
Delilah's 3 attempts to deceive Samson	After each lie, he slowly digressed into a complete submission to his enemy		

20. Look at the cost of his sin:

    a.   He lost God's anointing
    b.   Was deceived by someone he loved
    c.   He lost his vision (both natural and spiritual)
    d.   Brought to Gaza – strong, fortified. He was captured by Satan
    e.   Bound with brass – God's judgment. His hands being bound means he could no more do the works of the Lord. His feet being bound means he could no more walk with the Lord.
    f.   Grind in prison – this was humiliating to Samson because it was the work of women and slaves.
    g.   He was made to act as a clown.
    h.   He needed the help of a little child in the end.
    i.   Apart from all this, the tremendous heart ached and broken heart he must have had.

21. This story is the principle of Ichabod (I Samuel 4:21-22 – *"And she named the child I-chabod, saying, The glory is departed from Israel: because the ark of God was taken, and because of her father in law and her husband. And she said, The glory is departed from Israel: for the ark of God is taken."*)
22. This story is also the principle of strange fire (Leviticus 10:1-3 – *"1And Nadab and Abihu, the sons of Aaron, took either of them his censer, and put fire therein, and put incense thereon, and offered strange fire before the LORD, which he commanded them not. 2And there went out fire from the LORD, and devoured them, and they died before the LORD. 3Then Moses said unto Aaron, This is it that the LORD spake, saying, I will be sanctified in them that come nigh me, and before all the people I will be glorified. And Aaron held his peace."*)

23. *"How are the mighty fallen, and the weapons of war perished!"* (II Samuel 1:27)

    a.   Romans 12:3 – *"For I say, through the grace given unto me, to every man that is among you, <u>not to think of himself more highly than he ought to think</u>; but to think soberly, according as God hath dealt to every man the measure of faith."*

b. Proverbs 16:18 – "_Pride_ goeth before destruction, and an haughty spirit before a fall."
c. Jeremiah 9:23 – "Thus saith the LORD, Let not the wise man glory in his wisdom, _neither let the mighty man glory in his might_, let not the rich man glory in his riches:"
d. I Corinthians 10:11-12 – "Now all these things happened unto them for ensamples: and they are written for our admonition, upon whom the ends of the world are come. Wherefore let him that thinketh he standeth _take heed lest he fall_."

24. Though judgment tarries, it will come. Many men and women, because God doesn't immediately expose them, think it is alright (Ecclesiastes 8:11 – "_Because sentence against an evil work is not executed speedily, therefore the heart of the sons of men is fully set in them to do evil_"), or, crazy as it may seem, that God is actually blessing their disobedience of whatever kind, or that they are simply too special. It is the truth that God uses flawed men of which we all are, at least now, but He expects them to be like Him (Matthew 11:28-30), or at least like David, who though terribly flawed, always was truly sorry for his sins.
25. The story of Samson is a sad one, but ultimately shows us the way to redemption and restoration, and how that the "_gifts and calling of God are without repentance_" (Romans 11:29).
26. This story also clearly shows that the way to life, redemption, forgiveness, and paying back your arch enemy, and winning in the end, is through our own deaths, be it natural or spiritual.
27. Samson judged Israel twenty years. Twenty in Scripture is the number for expectancy.
28. He was buried between Zorah and Eshtaol, the same place his father was buried. Zorah in Hebrew means – a place of hornets, a place for troublesome men. Eshtaol means – women requesting, I will be entreated.

E. More revelation and facts about Samson

1. This wasn't the first harlot Samson fell for (Judges 16:1-3)
2. Samson was betrayed by his own lusts.

a. Numbers 11:4 – "And the mixt multitude that was among them fell a lusting: and the children of Israel also wept again, and said, Who shall give us flesh to eat?"
b. Mark 4:18-19 – "And these are they which are sown among thorns; such as hear the word, And the cares of this world, and the deceitfulness of riches, and the lusts of other things entering in, choke the word, and it becometh unfruitful."
c. John 8:44 – "Ye are of your father the devil, and the lusts of your father ye will do. He was a murderer from the beginning, and abode not in the truth, because there is no truth in him. When he speaketh a lie, he speaketh of his own: for he is a liar, and the father of it."
d. Romans 1:24 – "Wherefore God also gave them up to uncleanness through the lusts of their own hearts, to dishonour their own bodies between themselves:"
e. Romans 6:12-14 – "12Let not sin therefore reign in your mortal body, that ye should obey it in the lusts thereof. 13Neither yield ye your members as instruments of unrighteousness unto sin: but yield yourselves unto God, as those that are alive from the dead, and your members as instruments of righteousness unto God. 14For sin shall not have dominion over you: for ye are not under the law, but under grace."
f. Romans 13:14 – "But put ye on the Lord Jesus Christ, and make not provision for the flesh, to fulfil the lusts thereof."
g. Ephesians 2:1-3 – "1And you hath he quickened, who were dead in trespasses and sins; 2Wherein in time past ye walked according to the course of this world, according to the prince of the power of the air, the spirit that now worketh in the children of disobedience: 3Among whom also we all had our conversation in times past in the lusts of our flesh, fulfilling the desires of the flesh and of the mind; and were by nature the children of wrath, even as others."
h. Ephesians 4:22 – "That ye put off concerning the former conversation the old man, which is corrupt according to the deceitful lusts;"
i. II Timothy 2:22 – "Flee also youthful lusts: but follow righteousness, faith, charity, peace, with them that call on the Lord out of a pure heart."

j.   Titus 2:12 – *"Teaching us that, denying ungodliness and worldly lusts, we should live soberly, righteously, and godly, in this present world;"*

k.   James 4:1-3 – *"¹From whence come wars and fightings among you? come they not hence, even of your lusts that war in your members? ²Ye lust, and have not: ye kill, and desire to have, and cannot obtain: ye fight and war, yet ye have not, because ye ask not. ³Ye ask, and receive not, because ye ask amiss, that ye may consume it upon your lusts."*

l.   I Peter 2:11 – *"Dearly beloved, I beseech you as strangers and pilgrims, abstain from fleshly lusts, which war against the soul"*

m.   I Peter 4:1-4 – *"¹Forasmuch then as Christ hath suffered for us in the flesh, arm yourselves likewise with the same mind: for he that hath suffered in the flesh hath ceased from sin; ²That he no longer should live the rest of his time in the flesh to the lusts of men, but to the will of God. ³For the time past of our life may suffice us to have wrought the will of the Gentiles, when we walked in lasciviousness, lusts, excess of wine, revellings, banquetings, and abominable idolatries: ⁴Wherein they think it strange that ye run not with them to the same excess of riot, speaking evil of you:"*

n.   II Peter 3:3 – *"Knowing this first, that there shall come in the last days scoffers, walking after their own lusts,"*

o.   Jude 16-18 – *"¹⁶These are murmurers, complainers, walking after their own lusts; and their mouth speaketh great swelling words, having men's persons in admiration because of advantage. ¹⁷But, beloved, remember ye the words which were spoken before of the apostles of our Lord Jesus Christ; ¹⁸How that they told you there should be mockers in the last time, who should walk after their own ungodly lusts."*

p.   James 1:14-15 – *"But every man is tempted, when he is drawn away of his own lust, and enticed. Then when lust hath conceived, it bringeth forth sin: and sin, when it is finished, bringeth forth death."*

3.   His first mistake was taking a wife outside the kingdom. She was a daughter of Timnath (Judges 14:1). Definition of Timnath – portion assigned, separated, a gift; from a root meaning – to allot, to divide. It is obvious that women were a constant source of trouble for him (Judges 14-16).

4.   There is never a time when one's service to God is more endangered then when fleshly desires and worldly relationships are given a place higher than the Lord in our hearts.

   a.   Love of the world

      1)   I John 2:15-17 – *"¹⁵Love not the world, neither the things that are in the world. If any man love the world, the love of the Father is not in him. ¹⁶For all that is in the world, the lust of the flesh, and the lust of the eyes, and the pride of life, is not of the Father, but is of the world. ¹⁷And the world passeth away, and the lust thereof: but he that doeth the will of God abideth for ever."*

      2)   II Corinthians 6:14-18 – *"¹⁴Be ye not unequally yoked together with unbelievers: for what fellowship hath righteousness with unrighteousness? and what communion hath light with darkness? ¹⁵And what concord hath Christ with Belial? or what part hath he that believeth with an infidel? ¹⁶And what agreement hath the temple of God with idols? for ye are the temple of the living God; as God hath said, I will dwell in them, and walk in them; and I will be their God, and they shall be my people. ¹⁷Wherefore come out from among them, and be ye separate, saith the Lord, and touch not the unclean thing; and I will receive you..."*

   b.   The flesh

      1)   I Peter 2:11 – *"Dearly beloved, I beseech you as strangers and pilgrims, abstain from fleshly lusts, which war against the soul;"*

      2)   Matthew 26:41 – *"Watch and pray, that ye enter not into temptation: the spirit indeed is willing, but the flesh is weak."*

       3) Romans 6:19 – *"I speak after the manner of men because of the infirmity of your flesh: for as ye have yielded your members servants to uncleanness and to iniquity unto iniquity; even so now yield your members servants to righteousness unto holiness."*

       4) Romans 7:18 – *"For I know that in me (that is, in my flesh,) dwelleth no good thing: for to will is present with me; but how to perform that which is good I find not."*

       5) Romans 8:1-13

5. He was of the tribe of Dan – Judge
6. He was dedicated to God at his birth
7. He was brought up by godly parents (Judges 13). His father's name was Manoah, which means – rest, quiet, consolation to parents.
8. It seems he never took seriously his anointing and his supernatural gifts.
9. Samson was a man who, though called by God & anointed, always fought his battles alone.
10. Samson's lifestyle was one of uncontrollable desires and rebellion.

11. He was also a Nazarite (Hebrew – separated, consecrated, abstain, to hold aloof, devoted crown). By taking a Nazarite vow, he was to abstain from unclean food and drinks, he was to be pure, and he was set apart for sacred purposes. The vow of the Nazarite (Numbers 6:1-8) is defined below:

    a. It was voluntary
    b. Could be a man or woman
    c. Abstain from wine and grapes (symbolic of natural pleasures)
    d. Never to cut one's hair (representing their covering). A Nazarite was to be totally separated and covered by the Lord.
    e. They were to be separated from dead bodies – This is symbolic of anything dead, both natural or spiritual (Numbers 19, Ezekiel 44:25, Hebrews 6:1).
    f. They were to be separated from their families.

12. Even though Samson failed God, deceived himself, allowed his passions to control him, disappointed his parents, brought trouble to his people, broke his vow, was unequally yoked with unbelievers, he is still mentioned in the fall of fame of faith (Hebrews 11:32 – *"And what shall I more say? for the time would fail me to tell of Gedeon, and of Barak, and of Samson, and of Jephthae; of David also, and Samuel, and of the prophets"*)
13. Samson was in lust, not in love with Delilah.
14. Whoredom is one of those things that takes away a man's heart.
15. The shame of his life is he had fallen so far that he didn't even know God had departed from him.

16. The consequences of adultery (natural and spiritual) – Adultery simply put is sexual relations involving at least one partner who is married to someone else. This breaks the marriage covenant and is condemned in Scripture. Jesus extended the term when He spoke of it as adultery of the heart, when someone has inner lust without actually committing physical adultery (Matthew 5:28 – *"But I say unto you, That whosoever looketh on a woman to lust after her hath committed adultery with her already in his heart."*). It can also represent spiritual adultery which means worshipping or having any idol in our hearts other than the Lord Jesus. The Hebrew word for adultery is *na'aph* which means – woman that breaketh wedlock, to apostatize.

    a. Exodus 20:14 – *"Thou shalt not commit adultery."*
    b. Leviticus 20:10 – *"And the man that committeth adultery with another man's wife, even he that committeth adultery with his neighbour's wife, the adulterer and the adulteress shall surely be put to death."*
    c. Proverbs 6:32-34 – *"32But whoso committeth adultery with a woman lacketh understanding: he that doeth it destroyeth his own soul. 33A wound and dishonour shall he get; and his reproach shall not be wiped away. 34For jealousy is the rage of a man: therefore he will not spare in the day of vengeance."*

d. Jeremiah 3:8-14 – "*8And I saw, when for all the causes whereby backsliding Israel committed adultery I had put her away, and given her a bill of divorce; yet her treacherous sister Judah feared not, but went and played the harlot also. 9And it came to pass through the lightness of her whoredom, that she defiled the land, and committed adultery with stones and with stocks. 10And yet for all this her treacherous sister Judah hath not turned unto me with her whole heart, but feignedly, saith the LORD. 11And the LORD said unto me, The backsliding Israel hath justified herself more than treacherous Judah…14Turn, O backsliding children, saith the LORD; for I am married unto you: and I will take you one of a city, and two of a family, and I will bring you to Zion.*"

e. Jeremiah 7:9-11 – "*9Will ye steal, murder, and commit adultery, and swear falsely, and burn incense unto Baal, and walk after other gods whom ye know not; 10And come and stand before me in this house, which is called by my name, and say, We are delivered to do all these abominations? 11Is this house, which is called by my name, become a den of robbers in your eyes? Behold, even I have seen it, saith the LORD.*"

f. Jeremiah 23:14 – "*I have seen also in the prophets of Jerusalem an horrible thing: they commit adultery, and walk in lies: they strengthen also the hands of evildoers, that none doth return from his wickedness: they are all of them unto me as Sodom, and the inhabitants thereof as Gomorrah.*"

g. Matthew 5:28-32 – "*28But I say unto you, That whosoever looketh on a woman to lust after her hath committed adultery with her already in his heart. 29And if thy right eye offend thee, pluck it out, and cast it from thee: for it is profitable for thee that one of thy members should perish, and not that thy whole body should be cast into hell. 30And if thy right hand offend thee, cut if off, and cast it from thee: for it is profitable for thee that one of thy members should perish, and not that thy whole body should be cast into hell. 31It hath been said, Whosoever shall put away his wife, let him give her a writing of divorcement: 32But I say unto you, That whosoever shall put away his wife, saving for the cause of fornication, causeth her to commit adultery: and whosoever shall marry her that is divorced committeth adultery.*"

h. Matthew 19:9-12

i. John 8:1-11 – Jesus response to woman caught in the act of adultery

j. Romans 2:19-24 – "*…22Thou that sayest a man should not commit adultery, dost thou commit adultery? thou that abhorrest idols, dost thou commit sacrilege?…*"

k. Galatians 5:19 – "*Now the works of the flesh are manifest, which are these; Adultery, fornication, uncleanness, lasciviousness,*"

l. II Peter 2:9-22

m. Revelation 2:20-23 – "*20Notwithstanding I have a few things against thee, because thou sufferest that woman Jezebel, which calleth herself a prophetess, to teach and to seduce my servants to commit fornication, and to eat things sacrificed unto idols. 21And I gave her space to repent of her fornication; and she repented not. 22Behold, I will cast her into a bed, and them that commit adultery with her into great tribulation, except they repent of their deeds…*"

n. Proverbs 5:4-5, 9-11 – "*4But her end is bitter as wormwood, sharp as a twoedged sword. 5Her feet go down to death; her steps take hold on hell…9Lest thou give thine honour unto others, and thy years unto the cruel: 10Lest strangers be filled with thy wealth; and thy labours be in the house of a stranger; 11And thou mourn at the last, when thy flesh and thy body are consumed,*"

o. Proverbs 6:26-29 – "*26For by means of a whorish woman a man is brought to a piece of bread: and the adulteress will hunt for the precious life. 27Can a man take fire in his bosom, and his clothes not be burned? 28Can one go upon hot coals, and his feet not be burned? 29So he that goeth in to his neighbour's wife; whosoever toucheth her shall not be innocent.*"

p. Job 31:11-12 – "*11For this is an heinous crime; yea, it is an iniquity to be punished by the judges. 12For it is a fire that consumeth to destruction, and would root out all mine increase.*:

q. Hebrews 13:4 – "*Marriage is honourable in all, and the bed undefiled: but whoremongers and adulterers God will judge.*"

r. Proverbs 7:22-27

s. Job 24:15 – "*The eye also of the adulterer waiteth for the twilight, saying, No eye shall see me: and disguiseth his face.*"

t. II Samuel 12:11-12
u. I Corinthians 6:9
v. Malachi 3:5
w. Proverbs 30:20 – *"Such is the way of an adulterous woman; she eateth, and wipeth her mouth, and saith, I have done no wickedness."*

17. Samson judges Israel 20 years. 20 is the number for expectancy.
18. In His life he, slew a lion, killed 2030 Philistines, killed 100 men, burned 300 foxes, could break the strongest of bonds, carried off the gates of Gaza all by himself, brought down the temple of Dagon.
19. As long as Samson kept his Nazarite vow, he was unconquerable.
20. He performed all his acts by himself – He never called for the armies of Israel, he asked for no assistance, and he did everything single-handedly and alone.
21. His life consisted of a noble beginning, a supernatural call at birth, doing great deeds for God, allowing lusts to overcome him, mocking his anointing, being seduced by a woman, being captured and imprisoned and losing his vision, being made to look and act like a fool, destroying his enemies in the end, and glorifying God in his death.

III. The Actual Story Found In Judges 16:4-21 – Verse by Verse Analysis

A. Verse 4 – *"And it came to pass afterward, that he loved a woman in the valley of Sorek, whose name was Delilah."*

1. The Scriptures forbid loving the world

    a. Matthew 16:26 – *"For what is a man profited, if he shall gain the whole world, and lose his own soul? or what shall a man give in exchange for his soul?"*
    b. Mark 4:18-19 – *"And these are they which are sown among thorns; such as hear the word, And the cares of this world, and the deceitfulness of riches, and the lusts of other things entering in, choke the word, and it becometh unfruitful."*
    c. John 3:19 – *"And this is the condemnation, that light is come into the world, and men loved darkness rather than light, because their deeds were evil."*
    d. John 12:25-26 – *"He that loveth his life shall lose it; and he that hateth his life in this world shall keep it unto life eternal. If any man serve me, let him follow me; and where I am, there shall also my servant be: if any man serve me, him will my Father honour."*
    e. Romans 12:2 – *"And be not conformed to this world: but be ye transformed by the renewing of your mind, that ye may prove what is that good, and acceptable, and perfect, will of God."*
    f. John 15:18-19 – *"If the world hate you, ye know that it hated me before it hated you. If ye were of the world, the world would love his own: but because ye are not of the world, but I have chosen you out of the world, therefore the world hateth you."*
    g. Philippians 2:15 – *"That ye may be blameless and harmless, the sons of God, without rebuke, in the midst of a crooked and perverse nation, among whom ye shine as lights in the world;"*
    h. James 1:27 – *"Pure religion and undefiled before God and the Father is this, To visit the fatherless and widows in their affliction, and to keep himself unspotted from the world."*
    i. James 4:4 – *"Ye adulterers and adulteresses, know ye not that the friendship of the world is enmity with God? whosoever therefore will be a friend of the world is the enemy of God."*
    j. I John 2:15-17 – *"[15]Love not the world, neither the things that are in the world. If any man love the world, the love of the Father is not in him. [16]For all that is in the world, the lust of the flesh, and the lust of the eyes, and the pride of life, is not of the Father, but is of the world. [17]And the world passeth away, and the lust thereof: but he that doeth the will of God abideth for ever."*

2. The Scriptures forbid marrying someone in the world or even having a relationship with someone in it.

a. Ezra 10:2-3 – "...We have trespassed against our God, and have taken strange wives of the people of the land: yet now there is hope in Israel concerning this thing. Now therefore let us make a covenant with our God to put away all the wives, and such as are born of them, according to the counsel of my lord, and of those that tremble at the commandment of our God; and let it be done according to the law."

b. II Corinthians 6:14-18 – "14Be ye not unequally yoked together with unbelievers: for what fellowship hath righteousness with unrighteousness? and what communion hath light with darkness? 15And what concord hath Christ with Belial? or what part hath he that believeth with an infidel? 16And what agreement hath the temple of God with idols? for ye are the temple of the living God; as God hath said, I will dwell in them, and walk in them; and I will be their God, and they shall be my people. 17Wherefore come out from among them, and be ye separate, saith the Lord, and touch not the unclean thing; and I will receive you, 18And will be a Father unto you, and ye shall be my sons and daughters, saith the Lord Almighty."

c. Ezra 9:1-3, 11-12

d. Ezra 10:10-14, 17-19

e. Nehemiah 3:23-30

f. Numbers 11:4 – "And the mixt multitude that was among them fell a lusting: and the children of Israel also wept again, and said, Who shall give us flesh to eat?"

g. Joshua 9:3-23

h. Deuteronomy 7:1-6

i. Isaiah 52:11 – "Depart ye, depart ye, go ye out from thence, touch no unclean thing; go ye out of the midst of her; be ye clean, that bear the vessels of the LORD."

j. Judges 14:3 – "Then his father and his mother said unto him, Is there never a woman among the daughters of thy brethren, or among all my people, that thou goest to take a wife of the uncircumcised Philistines? And Samson said unto his father, Get her for me; for she pleaseth me well."

k. Exodus 34:11-16

B. Verse 5 – "And the lords of the Philistines came up unto her, and said unto her, Entice him, and see wherein his great strength lieth, and by what means we may prevail against him, that we may bind him to afflict him: and we will give thee every one of us eleven hundred pieces of silver."

1. "lords of the Philistines" – these natural leaders were the arch enemies of God's people. Delilah was joined unto them. Other translations include, "rulers", "tyrants", "chiefs", "Philistine rulers", "five heads of the Philistine nation", "princes of the Philistines", "five Philistine kings"

2. "Entice him" – Hebrew word for entice, pathah – to open, to make simple in a sinister way, to delude, to allure, deceive, flatter, persuade. Other translations include, "see if you can lure him...", "seduce him", "coax him into telling you", "find out", "trick him", "persuade him", "make use of your power over him", "deceive him".

3. We are warned in Scripture about being enticed

a. Proverbs 1:10 – "My son, if sinners entice thee, consent thou not."

b. Psalms 5:8-10 – "8Lead me, O LORD, in thy righteousness because of mine enemies; make thy way straight before my face. 9For there is no faithfulness in their mouth; their inward part is very wickedness; their throat is an open sepulchre; they flatter with their tongue. 10Destroy thou them, O God; let them fall by their own counsels; cast them out in the multitude of their transgressions; for they have rebelled against thee."

c. Proverbs 6:23-27 – "23For the commandment is a lamp; and the law is light; and reproofs of instruction are the way of life: 24To keep thee from the evil woman, from the flattery of the tongue of a strange woman. 25Lust not after her beauty in thine heart; neither let her take thee with her eyelids. 26For by means of a whorish woman a man is brought to a piece of bread: and *the adulteress will hunt for the precious life. ²⁷Can a man take fire in his bosom, and his clothes not be burned?"*

d. Psalms 12:1-3
e. Proverbs 7:5-27
f. Proverbs 26:28 – *"A lying tongue hateth those that are afflicted by it; and a flattering mouth worketh ruin."*
g. Ephesians 6:11-13
h. I Peter 5:8 – *"Be sober, be vigilant; because your adversary the devil, as a roaring lion, walketh about, seeking whom he may devour:"*
i. John 10:10 – *"The thief cometh not, but for to steal, and to kill, and to destroy: I am come that they might have life, and that they might have it more abundantly."*
j. II Peter 2:10, 14, 18-22 – *"¹⁰But chiefly them that walk after the flesh in the lust of uncleanness, and despise government. Presumptuous are they, selfwilled, they are not afraid to speak evil of dignities...¹⁴Having eyes full of adultery, and that cannot cease from sin; beguiling unstable souls: an heart they have exercised with covetous practices; cursed children...¹⁸Servants, be subject to your masters with all fear; not only to the good and gentle, but also to the froward. ¹⁹For this is thankworthy, if a man for conscience toward God endure grief, suffering wrongfully. ²⁰For what glory is it, if, when ye be buffeted for your faults, ye shall take it patiently? but if, when ye do well, and suffer for it, ye take it patiently, this is acceptable with God. ²¹For even hereunto were ye called: because Christ also suffered for us, leaving us an example, that ye should follow his steps: ²²Who did no sin, neither was guile found in his mouth:"*
k. James 1:14-15 – *"But every man is tempted, when he is drawn away of his own lust, and enticed. Then when lust hath conceived, it bringeth forth sin: and sin, when it is finished, bringeth forth death."*
l. I John 2:16-17
m. Galatians 5:16 – *"This I say then, Walk in the Spirit, and ye shall not fulfil the lust of the flesh."*
n. I Corinthians 10:6 – *"Now these things were our examples, to the intent we should not lust after evil things, as they also lusted."*
o. Romans 13:14 – *"But put ye on the Lord Jesus Christ, and make not provision for the flesh, to fulfil the lusts thereof."*
p. Galatians 5:24 – *"And they that are Christ's have crucified the flesh with the affections and lusts."*
q. II Timothy 2:22 – *"Flee also youthful lusts: but follow righteousness, faith, charity, peace, with them that call on the Lord out of a pure heart."*
r. Titus 3:3-5 – *"³For we ourselves also were sometimes foolish, disobedient, deceived, serving divers lusts and pleasures, living in malice and envy, hateful, and hating one another. ⁴But after that the kindness and love of God our Saviour toward man appeared, ⁵Not by works of righteousness which we have done, but according to his mercy he saved us, by the washing of regeneration, and renewing of the Holy Ghost;"*
s. I Peter 2:11 – *"Dearly beloved, I beseech you as strangers and pilgrims, abstain from fleshly lusts, which war against the soul;"*
t. I Peter 4:1-3 – *"¹Forasmuch then as Christ hath suffered for us in the flesh, arm yourselves likewise with the same mind: for he that hath suffered in the flesh hath ceased from sin; ²That he no longer should live the rest of his time in the flesh to the lusts of men, but to the will of God. ³For the time past of our life may suffice us to have wrought the will of the Gentiles, when we walked in lasciviousness, lusts, excess of wine, revellings, banquetings, and abominable idolatries:"*
u. I Corinthians 10:13 – *"There hath no temptation taken you but such as is common to man: but God is faithful, who will not suffer you to be tempted above that ye are able; but will with the temptation also make a way to escape, that ye may be able to bear it."*
v. James 1:12 – *"Blessed is the man that endureth temptation: for when he is tried, he shall receive the crown of life, which the Lord hath promised to them that love him."*
w. Luke 22:40, 46 – *"And when he was at the place, he said unto them, Pray that ye enter not into temptation...Why sleep ye? rise and pray, lest ye enter into temptation."*

x. Luke 8:13 – *"They on the rock are they, which, when they hear, receive the word with joy; and these have no root, which for a while believe, and in time of temptation fall away."*

y. Luke 4:13 – *"And when the devil had ended all the temptation, he departed from him for a season."*

z. Matthew 26:41 – *"Watch and pray, that ye enter not into temptation: the spirit indeed is willing, but the flesh is weak."*

4. The Scriptures are clear on this matter

a. II Peter 2:9 – *"The Lord knoweth how to deliver the godly out of temptations, and to reserve the unjust unto the day of judgment to be punished:"*

b. Luke 22:28 – *"Ye are they which have continued with me in my temptations."*

c. I John 2:25-29 – *"25And this is the promise that he hath promised us, even eternal life. 26These things have I written unto you concerning them that seduce you. 27But the anointing which ye have received of him abideth in you, and ye need not that any man teach you: but as the same anointing teacheth you of all things, and is truth, and is no lie, and even as it hath taught you, ye shall abide in him. 28And now, little children, abide in him; that, when he shall appear, we may have confidence, and not be ashamed before him at his coming. 29If ye know that he is righteous, ye know that every one that doeth righteousness is born of him."*

d. Revelation 2:20 – *"Notwithstanding I have a few things against thee, because thou sufferest that woman Jezebel, which calleth herself a prophetess, to teach and to seduce my servants to commit fornication, and to eat things sacrificed unto idols."*

e. I Timothy 4:1 – *"Now the Spirit speaketh expressly, that in the latter times some shall depart from the faith, giving heed to seducing spirits, and doctrines of devils;"*

5. Continuing in verse 5, *"...and see wherein his great strength lieth..."* – other translations:

a. *"...see in what his great strength lies..."*
b. *"...wherein his great power is..."*
c. *"...the secret of his great strength..."*
d. *"...what makes him so strong..."*
e. *"...discover what's behind his great strength..."*
f. *"...find out where his great strength comes..."*
g. *"...find out what makes Samson so strong..."*
h. *"...find out what makes his strength so great..."*

6. The source of Samson's strength and our strength as well comes from:

a. The Lord Himself gives us strength

1) Genesis 49:24 – *"But his bow abode in strength, and the arms of his hands were made strong by the hands of the mighty God of Jacob; (from thence is the shepherd, the stone of Israel:)"*

2) Deuteronomy 31:6 – *"Be strong and of a good courage, fear not, nor be afraid of them: for the LORD thy God, he it is that doth go with thee; he will not fail thee, nor forsake thee."*

3) Joshua 1:6-9

4) II Chronicles 16:9 – *"For the eyes of the LORD run to and fro throughout the whole earth, to shew himself strong in the behalf of them whose heart is perfect toward him..."*

5) II Chronicles 32:7-8

6) Nehemiah 1:10 – *"Now these are thy servants and thy people, whom thou hast redeemed by thy great power, and by thy strong hand."*

7) Psalms 24:8 – *"Who is this King of glory? The LORD strong and mighty, the LORD mighty in battle."*

8) Psalms 61:3 – *"For thou hast been a shelter for me, and a strong tower from the enemy."*

9) Psalms 71:3-7
10) Psalms 80:15-17
11) Psalms 136:11-12
12) Isaiah 27:1 – *"In that day the LORD with his sore and great and strong sword shall punish leviathan the piercing serpent, even leviathan that crooked serpent; and he shall slay the dragon that is in the sea."*
13) Isaiah 35:4 – *"Say to them that are of a fearful heart, Be strong, fear not: behold, your God will come with vengeance, even God with a recompence; he will come and save you."*
14) Isaiah 40:26-31
15) Jeremiah 32:21
16) Jeremiah 50:33-34
17) Daniel 11:32 – *"...the people that do know their God shall be strong, and do exploits."*
18) Joel 2:11 – *"And the LORD shall utter his voice before his army: for his camp is very great: for he is strong that executeth his word: for the day of the LORD is great and very terrible; and who can abide it?"*
19) Nahum 1:7-8
20) Haggai 2:4-5
21) Zechariah 9:12-17
22) II Corinthians 10:4 – *"(For the weapons of our warfare are not carnal, but mighty through God to the pulling down of strong holds;)"*
23) II Corinthians 12:9-10
24) Ephesians 6:10 – *"Finally, my brethren, be strong in the Lord, and in the power of his might."*
25) Hebrews 11:34 – *"Quenched the violence of fire, escaped the edge of the sword, out of weakness were made strong, waxed valiant in fight, turned to flight the armies of the aliens."*
26) II Chronicles 1:1 – *"And Solomon the son of David was strengthened in his kingdom, and the LORD his God was with him, and magnified him exceedingly."*
27) Ephesians 3:16 – *"That he would grant you, according to the riches of his glory, to be strengthened with might by his Spirit in the inner man;"*
28) Colossians 1:11
29) II Timothy 4:17 – *"Notwithstanding the Lord stood with me, and strengthened me; that by me the preaching might be fully known, and that all the Gentiles might hear: and I was delivered out of the mouth of the lion."*
30) Exodus 13:3, 14-16
31) Exodus 15:2, 13
32) Deuteronomy 33:25-29
33) I Samuel 2:4-10
34) I Samuel 15:29
35) II Samuel 22:33, 40
36) I Chronicles 16:11 – *"Seek the LORD and his strength, seek his face continually."*
37) I Chronicles 16:27 – *"...strength and gladness are in his place."*
38) I Chronicles 29:12
39) Job 12:13, 16, 36:4
40) Psalms 8:2 – *"Out of the mouth of babes and sucklings hast thou ordained strength because of thine enemies, that thou mightest still the enemy and the avenger."*
41) Psalms 18:1-2, 32, 39
42) Psalms 19:14, 20:6, 22:19
43) Psalms 27:1, 28:7-8 29:11
44) Psalms 31:4, 37:39
45) Psalms 43:2, 46:1
46) Psalms 59:17 – *"Unto thee, O my strength, will I sing..."*
47) Psalms 62:7
48) Psalms 68:28, 34-35, 73:26

49) Psalms 81:1, 84:5, 7
50) Psalms 118:14 – *"The LORD is my strength and song, and is become my salvation."*
51) Psalms 138:3 – *"In the day when I cried thou answeredst me, and strengthenedst me with strength in my soul."*
52) Psalms 140:7
53) Psalms 144:1 – *"Blessed be the LORD my strength, which teacheth my hands to war, and my fingers to fight:"*
54) Isaiah 12:2
55) Isaiah 25:4 – *"For thou hast been a strength to the poor, a strength to the needy in his distress, a refuge from the storm, a shadow from the heat, when the blast of the terrible ones is as a storm against the wall."*
56) Isaiah 26:4, 49:5
57) Jeremiah 16:19
58) Joel 3:16
59) Habakkuk 3:19
60) Hebrews 11:11 – *"Through faith also Sara herself received strength to conceive seed, and was delivered of a child when she was past age, because she judged him faithful who had promised."*

b. His anointing gives strength. This is where Samson's great strength lay.

1) Exodus 29:7, 21 – *"⁷Then shalt thou take the anointing oil, and pour it upon his head, and anoint him. ²¹And thou shalt take of the blood that is upon the altar, and of the anointing oil, and sprinkle it upon Aaron, and upon his garments, and upon his sons, and upon the garments of his sons with him: and he shall be hallowed, and his garments, and his sons, and his sons' garments with him."*

2) Exodus 30:25-31

1) Exodus 40:9-15
2) Leviticus 8:10-12, 30
3) Leviticus 21:10-12
4) Numbers 18:8

3) Isaiah 10:27 – *"And it shall come to pass in that day, that his burden shall be taken away from off thy shoulder, and his yoke from off thy neck, and the yoke shall be destroyed because of the anointing."*

4) James 5:14-15
5) I John 2:27 – *"But the anointing which ye have received of him abideth in you, and ye need not that any man teach you: but as the same anointing teacheth you of all things, and is truth, and is no lie, and even as it hath taught you, ye shall abide in him."*
6) Psalms 23:5 – *"Thou preparest a table before me in the presence of mine enemies: thou anointest my head with oil; my cup runneth over."*
7) I Samuel 2:10 – *"The adversaries of the LORD shall be broken to pieces; out of heaven shall he thunder upon them: the LORD shall judge the ends of the earth; and he shall give strength unto his king, and exalt the horn of his anointed."*
8) I Samuel 10:1 – *"Then Samuel took a vial of oil, and poured it upon his head, and kissed him, and said, Is it not because the LORD hath anointed thee to be captain over his inheritance?"*
9) I Samuel 16:13 – *"Then Samuel took the horn of oil, and anointed him in the midst of his brethren: and the Spirit of the LORD came upon David from that day forward..."*

10) II Samuel 5:17 – *"But when the Philistines heard that they had anointed David king over Israel, all the Philistines came up to seek David; and David heard of it, and went down to the hold."*

11) I Chronicles 16:22 – *"Saying, Touch not mine anointed, and do my prophets no harm."*

12) II Chronicles 22:7

13) Psalms 18:50 – *"Great deliverance giveth he to his king; and sheweth mercy to his anointed, to David, and to his seed for evermore."*

14) Psalms 20:6 – *"Now know I that the LORD saveth his anointed; he will hear him from his holy heaven with the saving strength of his right hand."*

15) Psalms 28:8

16) Psalms 89:20-24

17) Psalms 132:17-18 – *"There will I make the horn of David to bud: I have ordained a lamp for mine anointed. His enemies will I clothe with shame: but upon himself shall his crown flourish."*

18) Isaiah 45:1 – *"Thus saith the LORD to his anointed, to Cyrus, whose right hand I have holden, to subdue nations before him; and I will loose the loins of kings, to open before him the two leaved gates; and the gates shall not be shut;"*

19) Isaiah 61:1-3 – *"¹The Spirit of the Lord GOD is upon me; because the LORD hath anointed me to preach good tidings unto the meek; he hath sent me to bind up the brokenhearted, to proclaim liberty to the captives, and the opening of the prison to them that are bound; ²To proclaim the acceptable year of the LORD, and the day of vengeance of our God; to comfort all that mourn; ³To appoint unto them that mourn in Zion, to give unto them beauty for ashes, the oil of joy for mourning, the garment of praise for the spirit of heaviness; that they might be called trees of righteousness, the planting of the LORD, that he might be glorified."* (Luke 4:18-21)

20) Habakkuk 3:13 – *"Thou wentest forth for the salvation of thy people, even for salvation with thine anointed; thou woundedst the head out of the house of the wicked, by discovering the foundation unto the neck. Selah."*

21) Acts 10:38 – *"How God anointed Jesus of Nazareth with the Holy Ghost and with power: who went about doing good, and healing all that were oppressed of the devil; for God was with him."*

22) I Samuel 9:16

23) Revelation 3:18 – *"I counsel thee to buy of me gold tried in the fire, that thou mayest be rich; and white raiment, that thou mayest be clothed, and that the shame of thy nakedness do not appear; and anoint thine eyes with eyesalve, that thou mayest see."*

c. God's name (character) is given to deliver us, to help us, and to strengthen us

1) Exodus 34:5-8 – *"⁵And the LORD descended in the cloud, and stood with him there, and proclaimed the name of the LORD. ⁶And the LORD passed by before him, and proclaimed, The LORD, The LORD God, merciful and gracious, longsuffering, and abundant in goodness and truth, ⁷Keeping mercy for thousands, forgiving iniquity and transgression and sin, and that will by no means clear the guilty; visiting the iniquity of the fathers upon the children, and upon the children's children, unto the third and to the fourth generation. ⁸And Moses made haste, and bowed his head toward the earth, and worshipped."*

2) I Samuel 17:45 – *"Then said David to the Philistine, Thou comest to me with a sword, and with a spear, and with a shield: but I come to thee in the name of the LORD of hosts, the God of the armies of Israel, whom thou hast defied."*

3) I Kings 18:24, 32-39

4) Psalms 20:7 – *"Some trust in chariots, and some in horses: but we will remember the name of the LORD our God."*

5) Psalms 102:15 – *"So the heathen shall fear the name of the LORD, and all the kings of the earth thy glory."*

6) Psalms 116:4-8

7) Psalms 118:10-12
8) Psalms 124:6-8 – *"...Our help is in the name of the LORD..."*
9) Proverbs 18:10 – *"The name of the LORD is a strong tower: the righteous runneth into it, and is safe."*
10) Isaiah 30:27-30
11) Isaiah 59:19
12) Joel 2:32
13) Romans 10:13 – *"For whosoever shall call upon the name of the Lord shall be saved."*
14) Colossians 3:17
15) Exodus 15:3 – *"The LORD is a man of war: the LORD is his name."*
16) Matthew 1:21-23 – *"And she shall bring forth a son, and thou shalt call his name JESUS: for he shall save his people from their sins...and they shall call his name Emmanuel, which being interpreted is, God with us."*
17) Acts 3:16 – *"And his name through faith in his name hath made this man strong, whom ye see and know..."*
18) II Chronicles 14:11-14
19) Psalms 5:11-12
20) Psalms 44:5 – *"Through thee will we push down our enemies: through thy name will we tread them under that rise up against us."*
21) Psalms 54:1 – *"Save me, O God, by thy name, and judge me by thy strength."*
22) Isaiah 63:16
23) Luke 10:17 – *"And the seventy returned again with joy, saying, Lord, even the devils are subject unto us through thy name."*
24) Luke 11:2

d. God is the one who fights our battles (including Samson's)

1) II Chronicles 32:8 – *"With him is an arm of flesh; but with us is the LORD our God to help us, and to fight our battles..."*
2) Deuteronomy 20:1-4 – *"¹When thou goest out to battle against thine enemies, and seest horses, and chariots, and a people more than thou, be not afraid of them: for the LORD thy God is with thee, which brought thee up out of the land of Egypt. ²And it shall be, when ye are come nigh unto the battle, that the priest shall approach and speak unto the people, ³And shall say unto them, Hear, O Israel, ye approach this day unto battle against your enemies: let not your hearts faint, fear not, and do not tremble, neither be ye terrified because of them; ⁴For the LORD your God is he that goeth with you, to fight for you against your enemies, to save you."*
3) II Chronicles 20:15-17
4) I Samuel 17:47 – *"And all this assembly shall know that the LORD saveth not with sword and spear: for the battle is the LORD's, and he will give you into our hands."*
5) II Samuel 22:40 – *"For thou hast girded me with strength to battle: them that rose up against me hast thou subdued under me."* (Psalms 18:39)
6) I Chronicles 5:20-22
7) Psalms 140:7 – *"O GOD the Lord, the strength of my salvation, thou hast covered my head in the day of battle."*
8) Proverbs 21:31 – *"The horse is prepared against the day of battle: but safety is of the LORD."*
9) Zechariah 14:2-3

e. The Lord fights for us His people

1) Exodus 14:14, 25 – *"The LORD shall fight for you, and ye shall hold your peace...And took off their chariot wheels, that they drave them heavily: so that the Egyptians said, Let us flee from the face of Israel; for the LORD fighteth for them against the Egyptians."*

2) Deuteronomy 1:30 – *"The LORD your God which goeth before you, he shall fight for you, according to all that he did for you in Egypt before your eyes;"*

3) Deuteronomy 3:22 – *"Ye shall not fear them: for the LORD your God he shall fight for you."*

4) Deuteronomy 20:4 – *"For the LORD your God is he that goeth with you, to fight for you against your enemies, to save you."*

5) II Chronicles 20:17 – *"Ye shall not need to fight in this battle: set yourselves, stand ye still, and see the salvation of the LORD with you, O Judah and Jerusalem: fear not, nor be dismayed; to morrow go out against them: for the LORD will be with you."*

6) II Chronicles 32:8

7) Nehemiah 4:14, 20 – *"And I looked, and rose up, and said unto the nobles, and to the rulers, and to the rest of the people, Be not ye afraid of them: remember the Lord, which is great and terrible, and fight for your brethren, your sons, and your daughters, your wives, and your houses...In what place therefore ye hear the sound of the trumpet, resort ye thither unto us: our God shall fight for us."*

8) Psalms 56:2-3 – *"Mine enemies would daily swallow me up: for they be many that fight against me, O thou most High. What time I am afraid, I will trust in thee."*

9) Zechariah 14:3

10) Joshua 23:10 – *"One man of you shall chase a thousand: for the LORD your God, he it is that fighteth for you, as he hath promised you."*

7. Continuing in Judges 16:5, *"...and by what means we may prevail against him, that we may bind him to afflict him..."*

   a. Other translations:

   "...we may overpower him that we may bind him to subdue him..."
   "...tie him up and subdue him..."
   "...how he can be overpowered and tied up securely..."
   "...that we might bind him to humble him..."
   "...we can overpower him and capture him and tie him up..."
   "...we can subdue him and humiliate him..."
   "...we want to tie him up in order to torture him..."
   "...subdue him and put him in chains..."
   "...how we may get the better of him and put bands on him so that we may make him feeble..."
   "...tie him up and make him helpless..."

   b. God has a shield around us, Job 1:10 – *"Hast not thou made an hedge about him, and about his house, and about all that he hath on every side? thou hast blessed the work of his hands, and his substance is increased in the land."*

      1) Genesis 15:1 – *"After these things the word of the LORD came unto Abram in a vision, saying, Fear not, Abram: I am thy shield, and thy exceeding great reward."*

      2) Deuteronomy 33:29 – *"Happy art thou, O Israel: who is like unto thee, O people saved by the LORD, the shield of thy help, and who is the sword of thy excellency! and thine enemies shall be found liars unto thee; and thou shalt tread upon their high places."*

      3) II Samuel 22:3, 36 – *"The God of my rock; in him will I trust: he is my shield, and the horn of my salvation, my high tower, and my refuge, my saviour; thou savest me from violence...Thou hast also given me the shield of thy salvation: and thy gentleness hath made me great."* (Psalms 18:35)

      4) Psalms 3:3 – *"But thou, O LORD, art a shield for me; my glory, and the lifter up of mine head."*

      5) Psalms 5:12 – *"For thou, LORD, wilt bless the righteous; with favour wilt thou compass him as with a shield."*

6) Psalms 28:7 – *"The LORD is my strength and my shield; my heart trusted in him, and I am helped: therefore my heart greatly rejoiceth; and with my song will I praise him."*

7) Psalms 33:20 – *"Our soul waiteth for the LORD: he is our help and our shield."*

8) Psalms 59:11 – *"Slay them not, lest my people forget: scatter them by thy power; and bring them down, O Lord our shield."*

9) Psalms 84:9-11 – *"⁹Behold, O God our shield, and look upon the face of thine anointed. ¹⁰For a day in thy courts is better than a thousand. I had rather be a doorkeeper in the house of my God, than to dwell in the tents of wickedness. ¹¹For the LORD God is a sun and shield: the LORD will give grace and glory: no good thing will he withhold from them that walk uprightly."*

10) Psalms 115:9-11

11) Psalms 119:114 – *"Thou art my hiding place and my shield: I hope in thy word."*

12) Psalms 144:2

13) Psalms 30:5

14) Ecclesiastes 10:8 – *"He that diggeth a pit shall fall into it; and whoso breaketh an hedge, a serpent shall bite him."*

15) Isaiah 5:5 – *"And now go to; I will tell you what I will do to my vineyard: I will take away the hedge thereof, and it shall be eaten up; and break down the wall thereof, and it shall be trodden down:"*

16) Ezekiel 22:30 – *"And I sought for a man among them, that should make up the hedge, and stand in the gap before me for the land, that I should not destroy it: but I found none."*

17) Mark 12:1

18) Nehemiah 2:17

19) Nehemiah 4:3-6

20) Proverbs 24:31 – *"And, lo, it was all grown over with thorns, and nettles had covered the face thereof, and the stone wall thereof was broken down."*

21) Zechariah 5:5

22) Psalms 140:7

23) Isaiah 59:19 – *"...When the enemy shall come in like a flood, the Spirit of the LORD shall lift up a standard against him."*

24) I Corinthians 10:13 – *"There hath no temptation taken you but such as is common to man: but God is faithful, who will not suffer you to be tempted above that ye are able; but will with the temptation also make a way to escape, that ye may be able to bear it."*

c. We must give Satan no room. Satan can only bind us if we let him, by giving a reason or excuse, or a place to enter in our lives.

1) Job 4:11 – *"The old lion perisheth for lack of prey, and the stout lion's whelps are scattered abroad."*

2) Song of Solomon 2:15 – *"Take us the foxes, the little foxes, that spoil the vines: for our vines have tender grapes."*

3) Ephesians 4:26-27 – *"Be ye angry, and sin not: let not the sun go down upon your wrath: Neither give place to the devil."*

4) John 14:30 – *"Hereafter I will not talk much with you: for the prince of this world cometh, and hath nothing in me."*

5) I John 5:18 – *"We know that whosoever is born of God sinneth not; but he that is begotten of God keepeth himself, and that wicked one toucheth him not."*

6) Proverbs 1:17 – *"Surely in vain the net is spread in the sight of any bird."*

7) James 4:7 – *"Submit yourselves therefore to God. Resist the devil, and he will flee from you."*

8) I Peter 5:8 – *"Be sober, be vigilant; because your adversary the devil, as a roaring lion, walketh about, seeking whom he may devour:"*

9) Ephesians 6:10-18

d. Satan will try to overcome us, deceive us, and then bind us

1) I Chronicles 21:1 – *"And Satan stood up against Israel, and provoked David to number Israel."*
2) Job 1:6-12, 2:1-7
3) Matthew 16:21-23
4) Mark 4:15 – *"And these are they by the way side, where the word is sown; but when they have heard, Satan cometh immediately, and taketh away the word that was sown in their hearts."*
4) Luke 13:16 – *"And ought not this woman, being a daughter of Abraham, whom Satan hath bound, lo, these eighteen years, be loosed from this bond on the sabbath day?"*
5) Luke 22:31 – *"And the Lord said, Simon, Simon, behold, Satan hath desired to have you, that he may sift you as wheat:"*
6) Acts 5:3 – *"But Peter said, Ananias, why hath Satan filled thine heart to lie to the Holy Ghost, and to keep back part of the price of the land?"*
7) II Corinthians 2:11 – *"Lest Satan should get an advantage of us: for we are not ignorant of his devices."*
8) II Corinthians 11:14 – *"And no marvel; for Satan himself is transformed into an angel of light."*
9) II Thessalonians 2:9-10 – *"Even him, whose coming is after the working of Satan with all power and signs and lying wonders, And with all deceivableness of unrighteousness in them that perish; because they received not the love of the truth, that they might be saved."*
10) Revelation 12:9 – *"And the great dragon was cast out, that old serpent, called the Devil, and Satan, which deceiveth the whole world: he was cast out into the earth, and his angels were cast out with him."*
11) Revelation 20:7-8
12) Psalms 124:7 – *"Our soul is escaped as a bird out of the snare of the fowlers: the snare is broken, and we are escaped."*
13) II Timothy 2:26 – *"And that they may recover themselves out of the snare of the devil, who are taken captive by him at his will."*
14) II Peter 2:19-20
15) Revelation 11:7 (Revelation 13:7)
16) I Thessalonians 3:5
17) Matthew 4:1-11
18) Genesis 3:1-5
19) John 8:44 – *"Ye are of your father the devil, and the lusts of your father ye will do. He was a murderer from the beginning, and abode not in the truth, because there is no truth in him. When he speaketh a lie, he speaketh of his own: for he is a liar, and the father of it."*
20) John 10:10 – *"The thief cometh not, but for to steal, and to kill, and to destroy..."*
21) Acts 10:38
22) Acts 13:8-11
23) Ephesians 6:11
24) I Peter 5:8
25) II Corinthians 11:3
26) John 13:2
27) I Timothy 3:6-7 – *"Not a novice, lest being lifted up with pride he fall into the condemnation of the devil. Moreover he must have a good report of them which are without; lest he fall into reproach and the snare of the devil."*
28) Revelation 20:2, 10

8. Continuing in Judges 16:5 – *"...and we will give thee every one of us eleven hundred pieces of silver."* – <u>She was paid to rob Samson of his anointing.</u> Judas sold out Jesus for 30 pieces of silver. Other translations of this part of verse 5:

"...each man's company will give you a hundred shekels of silver."

139

"...each one of us will give you twenty-eight pounds of silver."

C. Verse 6 – *"And Delilah said to Samson, Tell me, I pray thee, wherein thy great strength lieth, and wherewith thou mightest be bound to afflict thee."* – Other translations:

    "...bound to subdue."
    "...Tell me the secret of your great strength, and how you can be tied up and subdued."
    "...Tell me what makes you so strong and what it would take to tie you up securely."

D. Verse 16 – *"And it came to pass, when she pressed him daily with her words, and urged him, so that his soul was vexed unto death;"*

    1. Other translations:

        "...nagged him daily, and kept urging him..."
        "...she so pestered him with these words, day after day..."
        "...she persisted with her questions, and allowed him not to rest..."
        "...wearied to death."
        "...till he grew tired to death of it."
        "...she crushed his spirit all together."

    2. *"...she pressed him daily..."*

        a. Proverbs 7:6-23
        b. Psalms 56:1-2 – *"Be merciful unto me, O God: for man would swallow me up; he fighting daily oppresseth me. Mine enemies would daily swallow me up: for they be many that fight against me, O thou most High."*
        c. Psalms 88:17 – *"They came round about me daily like water; they compassed me about together."*
        d. Psalms 42:10 – *"As with a sword in my bones, mine enemies reproach me; while they say daily unto me, Where is thy God?"*
        e. Jeremiah 20:7-8 – *"O LORD, thou hast deceived me, and I was deceived: thou art stronger than I, and hast prevailed: I am in derision daily, every one mocketh me. For since I spake, I cried out, I cried violence and spoil; because the word of the LORD was made a reproach unto me, and a derision, daily."*
        f. Proverbs 21:9 – *"It is better to dwell in a corner of the housetop, than with a brawling woman in a wide house."*
        g. Ecclesiastes 7:26 – *"And I find more bitter than death the woman, whose heart is snares and nets, and her hands as bands: whoso pleaseth God shall escape from her; but the sinner shall be taken by her."*
        h. Daniel 7:25 – *"And he shall speak great words against the most High, and shall wear out the saints of the most High..."*

E. Verse 17 – *"<u>That he told her all his heart</u>, and said unto her. There hath not come a rasor upon mine head; for I have been a Nazarite unto God from my mother's womb: if I be shaven, then my strength will go from me, and I shall become weak, and be like any other man."* – Other translations:

    "...opened to her his whole heart..."
    "...at last he told her the truth..."
    "...told her all the secret..."

F. Verse 20 – *"And she said, The Philistines be upon thee, Samson. And he awoke out of his sleep, and said, I will go out as at other times before, and shake myself. And <u>he wist not that the LORD was departed from him</u>."* – Other translations:

140

"...I will break free and shake myself clear..."
"...I will go out as usual..."
"...the Lord had left him."
"...had turned away from him."
"...that the eternal had left him."

G. Verse 21 – *"But the Philistines took him, and put out his eyes, and brought him down to Gaza, and bound him with fetters of brass; and he did grind in the prison house."*

1. Samson was sold out by Delilah. She is a stealer of the anointing using the spirit of seduction. Her name in Hebrew means – delicate and comes from a root meaning – to be brought low, to hang down, to be languid.
2. Samson is a type of the church. His name in Hebrew means – little sun, splendid sun, great joy and happiness, like the sun, distinguished, strong, a perfect servant, sun-man.
3. *"But the Philistines took him"* – Samson was taken away by the enemy, a type of Satan deceiving, defeating, and overcoming the church.
4. *"put out his eyes"* – vision lost, natural and spiritual
5. *"brought him down"* – Samson was humbled
6. *"to Gaza"* – strong, fortified; Gaza is a type of being under Babylon's system
7. *"bound him with fetters of brass"* – one who was used to be free is now bound. Fetters represents anything that binds us (sin, issues, attributes, characteristics). Brass represents the judgment of God on sin.

8. *"he did grind in the prison house"* – going in circles, treading in prison

   a. Deuteronomy 2:3 – *"Ye have compassed this mountain long enough: turn you northward."*
   b. Acts 2:40 – *"...Save yourselves from this untoward generation."*

H. Verse 22 – *"Howbeit the hair of his head began to grow again after he was shaven."*

1. The promise of restoration
2. A chance to renew your vow (Nazarite)
3. Romans 11:29 – *"For the gifts and calling of God are without repentance."*

I. Verse 23-24 – *"23Then the lords of the Philistines gathered them together for to offer a great sacrifice unto Dagon their god, and to rejoice: for they said, Our god hath delivered Samson our enemy into our hand. 24And when the people saw him, they praised their god: for they said, Our god hath delivered into our hands our enemy, and the destroyer of our country, which slew many of us."* – The enemy is celebrating too soon

1. Esther 7:10 – *"So they hanged Haman on the gallows that he had prepared for Mordecai..."*
2. I Corinthians 2:8 – *"Which none of the princes of this world knew: for had they known it, they would not have crucified the Lord of glory."*
3. Dagon – their fish god; Dagon had nothing to do with it.

J. Verse 25 – *"And it came to pass, when their hearts were merry, that they said, Call for Samson, that he may make us sport. And they called for Samson out of the prison house; and he made them sport: and they set him between the pillars."*

1. Other translations of, *"that he may make us sport"*: *"and he doth play for us"*, *"to entertain us"*, *"amuse us"*, *"that he may perform for us"*, *"so we can have some fun with him"*
2. Pillars – foundation that holds up their demonic house; what fools.

K. Verse 26 – *"And Samson said unto the lad that held him by the hand, Suffer me that I may feel the pillars whereupon the house standeth, that I may lean upon them."*

1. Principle of "the lad" – this little lad is a type of a company within the local church, to lead it out of its bondage and blindness.

    a. Hebrew definition of lad – a boy, a servant, child
    b. Isaiah 11:6 – *"...a little child shall lead them."*
    c. Matthew 18:2-4 – *"²And Jesus called a little child unto him, and set him in the midst of them, ³And said, Verily I say unto you, Except ye be converted, and become as little children, ye shall not enter into the kingdom of heaven. ⁴Whosoever therefore shall humble himself as this little child, the same is greatest in the kingdom of heaven."*
    d. John 6:9 – *"There is a lad here, which hath five barley loaves, and two small fishes: but what are they among so many?"*
    e. The lad held him by the hand. This company must show the way. Their comforting presence shall lead the church out of bondage.

2. Samson wanted to be led to the pillars whereupon the house standeth. He wanted to bring it down from the foundations.

L. Verse 27 – *"Now the house was full of men and women; and all the lords of the Philistines were there; and there were upon the roof about three thousand men and women, that beheld while Samson made sport"*

1. This is a type of the end of the kingdom of darkness and the world.
2. As he was acting the clown, he had a great purpose in mind.
3. Like David when he acted crazy to a heathen king (I Samuel 21:10-15)

M. Verse 28 – *"And Samson called unto the LORD, and said, O Lord GOD, remember me, I pray thee, and strengthen me, I pray thee, only this once, O God, that I may be at once avenged of the Philistines for my two eyes."*

1. Samson calls upon the Lord
2. God has now restored Samson's repentant heart, anoints him again, and avenges him of his (our) enemy.
3. "Remember me" – God will never leave us or forsake us
4. Avenge your people
5. Samson wanted revenge for his lost vision

N. Verse 29 – *"And Samson took hold of the two middle pillars upon which the house stood, and on which it was borne up, of the one with his right hand, and of the other with his left."*

1. The right hand and the left – this is a type of the church working together as well as the two hands of God (His dealings).
2. He tool hold once again. Once again he is able to lay hold on the powers of darkness.

O. Verse 30 – *"And Samson said, Let me die with the Philistines. And he bowed himself with all his might; and the house fell upon the lords, and upon all the people that were therein. So the dead which he slew at his death were more than they which he slew in his life."*

1. The principle of dying to bring forth life

    a. John 12:24 – *"Verily, verily, I say unto you, Except a corn of wheat fall into the ground and die, it abideth alone: but if it die, it bringeth forth much fruit."*

b. I Corinthians 15:31 – *"I protest by your rejoicing which I have in Christ Jesus our Lord, I die daily."*

c. Psalms 116:15 – *"Precious in the sight of the LORD is the death of his saints."*

2. It takes this kind of commitment to be willing to die with your enemies. He had learned death was the only way to true life.

a. John 12:25 – *"He that loveth his life shall lose it; and he that hateth his life in this world shall keep it unto life eternal."*

b. He showed a true heart of repentance – II Corinthians 7:9-11 – *"⁹Now I rejoice, not that ye were made sorry, but that ye sorrowed to repentance: for ye were made sorry after a godly manner, that ye might receive damage by us in nothing. ¹⁰For godly sorrow worketh repentance to salvation not to be repented of: but the sorrow of the world worketh death. ¹¹For behold this selfsame thing, that ye sorrowed after a godly sort, what carefulness it wrought in you, yea, what clearing of yourselves, yea, what indignation, yea, what fear, yea, what vehement desire, yea, what zeal, yea, what revenge! In all things ye have approved yourselves to be clear in this matter."*

P. Verse 31 – *"Then his brethren and all the house of his father came down, and took him, and brought him up, and buried him between Zorah and Eshtaol in the burying place of Manoah his father. And he judged Israel twenty years."*

1. God restores

a. Joel 2:25 – *"And I will restore to you the years that the locust hath eaten, the cankerworm, and the caterpiller, and the palmerworm, my great army which I sent among you."*

b. Jeremiah 30:17 – *"For I will restore health unto thee, and I will heal thee of thy wounds, saith the LORD; because they called thee an Outcast, saying, This is Zion, whom no man seeketh after."*

c. Psalms 23:3 – *"He restoreth my soul: he leadeth me in the paths of righteousness for his name's sake."*

d. Ruth 4:15 – *"And he shall be unto thee a restorer of thy life, and a nourisher of thine old age: for thy daughter in law, which loveth thee, which is better to thee than seven sons, hath born him."*

2. He is fully restored back to the family of God, Luke 15:22 – *"But the father said to his servants, Bring forth the best robe, and put it on him; and put a ring on his hand, and shoes on his feet:"* – End result of the parable of the prodigal son.

Lesson 21
The Story of Jael

I. Judges 4:1 - *"And the children of Israel again did evil in the sight of the LORD, when Ehud was dead."* – Israel became more dependent upon men rather than upon God, and when those men passed away, they fell into sin.

Just as usual, Israel backslid, they fell into sin and stayed in sin until they needed the Lord for help. And just as usual, God sent them a deliverer. As long as that deliverer was alive, Israel did alright. I believe that is also indicative of the body of Christ; we have aligned ourselves so much with men of God, that as long as those men are doing ok, we're alright. But when something happens to them, our faith is shipwrecked. The body of Christ can be much like Israel; when Israel had a leader who was strong, dynamic and charismatic, they were alright. But when the man passed, so did their walk with God. Then after a long period of time, they would begin to cry out to the Lord and God would send them a deliverer. We need to grow up and be delivered from that. We do however, ought to respond and honour the office of God; however, we shouldn't be in bondage to them.

We should not be standing in the revelation of another man; we need to get our own revelation. Our walk with Jesus cannot be wrapped and tangled up in a man, it's got to be in Jesus. Ehud's name means *"join together in he who praises"* or to elaborate, it speaks of being joined together with the praise leader rather than with the one who is to be praised: Jesus. Some people cannot worship unless a certain man is the one to lead worship. They depend upon a man to take them into worship. That's alright if you're a babe in Christ. We're under tutors and governors for a time, but eventually, there should be a time appointed in our lives when we break through and are able to feed ourselves and enter into worship by ourselves.

This story in Judges 4 is of a woman who exemplifies such independence. Her name was Jael. She was wild, she was bold and brave, and she did not depend or wait upon a man for deliverance. When the opportune time came to her to defeat the enemy, she did it right then and there, and she did it herself. Let's search the Scriptures to understand what this story is meant to teach us in our own lives and how we ourselves ought to follow the example of Jael.

II. Judges 4:2-3 - *"And the LORD sold them into the hand of Jabin king of Canaan, that reigned in Hazor; the captain of whose host was Sisera, which dwelt in Harosheth of the Gentiles. And the children of Israel cried unto the LORD: for he had nine hundred chariots of iron; and twenty years he mightily oppressed the children of Israel."*

A. Sisera - As the captain of Israel's enemies, Sisera is a type of satan. His name means *"a crane, a bird of seeing, one who binds with chains, one who sets the battle array"*. What this means is Sisera was a man who brought people into bondage by using their evident weaknesses as a weapon against them; he used what he *saw* to be true against them. This is exactly what satan does, but he is not omniscient; he doesn't know any more than what we show him. The truth is, if we would keep our mouths shut, he wouldn't know a whole lot. He is a crane of seeing; he's watching and waiting like a roaring lion. He is watching and listening so that he can find something to trap us in.

  1. Luke 22:31 – Jesus said to Peter, *"...satan hath desired to have you, that he may sift you as wheat."* – satan is sifting you and going through your life. He is looking for a way to capture, manipulate or torment you.

    a. John 14:30 – Jesus said, *"... for the prince of this world cometh, and hath nothing in me."* - satan searched through Jesus' life and found nothing that he could hold against him. This shall be true for us also.

b. Job 4:11 - *"The old lion perisheth for lack of prey..."* If he can't find something to eat in us, he goes hungry. If we don't tell him about our life, he goes hungry. We should never feed or satisfy the devil.

Just as Sisera did to Israel, Satan also sets up the battle in a way that is meant to scare us and intimidate us. He also walks to and fro in the earth, walking up and down in it to find something that will enable him to bind us in chains.

B. *"...and twenty years he mightily oppressed the children of Israel."*

1. The number 20 in the Scriptures is the number of "expectancy". Satan (Sisera) is tormenting God's people. He wants us bound up, tormented and oppressed. But there is an expectancy for deliverance to come!

And what happens in this story? God brings a prophetess named Deborah to judge Israel.

C. Judges 4:4 - *"And Deborah, a prophetess, the wife of Lapidoth, she judged Israel at that time."* - That means she pastored Israel. How do I know? If they ever had problems, they brought their problems to the judge, and the judge gave the answer. That's basically nothing more or less than a pastor. Deborah pastored Israel. She called a man named Barak to come and help her to go fight Sisera (Judges 4:6).

1. Deborah means, *"an eloquent orator"*

2. Barak means, *"lightning and thunder"*

We have a lot of strong men of God that are full of lightning and thunder. And we also have a lot of women who are eloquent orators who can sing and speak, and it's beautiful. These men and women are of a remnant within the body of Christ, a people within a people. They're going to be the very people who get rid of Satan's works. Thank God for Deborah and Barak. We thank God for lightning and thunder and for eloquent orators. However, they are not the ones unto whom specifically the Lord has committed the "nail".

III. What do *"nails"* in the Word of God represent? Nails will play a significant part in the story of Jael. I am going to speak of what nails biblically represent and how they are important for the remnant people to have in order that they may deal with the devil once and for all.

A. Lucifer - Satan that was once Lucifer was the, *"...the anointed cherub that covereth..."* He led the worship in heaven for perhaps thousands of years and walked up and down in the midst of the stones of fire. He was right there before the glory of God, he walked in the glory. But Lucifer later resisted and rejected the glory of God and was cast out of the third heaven. Meanwhile, the earth was plunged into judgment and that's where Satan did his merchandising. Right now he has his domain in the second heaven, the seat of Satan, where he is ruling and reigning over his principalities, powers, thrones, dominions, rulers of darkness, wicked spirits and demons and so on.

The Bible talks in Revelation 12 about the man child. The Bible says that this man child is to be birthed out of this "woman", who is not Israel but the church. This man child is caught up to God and to His throne. The next thing we see happening in Revelation 12 is Satan being cast out of the second heaven.

1. Revelation 12:9 – *"And the great dragon was cast out, that old serpent, called the Devil, and Satan, which deceiveth the whole world: he was cast out into the earth, and his angels were cast out with him."* - Woe unto them who are on the earth because Satan is down there. There is an evident correlation between the man child going up and Satan going down. I want to be a part of that man child!

145

a. Isaiah 14:16 - *"They that see thee shall **narrowly look upon thee**, and consider thee, saying, **Is this the man that made the earth to tremble, that did shake kingdoms**"*. Once you've overcome fear, as the man child will, you will see Satan this way: little, weak, meaningless and ineffective.

There is a man child, a people who God is going to commit the nail to. However, it is not Deborah or Barak. They're doing a good job killing Satan's army, but God reserves the greatest responsibility for a little woman that no one has known or heard of.

B. Judges 4:8-9 – *"8And Barak said unto her, If thou wilt go with me, then I will go: but if thou wilt not go with me, then I will not go. 9And she said, I will surely go with thee: notwithstanding the journey that thou takest shall not be for thine honour; for the Lord shall sell Sisera into the hand of a woman. And Deborah arose, and went with Barak to Kedesh."* – This is still true today: we do things in the name of the Lord but we have been taking the credit. What we do will not be for our honour, it's not going to be about our ministry, it will be for the Kingdom of God. We are moving into a place where we're building the Kingdom of God. Truly all the glory is going to Jesus. Deborah warned Barak because men are susceptible in their pride. It is not about our pride, it's about Jesus. However, a woman doesn't mind sharing the credit, but man desires to have it. Therefore, as Deborah mentioned here, the Lord will deliver Sisera into the hand of a woman.

C. Judges 4:15-17 - *"15And the LORD discomfited Sisera, and all his chariots, and all his host, with the edge of the sword before Barak; so that Sisera lighted down off his chariot, and fled away on his feet. 16But Barak pursued after the chariots, and after the host, unto Harosheth of the Gentiles: and all the host of Sisera fell upon the edge of the sword; and there was not a man left. 17Howbeit Sisera fled away on his feet to the tent of Jael the wife of Heber the Kenite: **for there was peace between Jabin the king of Hazor and the house of Heber the Kenite.**"*

1. *"...for there was peace between Jabin the king of Hazor and the house of Heber the Kenite."* - Do you understand what this means? Her husband made a pact with Jabin who was Sisera's king. Many women today are living with men who are not walking with Jesus and many men are living with women who are not walking with Jesus. As a matter of fact, their husbands or wives may have even made a pact with Satan! This was the case here and that is why Sisera felt comfortable going into Heber's and Jael's tent.

2. Jael's name means, *"A wild goat, a climber, one who brings profit."* In layman's terms, this means, "anyone who doesn't follow the status quo". This is anyone who loves Jesus more than we do. They are recognized and labelled as rebels.

a. Mark 11:2, 4 – *"2And saith unto them, Go your way into the village over against you: and as soon as ye be entered into it, ye shall find a colt tied, whereon never man sat; loose him, and bring him... 4And they went their way, and found the colt tied by the door without in a place where two ways met; and they loose him."* - Like Jael, you're a wild goat; you're a wild colt whereon never man sat.

How many times have people said to you, "The problem with you is that you're rebellious"? I am not encouraging people to be rebellious or for them to be without authority, or to spiritually wander around, not submitted to anyone. I myself am submitted to leadership in my life. There is a place of submission to God where you truly are not rebellious, but are inevitably seen as rebellious in people's eyes. Yet there are still people who really are rebellious. They are not a wild colt, they are just wild and need to come under authority and be delivered.

The colt from Mark 11 was tied by the door where two ways met and it was loosed. The Bible says that was a colt upon whom never a man sat. There is a people on the earth today, biblically represented by this colt, who can't fit in. They won't fit in, yet they've tried. Jesus didn't fit in either and the Bible said that He died "outside the camp". When God brought his Word into the earth He did not bring it to the religious leaders or to those who were in responsible positions. The Bible also says that the Word of God came unto John in the wilderness. There is a people in the wilderness, a people who have been separated from the rest of the body. Either they had to go by choice or they were forced to go.

I remember George Haughton, a great Canadian pastor who wrote many books on the mysteries of the Kingdom of God. He was a great man of God in the Pentecostal Assemblies of Canada (the PAOC) during the latter rain movement then he later moved into the US. Because of his works, people started prophesying, singing in the spirit and laying hands on people. The PAOC resisted him. It reached a point where they made him feel so uncomfortable in his own church that one Sunday morning, while the worship was going on, he realized and knew he did not fit in anymore. He didn't know what to do, so he decided to walk out softly into the foyer.

George was looking at the people through the diamond shaped windows on the doors. Through the windows, he noticed the people having a great time, enjoying themselves inside. It was like when David in the Bible brought the arc in the first time. The glory was not there. All over the country people in the church are having "great times", enjoying themselves, yet they are unaware of the fact that the glory was not there with them. George felt very sad that he was separated from his brothers and sisters, yet he knew he had to leave. There was no other choice for him but to go. To stay would be like Jonathan who died in Saul's house, even though he recognized David was to be king, he stayed in a place that he needed to leave and then he died there. George had to leave and continue on in God, otherwise he would have spiritually died in the place where he was.

George stood in the foyer thinking to himself, "I'm separated. What is it about me that is so awful?" Have you ever thought that? He was told that he was rebellious and that he wouldn't listen and receive from the elders and those with authority. Then he turned around and saw Jesus there standing with him in the foyer, not in the sanctuary. He said to George, "Don't worry about it George, they don't want Me in there either."

3. Sometimes we have to leave the place that we were in, because God is separating us. We can no longer endure that phony earthly praise and worship. We can no longer handle the smart well-dressed man with the perfect hair, make up and fancy building. There is no glory there. We have come to the place where we have to have the meat of God's word. We have to have the glory. As a result, sometimes we become separated, either we're told to go or we leave by our choice; we've been tied by the door where two ways meet and now we are loosed. If you're a wild goat, you're still a climber; your nature is to keep moving onward and upward.

   a. Psalms 24:3 - *"Who shall ascend into the hill of the LORD?"* - Who went up the Mount of Transfiguration? Not the 70, not the whole 12, but only the 3: Peter, James and John. They climbed up the mountain to see the visitation of God.
   b. Jael is outside the camp. She's even living with a man who has made a pact with the enemy. Jael survived because she wasn't in bondage to her husband. Are you in bondage to anyone? Are you in bondage to religion?

D. Judges 4:18-19 - *"18And Jael went out to meet Sisera, and said unto him, Turn in, my lord, turn in to me; fear not. And when he had turned in unto her into the tent, she covered him with a mantle. 19And he said unto her, Give me, I pray thee, a little water to drink; for I am thirsty. And she opened a bottle of milk, and gave him drink, and covered him."* - It just takes the milk of the word to put satan asleep. You don't even need to have hidden manna, just milk.

   1. Mark 16:17 – *"In my name shall they cast out devils..."* – It doesn't require much to cast out devils. You can simply speak the name of Jesus to do it. We Christians think that the louder we are when casting demons out of people, the more the demons will obey us. On the contrary, the greatest power does not have to be screamed or yelled, it can simply be spoken softly through true authority. We don't see Jesus doing that. He simply spoke softly for the demons to leave and they

obeyed. That isn't hidden manna, that's obvious. Just a little bit of milk can cause the enemy to fall asleep.

E. Judges 4:20-21 - "*²⁰Again he said unto her, Stand in the door of the tent, and it shall be, when any man doth come and inquire of thee, and say, Is there any man here? that thou shalt say, No. ²¹Then Jael Heber's wife took a nail of the tent, and took an hammer in her hand, and went softly unto him, and smote the nail into his temples, and fastened it into the ground: for he was fast asleep and weary. So he died.*"

1. Your temples are in your head, the controlling aspect of your body, they represent government. The government of Satan is going to be destroyed by a little company outside the camp. Hallelujah! Not Deborah, not Barak but a little woman who is a wild goat and a climber and will bring deliverance from the enemy. She is a wild goat and a climber and she is also one who brings profit.

No one may see your destiny today, maybe no one can see what you will bring to the table at the harvest time, but God knows. Some of us may never even enter into our ministry until that very moment in the end. For 30 years, Jesus Himself did nothing until an exact moment in time. His ministry was only for three and a half years. The day is coming where you won't need Deborah or Barak signing papers to ordain you. Satan is going to come to your house. There will come a time, just like in verses Judges 4:16-17, (when the battle seemed to be over, but really, Sisera fled and hid), when everyone will wonder where Satan is, but you can say to them, "Oh he's just in my tent, nailed to the ground."

F. Nails

1. Ecclesiastes 12:11 - "*The words of the wise are as goads, and as nails fastened by the masters of assemblies, which are given from one shepherd.*"

    a. The modern day translation of this verse would be: The chief Shepherd and bishop of our souls, Jesus, gives wise words, the word of God, the masters of assemblies are pastors or teachers. They take those nails and they hammer them into the hearts of men. They hammer principles and truths into men's hearts. So these nails represent the Word of God. If we're going to be like Jael, we need to know the Word of God. Many don't read the Bible or search the Scriptures, they are a generation who live on experience and have no enduring substance inside of them.

        1) Hebrews 5:12 - "*For when for the time ye ought to be teachers, ye have need that one teach you again which be the first principles of the oracles of God; and are become such as have need of milk, and not of strong meat.*"

Jael knows how to use the Word correctly. Never can we give up the Word of God. Jesus answered Satan in the wilderness every single time, He spoke the Word of God to him. In the spirit realm our weapon is the Bible.

        2) Zechariah 10:1-6 "*Ask ye of the LORD rain in the time of the latter rain.*" - This latter rain is speaking of the last great move of God.

2. Zechariah 10:3-5 - "*³Mine anger was kindled against the shepherds, and I punished the goats: for the LORD of hosts hath visited his flock the house of Judah, and hath made them as his goodly horse in the battle. ⁴Out of him came forth the corner, out of him the nail, out of him the battle bow, out of him every oppressor together. ⁵And they shall be as mighty men, which tread down their enemies...*" - Out of Judah comes the nail. I believe that you must know the Word of God to be in this remnant company like this little woman Jael. The name Judah means, "praise." I also believe with certainty that you must be a worshipper or a praiser to defeat the enemy. Worship is an action, lifting hands, dancing, shouting, kneeling, bowing and clapping. It's always something with our bodies. Out of Judah comes the nail.

3. Isaiah 41 talks about raising up the righteous man from the east and the Lord coming forth in the last days. Isaiah 41:6-7 - "*6They helped every one his neighbour; and every one said to his brother, Be of good courage. 7So the carpenter encouraged the goldsmith, and he that smootheth with the hammer him that smote the anvil, saying, It is ready for the sodering: and he fastened it with nails, that it should not be moved.*"

    a. The revelation in relation to the nails here is flowing in a community of people. The day is coming when it will not be about "my ministry" anymore but, the carpenter is going to encourage the goldsmith and the goldsmith is going to encourage the blacksmith; everyone is going to be encouraging one another in their own ministry.

    b. Joel 2:7-8 – "*7They shall run like mighty men; they shall climb the wall like men of war; and they shall march every one on his ways, and they shall not break their ranks: 8Neither shall one thrust another; they shall walk every one in his path: and when they fall upon the sword, they shall not be wounded.*" - The army of the Lord will not break rank, neither will they jostle one another or smite or stab each other. Yet what is the body of Christ like today? Sadly, the body of Christ right now is like the opposite of this army in Joel 2. In the last days, there will be a people that operate and walk in their ministries together.

4. Isaiah 22:23 - "*And I will fasten him as a nail in a sure place; and he shall be for a glorious throne to his father's house.*" - A man can be a nail. This means that you can smite Satan with your very life. When he comes to you, he won't find anything crooked and your very life will smite him to the ground.

In the book of Job, Job held fast to his integrity in God, he was as a nail. But the book of Job isn't even about Job, it is about God proving to Satan that there can be and will be a people that hold fast as a nail to their integrity in God. And when they've lost everything, their children, their health, their property and all their possessions, instead of running away or freaking out, they will tear their garments, shave their heads and fall down upon the ground and say, "*The Lord gave, and the Lord hath taken away; blessed be the name of the Lord*" (Job 1:21).

5. In II Chronicles 3:9 it says that David prepared nails in abundance, "*9And the weight of the nails was fifty shekels of gold. And he overlaid the upper chambers with gold.*" - It says that the nails were purchased for 50 shekels of gold.

    a. 50 is the number of liberty and jubilee.
    b. Gold is the character of God.

Jael was a wild, loosed woman; she was not in bondage to her husband, she was free. In other words, she was liberated. With her nail of liberty and jubilee in the character of God, she smote Sisera to the earth, fastening that nail right through his head. We ourselves also ought to be wild and liberated, and with that same nail, we will destroy Satan's government and all his works. We will finish him to the end so that he can never touch the body of Christ again. The accuser and oppressor of the brethren will be cast down. We need to be like Jael.

Lesson 22
The Great Woman

Through the Scriptures, there is a thread of revelation that speaks of a <u>great</u> woman. I don't believe that this woman is natural but spiritual, or a representative of the true church. This great woman is spoken of as an allegory, as a type and as a symbol, though all the natural stories are ture and happened, we can still however derive great revelation from these true accounts of women by allowing the Holy Spirit to show us deeper truths beyond the literal. I believe this great woman is none other than the "Bride of Christ", God's great company of believers who have attained this great prize. She is made up of people from the Old and New Testament. Just as the New Testament bride will receive a great and special resurrection (Philippians 3:10-13 – "*10That I may know him, and the power of his resurrection, and the fellowship of his sufferings, being made conformable unto his death; 11If by any means I might attain unto the resurrection of the dead. 12Not as though I had already attained, either were already perfect: but I follow after, if that I may apprehend that for which also I am apprehended of Christ Jesus. 13Brethren, I count not myself to have apprehended: but this one thing I do, forgetting those things which are behind, and reaching forth unto those things which are before*", Hebrews 11:35 – "*Women received their dead raised to life again: and others were tortured, not accepting deliverance; that they might obtain a better resurrection*", I Corinthians 15:22-23, 41-42 – "*22For as in Adam all die, even so in Christ shall all be made alive. 23But every man in his own order: Christ the firstfruits; afterward they that are Christ's at his coming…41There is one glory of the sun, and another glory of the moon, and another glory of the stars: for one star differeth from another star in glory. 42So also is the resurrection of the dead. It is sown in corruption; it is raised in incorruption:*"), so also did the bride of the Old Testament have a special resurrection (Matthew 27:50-53 – "*50Jesus, when he had cried again with a loud voice, yielded up the ghost. 51And, behold, the veil of the temple was rent in twain from the top to the bottom; and the earth did quake, and the rocks rent; 52And the graves were opened; and many bodies of the saints which slept arose, 53And came out of the graves after his resurrection, and went into the holy city, and appeared unto many.*")

As we search the Scripture exhaustively to see this great thread of revelation, remember the Word says "*…that in the mouth of two or three witnesses every word may be established.*" (Matthew 18:16). I trust we will understand this "woman of all women" and aspire to be in that great company. Isn't it interesting that the entity God will be most proud of, that part of creation who will justify Him and His greatness, purpose, mercy, grace, kindness, and longsuffering, is a woman! I think because of this we should all know and believe God loves women and has called them to a mighty and high calling and that He especially wants them to be used in service of His Kingdom.

I.   The Great Woman As She Is Found Throughout Scripture

A.   II Kings 4:8-35

We have looked at this chapter in detail elsewhere in this book, but it is important to note that this widow was called a "great woman" because she had great spiritual substance in her life and ministered to the man of God. She fed and blessed him both naturally and spiritually and out of her was born a son (manchild) whom she embraced. This special son is none other than the manchild of Revelation 12:1-5. The union between God and this glorious bride will bring about the birthing of the "sons of God" in the last days. These will have the full image of Jesus Christ (Romans 8:28-30 – "*28And we know that all things work together for good to them that love God, to them who are the called according to his purpose. 29For whom he did foreknow, he also did predestinate to be conformed to the image of his Son, that he might be the firstborn among many brethren. 30Moreover whom he did predestinate, them he also called: and whom he called, them he also justified: and whom he justified, them he also glorified.*"). They will attain the "*measure of the stature of the fulness of Christ*" (Ephesians 4:13), and will ultimately become the perfect man (Ephesians 4:13). These will be the ones in whom Christ is fully formed (Galatians 4:19). These will grow up into Jesus in all things (Ephesians 4:15-16). They will stand complete in all the will of God (Colossians 4:12, 2:10).

B.   Song of Solomon 6:8-13 – "*8There are threescore queens, and fourscore concubines, and virgins without number. 9My dove, my undefiled is but one; she is the only one of her mother, she is the choice one of her that bare her. The daughters saw her, and blessed her; yea, the queens and the concubines, and they praised her. ¹⁰Who is she that looketh forth as the morning, fair as the moon, clear as the sun, and terrible as an army with banners? ¹¹I went down into the garden of nuts to see the fruits of the valley, and to see whether the vine flourished, and the pomegranates budded. ¹²Or ever I was aware, my soul made me like the chariots of Amminadib. ¹³Return, return, O Shulamite; return, return, that we may look upon thee. What will ye see in the Shulamite? As it were the company of two armies."* – Notice she stands out from among the rest.

1. Queens, concubines, virgins, and daughters speak of all other blood-bought believers.

   a. Queens – Those in the body who have a special revelation of Him but who are not chosen. There are threescore or sixty queens and sixty is the number for pride.
   b. Virgins – All of the members of the body of Christ and they are without number.
   c. Concubines – Those who have intimate experiences with God, but do not have a daily personal relationship with Him. There are fourscore or eighty concubines and eighty is the number for fulfilled life.
   d. Daughters – Family members with no deep revelation.

2. But the bride here is special because:

   a. She's the dove
   b. The undefiled
   c. Only one of her mother (the church)
   d. Choice one – Choice one in the Hebrew means beloved, pure, clean, clear and is from a root word which means to clarify, examine, select, chosen, purge out, polished, and purified.
   e. Looks like the morning (shining)
   f. Fair as the moon (reflecting the Son)
   g. Terrible as an army
   h. Two dancing companies (verse 13)
   i. Shulamite is the feminine form of Solomon which in the Hebrew means peace.

C. Psalms 45:9-16 – *"⁹Kings' daughters were among thy honourable women: upon thy right hand did stand the queen in gold of Ophir. ¹⁰Hearken, O daughter, and consider, and incline thine ear; forget also thine own people, and thy father's house; ¹¹So shall the king greatly desire thy beauty: for he is thy Lord; and worship thou him. ¹²And the daughter of Tyre shall be there with a gift; even the rich among the people shall intreat thy favour. ¹³The king's daughter is all glorious within: her clothing is of wrought gold. ¹⁴She shall be brought unto the king in raiment of needlework: the virgins her companions that follow her shall be brought unto thee. ¹⁵With gladness and rejoicing shall they be brought: they shall enter into the king's palace. ¹⁶Instead of thy fathers shall be thy children, whom thou mayest make princes in all the earth."*

Notice the King's daughter (same as the queen in gold of Ophir in verse 9) is set apart from all the other "virgins". They follow her and are virgins (representing born again believers in scripture) but they are not brought to the King in the same way. She is special because:

1. She's all glorious within
2. Her clothing is of wrought gold
3. She's the queen (bride)

Notice that she goes first, and then the companions and the virgins follow. This is how it will be in the resurrection. Every man will be raised in his own order (or rank).

D. Revelation 12:1-17

1. I believe the woman here represents the church – Reasons:

a. This is a prophetic book speaking of the future, not the past. I believe these events have yet to take place.

b. The manchild spoken of in verse 5, Jesus spoke of in Revelation 2:26-28. The manchild is simply the overcomers, not Jesus. They come out of the church, not Israel.

c. I believe also the language of verse one expresses the church

    1) Clothed with the sun – Notice it says "the moon under her feet." I believe the bride coming out of her is the moon, reflecting the light of the sun, or the triune God.

    2) Crown of twelve stars – Twelve speaks of divine order and government. Israel could never walk in divine government but spiritual Israel, the church, can and should. God's government in her life is complete. The twelve stars could also represent in some manner the twelve apostles, or twelve angels sent to minister for the body of Christ.

2. The manchild would then be a special company of believers. We see three divisions within the church here.

a. The woman who travails in birth – verse 1, 5, 6
b. The manchild – verse 5
c. The rest of the woman's seed – verse 17

3. The definitions

a. The woman is made up of all dedicated believers. Out of her comes a special group of overcomers. The woman consists of the 60-fold Christians in the world, those who love the Lord but who never pressed totally in to all that God had for them. They do not know the Lord intimately, and did not allow Him to form His image in them. They did not pay the price, nor did they attain to the bride.

b. The manchild consists of the 100-fold Christians. They are conformed to His image. They are the manifested sons of God. They have a wonderful, intimate, loving relationship with Him. They paid the price and have attained to all that God had for them.

c. The rest of her seed are the 30-fold Christians. They are the ones who backslid or just simply never went on with God. All they have is their salvation, and judgment is great for them.

4. Why is the manchild special? (Revelation 2:26-28)

a. They are overcomers
b. They keep His works unto the end
c. They are given authority
d. They rule all nations

e. Given the morning star

    1) II Peter 1:19
    2) Revelation 22:16
    3) Numbers 24:17-19

f. They are caught up to the throne and God

E. Matthew 25:1-13 – Here once again we see the bride coming out of the church. She is selected above the rest. She is ready, prepared with oil. Why is she special?

1. She is wise. The Greek word for wise means thoughtful, discreet, intelligent, prudent, sensible, wise and is from a root word that means to rein in, to curb, or to fence in. The Greek word for foolish means dull, stupid, heedless, or a blockhead.
2. She has oil in her vessel
3. She bought her oil (paid the price)
4. She is ready
5. She knows Him intimately

The five foolish virgins are Christians who are not full of the Holy Ghost, have not paid a price, and are not ready. Even though they cry, "open to us" (Luke 13:24-30), the Lord refuses because He does not know them. The Lord is speaking of an intimate knowing, as Adam "knew" Eve his wife. Because these foolish ones never took the time to get close to Jesus, they missed out on the greatest reward offered to man.

     F.   Proverbs 31:29 – *"Many daughters have done virtuously, but thou excellest them all."*

This virtuous woman is the bride. Notice it says *"many daughters have done virtuously, but thou excellest them all."* Doing virtuously is not enough, we must excel! What makes her special is found in verses 10-30.

     G.   John 2:1-11
     H.   Revelation 14:1-5

II. The Virtuous Woman Seen Elsewhere In Scripture

     A.   Scriptures

1. II John 1 – *"The elder unto the elect lady and her children, whom I love in the truth; and not I only, but also all they that have known the truth;"*
2. Ephesians 5:25-27 – *"25Husbands, love your wives, even as Christ also loved the church, and gave himself for it; 26That he might sanctify and cleanse it with the washing of water by the word, 27That he might present it to himself a glorious church, not having spot, or wrinkle, or any such thing; but that it should be holy and without blemish."*
3. Galatians 4:22-31
4. Revelation 19:7-9 – *"7Let us be glad and rejoice, and give honour to him: for the marriage of the Lamb is come, and his wife hath made herself ready. 8And to her was granted that she should be arrayed in fine linen, clean and white: for the fine linen is the righteousness of saints. 9And he saith unto me, Write, Blessed are they which are called unto the marriage supper of the Lamb. And he saith unto me, These are the true sayings of God."*
5. Revelation 21:2 – *"And I John saw the holy city, new Jerusalem, coming down from God out of heaven, prepared as a bride adorned for her husband."*
6. Ezekiel 16:2-14
7. Isaiah 52:1-2 – *"1Awake, awake; put on thy strength, O Zion; put on thy beautiful garments, O Jerusalem, the holy city: for henceforth there shall no more come into thee the uncircumcised and the unclean. 2Shake thyself from the dust; arise, and sit down, O Jerusalem: loose thyself from the bands of thy neck, O captive daughter of Zion."*
8. Isaiah 54:1-10
9. Hosea 2:14-23
10. Isaiah 62:1-5 – Hephzibah means – my delight is in her, and Beulah means – married
11. Isaiah 66:5-12
12. Isaiah 4:2-6
13. Song of Solomon 7:1-6
14. Song of Solomon 3:6, 6:10, 8:5
15. Song of Solomon 2:15, 6:3, 7:10

Lesson 23
The Virtuous Woman

I.   Proverbs 31:10-31

"¹⁰Who can find a <u>virtuous woman</u>? for her price is far above rubies. ¹¹The heart of her husband doth safely trust in her, so that he shall have no need of spoil. ¹²She will do him good and not evil all the days of her life. ¹³She seeketh wool, and flax, and worketh willingly with her hands. ¹⁴She is like the merchants' ships; she bringeth her food from afar. ¹⁵She riseth also while it is yet night, and giveth meat to her household, and a portion to her maidens. ¹⁶She considereth a field, and buyeth it: with the fruit of her hands she planteth a vineyard. ¹⁷She girdeth her loins with strength, and strengtheneth her arms. ¹⁸She perceiveth that her merchandise is good: her candle goeth not out by night. ¹⁹She layeth her hands to the spindle, and her hands hold the distaff. ²⁰She stretcheth out her hand to the poor; yea, she reacheth forth her hands to the needy. ²¹She is not afraid of the snow for her household: for all her household are clothed with scarlet. ²²She maketh herself coverings of tapestry; her clothing is silk and purple. ²³Her husband is known in the gates, when he sitteth among the elders of the land. ²⁴She maketh fine linen, and selleth it; and delivereth girdles unto the merchant. ²⁵Strength and honour are her clothing; and she shall rejoice in time to come. ²⁶She openeth her mouth with wisdom; and in her tongue is the law of kindness. ²⁷She looketh well to the ways of her household, and eateth not the bread of idleness. ²⁸Her children arise up, and call her blessed; her husband also, and he praiseth her. ²⁹Many daughters have done virtuously, but thou excellest them all. ³⁰Favour is deceitful, and beauty is vain: but a woman that feareth the LORD, she shall be praised. ³¹Give her of the fruit of her hands; and let her own works praise her in the gates" (Proverbs 31:10-31).

So many scholars and teachers treat this passage as a treatise on the so-called perfect woman or wife. I agree that literally much can be received and helpful in that respect, but however, I think the picturesque language, the symbolism, points to something far deeper and revelatory. This woman is none other than the "bride of Christ". Seen this way, a world of revelation is opened to us concerning God's holy pure bride. So though this can be used to describe a natural woman, it is without doubt, speaking of God's own true bride, made up of the body of Christ who are devoted to Jesus.

II.   The Virtuous Woman Is the Bride

    A.   Scriptures confirming this

        1.   Psalms 45:9-14 – *"⁹Kings' daughters were among thy honourable women: upon thy right hand did stand the queen in gold of Ophir..."*

        2.   Song of Solomon 6:9-10 – *"⁹My dove, my undefiled is but one; she is the only one of her mother, she is the choice one of her that bare her. The daughters saw her, and blessed her; yea, the queens and the concubines, and they praised her. ¹⁰Who is she that looketh forth as the morning, fair as the moon, clear as the sun, and terrible as an army with banners?"*

        3.   Song of Solomon 8:5-8 – *"⁵Who is this that cometh up from the wilderness, leaning upon her beloved?"*

        4.   Revelation 19:7-8 – *"⁷Let us be glad and rejoice, and give honour to him: for the marriage of the Lamb is come, and his wife hath made herself ready. ⁸And to her was granted that she should be arrayed in fine linen, clean and white: for the fine linen is the righteousness of saints."*

        5.   Revelation 21:2, 9 – *"And I John saw the holy city, new Jerusalem, coming down from God out of heaven, prepared as a bride adorned for her husband...And there came unto me one of the seven angels which had the seven vials full of the seven last plagues, and talked with me, saying, Come hither, I will shew thee the bride, the Lamb's wife."*

        6.   Matthew 25:1-10 – *"²⁵Then shall the kingdom of heaven be likened unto ten virgins, which took their lamps, and went forth to meet the bridegroom..."*

        7.   Hosea 2:14-20 – *"...¹⁶And it shall be at that day, saith the Lord, that thou shalt call me Ishi (Husband); and shalt call me no more Baali (Master)..."*

8. Isaiah 62:1-5 – "...5For as a young man marrieth a virgin, so shall thy sons marry thee: and as the bridegroom rejoiceth over the bride, so shall thy God rejoice over thee."

9. Isaiah 54:1-8 – "...5For thy Maker is thine husband; the Lord of hosts is his name; and thy Redeemer the Holy One of Israel; The God of the whole earth shall he be called. 6For the Lord hath called thee as a woman forsaken and grieved in spirit, and a wife of youth, when thou wast refused, saith thy God..."

10. Matthew 22:1-14 – "2The kingdom of heaven is like unto a certain king, which made a marriage for his son..."

11. Luke 14:16-24

12. Revelation 14:1-6 – "...4These are they which were not defiled with women; for they are virgins. These are they which follow the Lamb whithersoever he goeth. These were redeemed from among men, being the firstfruits unto God and to the Lamb..."

13. Songs of Solomon 7:10 – "I am my beloved's, and his desire is toward me." (Also Songs of Solomon 1:1-4, 3:1-8, 4, 5:1-9.)

All of the above Scriptures speak of that one true bride that God has been patiently waiting to give His Son. She will be perfect, complete, full of God's glory and manifest presence but most of all she will have His godly character. She will have the true image of God. This virtuous woman is the bride.

III. Verse by verse exposition of Proverbs 31:10-31

A. Verse 10 – "Who can find a virtuous woman? for her price is far above rubies." - The Hebrew word for virtuous, *chayil*, means a force (whether of men, means or other resources), an army, valor, strength. This word comes from a Hebrew root word (*chiyl*) which means to dance. These are interesting definitions in that they seem to point to the fact that this bride is an army, a force to be reckoned with because of its valor and strength. It also seems that she is a dancing bride.

1. Song of Solomon 6:13 – "Return, return, O Shulamite; return, return, that we may look upon thee. What will ye see in the Shulamite? As it were the company of two armies."

2. "Who can find a virtuous woman?" – Apparently there aren't many of them.

3. "Her price is far above..." – She is priceless, nothing can be compared to her.

4. "...rubies"

   a. Malachi 3:16-17 – "Then they that feared the LORD spake often one to another: and the LORD hearkened, and heard it, and a book of remembrance was written before him for them that feared the LORD, and that thought upon his name. And they shall be mine, saith the LORD of hosts, in that day when I make up my jewels; and I will spare them, as a man spareth his own son that serveth him."

   b. I Corinthians 3:10-14 – "...11For other foundation can no man lay than that is laid, which is Jesus Christ. 12Now if any man build upon this foundation gold, silver, precious stones, wood, hay, stubble; ..."

   c. Psalms 102:14 – "For thy servants take pleasure in her stones, and favour the dust thereof."

   d. Isaiah 54:11-14

   e. Revelation 21:9-11, 19

   f. Zechariah 9:12-17

   g. Ezekiel 16:6-14

   h. Isaiah 62:3

B. Verse 11 – "The heart of her husband doth safely trust in her, so that he shall have no need of spoil."

1. Jesus is her husband

   a. Isaiah 54:5 – "For thy Maker is thine husband; the LORD of hosts is his name; and thy Redeemer the Holy One of Israel; The God of the whole earth shall he be called."

   b. Hosea 2:7-8, 14-20

155

      c.   Revelation 21:2 – *"And I John saw the holy city, new Jerusalem, coming down from God out of heaven, prepared as a bride adorned for her husband."*

      d.   Isaiah 62:5 – *"For as a young man marrieth a virgin, so shall thy sons marry thee: and as the bridegroom rejoiceth over the bride, so shall thy God rejoice over thee."*

      e.   Matthew 25:1-10

      f.   John 3:29

      g.   Matthew 22:2-12

      h.   Revelation 19:7-9

      i.   Ephesians 5:32

      j.   Luke 12:36

2.   Her husband trusts her.

The type here of course is Jesus, our husband, trusting in us, His bride, with His whole heart. He can count on her. He knows she will be faithful. This is so important to God. Down through the ages, everything God created and blessed with wisdom, anointing, riches, responsibility, and the opportunity to have a unique relationship with Him, have rejected Him. Examples of this include Lucifer, one-third of the angelic host, Adam, Abraham, the priesthood of Israel, the children of Israel, His disciples, John the Baptist, and you and I.

      a.   God in this hour is bringing forth a people in whom He can trust, depend and rely on, knowing they will never usurp His authority or seek after vain glory. He will have this people. I pray we will be a part.

      b.   Deuteronomy 32:9

      c.   Ezekiel 16:8

      d.   John 15:16

      e.   Deuteronomy 7:7-8

3.   *"he shall have no need of spoil"* – He never needs to be concerned that she would mishandle His provision, glory and attributes. She is trustworthy and mature enough to handle God's household.

      a.   I Samuel 2:35

      b.   Luke 12:41-43

      c.   Psalms 101:6

      d.   Proverbs 25:13

      e.   I Corinthians 4:2

      f.   Matthew 25:21

      g.   Revelation 17:14

C.   Verse 12 – *"She will do him good and not evil all the days of her life."*

What is your testimony? Among Christians our testimony may be great, but what is our testimony among the world. A bride in the natural always wants to do good by her husband (at least we would hope so). You never uncover your mate before people in an ungodly way or do something that will bring a reproach upon your spouse. *"She will do him good and not evil all the days of her life."* This tells me there is a possibility that I can do evil to the cause of Christ. As the bride of Christ, she will represent Him in the earth. Are we doing Jesus good? Will Jesus say to us, *"Well done thou good and faithful servant?"* No matter what we do or how small our task, it is very important. A house wife's job is just as important, or a pastor's wife and her work is just as important as the person that stands behind the pulpit and ministers to thousands. Be faithful in everything you put your hands to and be faithful with what you have. If your job is to keep the children and you never have a public ministry, you will still get the same reward. Preachers don't get a greater reward because they are seen before men. God's eyes are on the faithful of the land. God requires faithfulness of His people. Every day you raise your child with love and every day you minister to your children, or your husband, or every day you work faithfully under your boss and you shine as a light in this world, you are doing Jesus good and not evil. How many times do we hear God's name being reproached because of what some man or woman has done, especially in this hour. It seems a week will not go by until we hear of another person that is in leadership in the body of Christ falling into sin, whether it is committing adultery, misusing God's money, etc.

In I Samuel, Hophni and Phinehas were the sons of Eli and were the Levitical priests that met with the people to receive their sacrifices at the temple to offer them to the Lord. The bible says they were stealing the best parts of the animals and God had specifically told them what they were supposed to do with the sacrifices. They were making a mockery of the sacrifices of God, and on top of that, they were laying with women who gathered at the assembly. It got so bad that the bible says, "*Wherefore the sin of the young men was very great before the LORD: for men abhorred the offering of the LORD*" (I Samuel 2:17). The people didn't even want to come to give sacrifice because they didn't trust Hophni and Phinehas, the "men of God". God's name was evil spoken of. Now we all have our weaknesses and fall, but when we fall, we repent and do what's right. Hophni and Phinehas never repented and were so presumptuous that they thought they could handle the ark of God, so God slew them.

You have to keep in mind, are you doing the Lord good every day? Paul said in Acts 24:16, "*And herein do I exercise myself, to have always a conscience void of offence toward God, and toward men.*" Matthew 5:8 says, "*Blessed are the pure in heart: for they shall see God.*" I'm not talking about seeing God in the second coming, but seeing God right now! If we keep our hearts pure every day, we can see the manifestation of God in our life right now. Do Him good! Let everyone else do evil. You do good! Don't bring reproach to His name. Let's suffer the reproach to do the right thing and be lights in this world. "*14Do all things without murmurings and disputings: 15That ye may be blameless and harmless, the sons of God, without rebuke, in the midst of a crooked and perverse nation, among whom ye shine as lights in the world; 16Holding forth the word of life; that I may rejoice in the day of Christ, that I have not run in vain, neither laboured in vain.*" (Philippians 2:14-16). We are to shine as lights in this perverse generation. Every day you wake up, determine to keep your heart pure today, walk with God, and hold forth the Word of life. The Word of God is not supposed to be just in your head, but in your lifestyle. We are to be a living epistle, "*known and read of all men*" (II Corinthians 3:2). Our goal is to live the Word of God. When you are younger in the Lord you fall more, struggle more with condemnation, but Jesus made a provision for every sin we will ever commit. Just keep repenting and getting up.

The Amplified version of verse twelve reads, "*She will comfort, encourage and do him only good as long as there is life within her.*" Do you have this kind of heart towards the Lord today?

1. Other Scriptures related to this verse:

   a. Psalms 37:3
   b. Psalms 125:4
   c. Proverbs 10:1
   d. Psalms 96:7-8
   e. I Samuel 3:1

D. Verse 13 – "*She seeketh wool, and flax, and worketh willingly with her hands.*"

Who has wool? Sheep do. God isn't looking for people who will build kingdom's after themselves. He is seeking shepherds who seek for the sheep. God the Father says, "*I will give you pastors according to mine heart, which shall feed you with knowledge and understanding.*" (Jeremiah 3:15). He tells Samuel, "*And I will raise me up a faithful priest, that shall do according to that which is in mine heart and in my mind: and I will build him a sure house; and he shall walk before mine anointed for ever.*" (I Samuel 2:35). The bride of Christ is seeking her brothers and sisters to bless them.

She also works willingly with her hands. Hands in Scripture, as we've seen many times before, always relates to our works. When Jesus was only 12 years old, He told His mother, "*Wist ye not that I must be about my Father's business?*" Do you do the will of God willingly or do you do it with a chip on your shoulder? Ezekiel said, "*I went in bitterness, in the heat of my spirit; but the hand of the LORD was strong upon me.*" (Ezekiel 3:14). Many times in my own life, I find that when God tells me to do something, I find that my will often does not line up with God's will for that day. He may want me to encounter somebody that I may not want to encounter. We many times avoid situations or people when God wants us right in the middle of them so we can overcome, minister, and do His will. The very person that can always seem to push our buttons is the very person God has His eye on to deal with us.

Consider Matthew 21:28-30 which says, "*A certain man had two sons; and he came to the first, and said, Son, go work to day in my vineyard. He answered and said, I will not: but afterward he repented, and went. And he came to the second, and said likewise. And he answered and said, I go, sir: and went not.*" God is so wonderful. He doesn't even care if we don't like what He wants us to do, even if you initially say I don't want to do that. I don't have to like everything God tells me to do. But I still need to do it.

The bride's will lines up with God's will. The bride is faithful and has an obedient heart to do the work of the Lord, wherever He may place her. Her life is not her own. We ourselves can't live our lives doing everything we want to do. When we are called upon to do something, what is our response? The bride's response is yes, I'll do it! As the bride of Christ, are we willing to work? God is looking for laborers and workers.

E. Verse 14 – "*She is like the merchants' ships; she bringeth her food from afar.*"

She is like a vessel loaded down with goods. This bride has whatever you need in her boat. People used to ask me, what kind of gift do you want from the Lord? My answer was always, I want whatever gift is necessary at the moment. If it is a gift of discernment or working of miracles or speaking in tongues, I want whatever is necessary. This bride is like a merchant's ship and she's bringing food from afar. She's bringing the provision of the Lord to God's people. Back in the old days, people had to wait for ships to bring their basic necessities. She is like this ship. She has everything on that ship that is necessary. Job 6:13 says, "*Is not my help in me?*" I John 2:27 says, "*But the anointing which ye have received of him abideth in you, and ye need not that any man teach you: but as the same anointing teacheth you of all things, and is truth, and is no lie, and even as it hath taught you, ye shall abide in him.*" We have the ability, as we learn to draw upon the anointing and Spirit within us, to minister to anybody. Every Christian should be like a merchant's ship, filled with the Word of God, filled with the presence of God, so whatever comes their way you can deal with it and have an answer. If somebody needs prayer for sickness, you can lay hands on them. If somebody needs counsel for their situation, you can counsel them because you have the Word of God in you, the greatest counselor in the universe.

    1. Our vessel should be filled and ready to give out.

        a. I Peter 3:15
        b. II Timothy 4:2
        c. Colossians 3:16
        d. Joel 2:32

F. Verse 15 – "*She riseth also while it is yet night, and giveth meat to her household, and a portion to her maidens.*"

    1. "*She riseth also while it is yet night*" – She is faithful and diligent to seek God, even in the night. Even in her darkest and hardest hour, she rises up and does the opposite of what the devil is trying to get her to do. She doesn't allow her circumstances to stop her.
    2. "*and giveth meat to her household, and a portion to her maidens*" – The household and maidens are the local church. She's the teacher, the one with the Word in her heart. When her brother has a need, she has the answer or the provision. She is willing to administer it.
    3. Luke 12:42-44 – If you are faithful in one thing, God will increase you into larger things.

G. Verse 16 – "*She considereth a field, and buyeth it: with the fruit of her hands she planteth a vineyard.*"

    1. The field represents the world as well as a place of ministry.

       a.   Matthew 13:38

       b.   John 4:35

       c.   Proverbs 24:27

       d.   Song of Solomon 7:11-12

2.   *"She considereth a field, and buyeth it"* – She is willing to pay the price to buy that field. She is willing to do whatever it takes for that ministry to be fruitful. She is committed to that end.

3.   Numbers 13:31-32

4.   *"with the fruit of her hands she planteth a vineyard"* – Once she's bought and established this field or ministry and God is causing it to grow, fruit will come forth. Out of that fruit will then come a vineyard or a place that is flowing with the presence of God. You can't plant a vineyard if you don't have the initial seeding to do it. The bride herself is full of the Holy Ghost and therefore when she goes, she is able to plant it and reap a harvest.

H.   Verse 17 – *"She girdeth her loins with strength, and strengtheneth her arms."*

"She girdeth her loins with strength" – Loins in the Scripture represent two things: I Peter 1:13 says, *"Wherefore gird up the loins of your mind"*. She has the mind of Christ and keeps her mind stayed on Jesus (Isaiah 26:3, Colossians 3:2, Philippians 2:5). Secondly, loins represent the reproductive cycle within a person. She is preparing for a birth or to have fruit come forth from her womb. It is like a natural woman doing things and preparing herself to give birth to a child. The same is true spiritually speaking. We have to prepare ourselves to birth children in the Lord and be strong enough to finish it (Luke 14:28). Even in the Kingdom of God concerning birthing children, you have to prepare yourself against that day.

She is strong. She feeds herself. A believer's strength comes from the Word of God and His Spirit. We will only be as strong as the level of Word we have in our lives and by how we've cultivated God's presence individually. *"and strengtheneth her arms"* – Arm and hands in Scripture represent the works of God.

I.   Verse 18 – *"She perceiveth that her merchandise is good: her candle goeth not out by night."*

"She perceiveth that her merchandise is good" – In verse 14, she is compared to a merchant's ship. A merchant ship represents someone who is filled with all kinds of treasures, gifts, callings, and talents. She perceives that her merchandise is good. In other words, she sees that what God has done in her and the gifts that He has placed in her are good things. If you know that God has given you something good, you want to give it away. God never gives you a gift just for you. He gives it so that you can give it away.

"her candle goeth not out by night." – Proverbs 20:27 says, *"The spirit of man is the candle of the LORD, searching all the inward parts of the belly."* We find also in I Samuel 3:3 that the candle in the tabernacle almost went out. This candle speaks of the flame of fire in her spirit-man. When the night comes many of us yield to the darkness rather than turning inwardly and allowing the spirit of God within us to literally blaze forth. Psalms 50:2 says, *"Out of Zion, the perfection of beauty, God hath shined."* Another translation of this says, *"...He blazes forth"*. Inside of you is Zion and it never ceases to amaze me that when trouble comes in so many people's lives, they go to things that will not bring an answer. We are always to go to the Lord first. The bride's candle doesn't go out at night. She's not one of those that Paul was speaking of in Ephesians 4:26-27, *"Be ye angry, and sin not: let not the sun go down upon your wrath: Neither give place to the devil."* Wrath represents our righteous indignation. The only way you can give place to the devil is when you let the sun go down on your righteous indignation. Her candle is not going out because she is trimming that wick, she's causing that flame to burn ever brightly, she's building up her most holy faith by praying in the Holy Ghost, and she's staying in the Word of God. If you do those things, I don't care what you go through, because ultimately, you will endure whatever it is. The bride is someone whose candle is shining.

J.   Verse 19 – *"She layeth her hands to the spindle, and her hands hold the distaff."*

Hands again represent our works or the works of God. This passage simply says to us that this is a faithful woman who is willing to work. The bride is not afraid of work. She lays her hands to something. Luke 9:62 says, "*And Jesus said unto him, No man, having put his hand to the plough, and looking back, is fit for the kingdom of God.*" Once you begin something, you need to finish it.

K.   Verse 20 – "*She stretcheth out her hand to the poor; yea, she reacheth forth her hands to the needy.*"

One of the characteristics of the bride is she has a giving heart, someone who is more concerned with others than she is herself. Selfishness reigns in the body of Christ, and the only way to stop that is by one believer at a time beginning to do selfless acts, giving and sharing all that they have with others and start a revolution.

The bride is considerate of the poor and needy, something God requires of His people. We must always keep within our hearts a response and a readiness to minister to the needy. Yes, you can be taken advantage of. Yes, people use and abuse it, but it doesn't matter. James 4:17 says "*Therefore to him that knoweth to do good, and doeth it not, to him it is sin.*" Proverbs 3:27 says, "*Withhold not good from them to whom it is due, when it is in the power of thine hand to do it.*" If you have money in your pocket and somebody in front of you has a need, you are honor bound by God to try to help meet that need. Whatever God gives us is to pass through us. We should be always remember to reach out to the poor and needy. So many people stretch out their hands and exalt people with power; they cater to rich people who could potentially benefit them in any way. On the other end, the bride reaches out and is willing to work, minister, and bless everybody, regardless of their social or economic status. Jesus never turned down the call of a lowly person. Lepers would call out to Him, women (who weren't allowed to speak many times) would call out to Him, blind people, widows, etc. Jesus was always touched by the needy. Lamentations 3:51 says, "*Mine eye affecteth mine heart because of all the daughters of my city.*" The eye gate in people is given to them to see the needs of others. If you see a need, reach out!

1.   I John 3:17
2.   Acts 2:45
3.   Proverbs 19:17
4.   Proverbs 21:13
5.   Proverbs 29:7
6.   Galatians 2:10

L.   Verse 21 – "*She is not afraid of the snow for her household: for all her household are clothed with scarlet.*"

Job 38:22 – "*Hast thou entered into the treasures of the snow?*" The treasures of the snow are symbolic of the "treasures of darkness" found elsewhere in Scripture (Isaiah 45:3). She is not afraid of the dealings of God. She is not afraid of any kind of happenings that might come to her or her household because, "*all her household are clothed with scarlet.*" Scarlet represents two things, the blood of Jesus, and sufferings. The bride will have suffered. The bride also knows that the blood of Jesus Christ is planted on the doorpost of her life. When you are in a position of authority you have to remember that the blood is also applied to the doorpost of her household. She's not afraid because she's taught her people well and right, teaching them about the dealings of God. They've gone through suffering and they know as I Peter 5:10 says, "*But the God of all grace, who hath called us unto his eternal glory by Christ Jesus, after that ye have suffered a while, make you perfect, stablish, strengthen, settle you.*" When you are teaching people about the dealings of God, you are preparing them and teaching them that suffering, as well as prosperity, is a way of life. "*In the day of prosperity be joyful, but in the day of adversity consider: God also hath set the one over against the other, to the end that man should find nothing after him*" (Ecclesiastes 7:14). These are the ways of God.

M.   Verse 22 – "*She maketh herself coverings of tapestry; her clothing is silk and purple.*"

"*She maketh herself coverings of tapestry*" – Everyday of our life, we are weaving a garment. Peaking of the resurrection, Paul puts it this way, "*There is one glory of the sun, and another glory of the moon, and another glory of the stars: for one star differeth from another star in glory. So also is the resurrection of the dead. It is sown in corruption; it is raised in incorruption:*" (I Corinthians 15:41-42). Our clothing in the ages to come is going to be to the degree that we've allowed God to work in our life. Some people will shine brightly, others not so brightly. Every day you and I are weaving a tapestry, a garment in our lives. It says of the bride in Psalms 45:13 that "*her clothing is of wrought gold*", meaning she has had the character of God worked into her life. The clothing of the bride in Revelation 19:7-9 is "*fine linen*". When it speaks to us of a tapestry, she realizes that everything that happens to her every day is important. At the end of each day you need to ask yourself, what have I woven today in my life? What is the clothing that I am working into my life? Did I do good today? Was I a blessing to others today? Did I do something to encourage another for no reason at all? God sees everything we do. We need to keep building and clothing ourselves with a tapestry or garment of fine linen. Remember in Matthew 22:2-14, when the Lord kicked out a man out of the wedding supper that didn't have a wedding garment on? It is the same principle.

"*...her clothing is silk and purple.*" – Silk is like linen and speaks of the righteousness of the saints or what she has attained in God. Purple in Scripture always speaks of royalty or riches. Her clothing is silk and purple which means that her lifestyle is one of righteousness and royalty.

N.   Verse 23 – "*Her husband is known in the gates, when he sitteth among the elders of the land.*"

Jesus again is her husband. She acknowledges that her husband has authority and that her husband is an elder. The bride understands her position in the Kingdom of God as it relates to the Lord Jesus. This also speaks of her deferring always to her husband. Jesus said in John 7:18, "*He that speaketh of himself seeketh his own glory: but he that seeketh his glory that sent him, the same is true, and no unrighteousness is in him.*" Jesus came not seeking His own glory, but the glory of His Father. In every one of our hearts there should be desire to bring glory to our Father and not to promote ourselves. It is amazing the lengths people will go to promote themselves. Ministers should not promote or speak of themselves. They should make it known, "The Lord be magnified"! In II Samuel 23 when David's mighty men did many great feats it reads, "*and the Lord wrought a great victory*".

O.   Verse 24 – "*She maketh fine linen, and selleth it; and delivereth girdles unto the merchant.*"

"*She maketh fine linen, and selleth it*". Fine linen is called the righteousness of the saints in Revelation 19:7. Her selling it means she is ministering righteousness. It is hard to minister righteousness if your lifestyle is not righteous. "*and delivereth girdles unto the merchant*" simply means the gifts that God gives His people, she's teaching and giving them instruction as to how to walk in those gifts. The bride, because she is mature and knows how to flow in the Spirit of God, is able to teach others properly. When it comes to growing in the gifts of God, people need to keep their girdle on. How many times do you see people trying to move in the Spirit of God without ever receiving instruction? Most of the time they get spooky and fall into error.

P.   Verse 25 – "*Strength and honour are her clothing; and she shall rejoice in time to come.*"

Clothing again is our righteousness, what we've attained to in God. Her lifestyle is one of strength and honor. The Lord said, "*for them that honour me I will honour, and they that despise me shall be lightly esteemed*" (I Samuel 2:30). Jesus said in John 12:26, "*if any man serve me, him will my Father honour.*" In Malachi 1:6 says, "*A son honoureth his father, and a servant his master: if then I be a father, where is mine honour? and if I be a master, where is my fear?*" The question then is do we honour the Lord with our life? Everybody sees your clothing. Everybody, if they have discernment, can see where you are at in God because it shows by the way you live your life. Do we honour the Lord with our mouth, with our mind, with our works, with our money, etc? If you honour the Lord with your life, you (like the bride), will rejoice in time to come, that is, in the day of the Lord. So many people think that lightning will strike one day and then they will do the will of God. They think one day I will start reading the bible and give myself to the Word of God and that day never comes. The end of a fool is not a good thing. Proverbs 5:12 says, "*How have I hated instruction, and my heart despised reproof.*" In other words, this person is saying if I only just listened and bowed my ear during my life and honored the Lord. Saul said at the end of his life in I Samuel 26:21, "*behold, I have played the fool, and have erred exceedingly.*"

Today is the day of salvation and time to honour the Lord. Even today, all day long, you will have choices to be nice to people, to be kind, to show goodness, to show favor, mercy, or you can choose to be surly, mean, unkind with your mouth, a gossiper, a scorner, and so many other things. *"Strength and honour are her clothing"*. What is your testimony? What are the clothes you wear?

1. Who does God give honor to?

   a. II Timothy 2:20-21 – Those who have gone through a purging of all that would foster wood and earth (flesh) in their lives. They have allowed Him to wash them of all that is ungodly. They have His divine nature (gold) and they are walking in their full redemption (silver).
   b. John 12:26 – Service to God brings honor. If we could only learn to serve God rather than ourselves, God would bring honor into our lives.
   c. Proverbs 15:33 – Humility brings the honor of God into our life. Proverbs 29:23 – God is looking for humble people who have left off being proud.
   d. Proverbs 20:3 – God gives honor to those who stay free from strife, arguing and contention.

"She shall rejoice in time to come." There will be a day of reward for the bride. Many times it seems that we are going through so much, allowing God to deal with us and bring changes into our lives. Most of the time it is painful, but it is better for this to happen now than to be caught not ready at His appearing. Be encouraged to press on, for our day of rejoicing <u>is</u> coming if we will hold fast and be faithful to the end.

Q. Verse 26 – *"She openeth her mouth with wisdom; and in her tongue is the law of kindness."*

You can't open your mouth with wisdom unless you have wisdom. Where does wisdom come from? Wisdom comes from the Word of God. Wisdom, Proverbs 4:7 says, *"is the principal thing; therefore get wisdom: and with all thy getting get understanding."* There is a difference between wisdom and knowledge. Knowledge is just a bunch of information and know-how. Wisdom is putting knowledge into practice. Someone who has wisdom doesn't just know how to do something, but walks in it. So many people have knowledge but they have no life experience. The bride has the wisdom of God. Out of her mouth comes wisdom because out of the abundance of the heart the mouth speaks. She has the Word of God, His wisdom, hidden in her heart.

Not only does the bride have wisdom but, *"in her tongue is the law of kindness"*. Far too many people do not have the law of kindness in their mouth. They are mean, surly, abrupt, rude, and critical. Why is it such a struggle to be kind? Is the law of kindness in your mouth? Let our speech always be seasoned with salt and with grace. I pray from this day forward that right before you open your mouth to say something stupid that you remember the words of Apostle Paul, *"study to be quiet"* (I Thessalonians 4:11), and Solomon that said, *"in the multitude of words there wanteth not sin"* (Proverbs 10:19). Solomon also said, *"Even a fool, when he holdeth his peace, is counted wise: and he that shutteth his lips is esteemed a man of understanding"* (Proverbs 17:28). The bride has learned the law (principle) of a right confession and to be kind and love her brothers and sisters. She has learned to bless with her mouth and not curse. The way to stay undefiled is to control our tongue (James 3:6).

R. Verse 27 – *"She looketh well to the ways of her household, and eateth not the bread of idleness."*

Ecclesiastes 10:18 says, *"By much slothfulness the building decayeth; and through idleness of the hands the house droppeth through."* Idleness is slothfulness, laziness. Because she is in authority of her household she cannot by idle and lazy. Also, every shepherd should look well to the ways of their flock. Every shepherd should know their sheep and should be *"diligent to know the state of thy flocks, and look well to thy herds"* (Proverbs 27:23). The bride does all this. She is diligent to take care of her household. She provides for and cares for them.

S. Verse 28 – *"Her children arise up, and call her blessed; her husband also, and he praiseth her."*

Anybody that has children knows that when you are in the middle of it and they are growing up, it can be a struggle. The first two or three years of a child's life is cute. But after that, it's on. For the next 18 years it is hard work for a parent. Get used to it. But one day, they will rise up and call you blessed. Your spiritual children will rise up one day and thank you for taking care of the ways of the household of God. Jesus Himself will have a good report of you, *"Well done, thou good and faithful servant: thou hast been faithful over a few things, I will make thee ruler over many things: enter thou into the joy of thy lord."* (Matthew 25:21, 23). There will be no greater reward than to hear King Jesus praise that bride. He does it because she is worthy of it.

T.   Verse 29 – *"Many daughters have done virtuously, but thou excellest them all."*

Song of Solomon 6:8-9 says *"⁸There are threescore queens, and fourscore concubines, and virgins without number. ⁹My dove, my undefiled is but one; she is the only one of her mother, <u>she is the choice one</u> of her that bare her. The daughters saw her, and blessed her; yea, the queens and the concubines, and they praised her."* This virtuous woman excels all the other woman. She is the bride of Christ.

U.   Verse 30 – *"Favour is deceitful, and beauty is vain: but a woman that feareth the LORD, she shall be praised."*

As the bride of Christ, be careful of flattery. Be careful of trying too hard to make your church building beautiful, putting the emphasis in the wrong place. The main defining characteristic of a place or a person is not what they look like or what the church looks like on the outside, but that they fear the Lord. The bride is not interested in complements and is not interested in being told how great or beautiful she is. Don't be impressed with flattery. That is what brought Lucifer down, when he saw he was beautiful. It said of Moses in Exodus 34:29 *"that Moses wist not that the skin of his face shone."* That is the bride of Christ. Jeremiah says in 9:23-24, *"Thus saith the LORD, Let not the wise man glory in his wisdom, neither let the mighty man glory in his might, let not the rich man glory in his riches: But let him that glorieth glory in this, that he understandeth and knoweth me, that I am the LORD which exercise lovingkindness, judgment, and righteousness, in the earth: for in these things I delight, saith the LORD."* The end of Ecclesiastes says, *"Let us hear the conclusion of the whole matter: Fear God, and keep his commandments: for this is the whole duty of man"* (Ecclesiastes 12:13).

One of the great characteristics of the bride is that she fears the Lord. This is one reason why she is praised. She is after Him and His favor, not the favor of man. The favor of man is deceitful and fickle, changing from day to day. The Bible says Jesus would not commit himself to man because He knew what was in man. One day they shouted "Hosanna, Hosanna" and the next day, "Crucify Him". We should seek the favor God gives.

V.   Verse 31 – *"Give her of the fruit of her hands; and let her own works praise her in the gates."*

There will be a day of reckoning, a day when God will reward the bride for all that she's done *"and then shall every man have praise of God"* (I Corinthians 4:5). She will be rewarded for all that she's suffered. She will be rewarded for all that she did when she didn't have to. She will be rewarded for all the dealings of God she endured and went through. There is coming a day that will end all days. When the last day of the Lord begins, when all things have been returned back to God the Father and God is all in all, we're going to live through the eternity of eternities dressed in the garment we've woven in this life. She will be rewarded for her works. Her works will praise her then, simply because she is the bride and is seated next to Jesus.

Lesson 24
Jesus And Women

Jesus' ministry took place between the Old and New Covenants. He was the *"mediator of the new covenant"* (Hebrew 12:24), so what He had to say and how He lived are vital to understanding what God's attitude towards women is. When Jesus came, He seemed to counter constantly what the Scribes, the Pharisees, and Doctors of the Law taught about the Old Testament. He often said, "It has been said" referring to the Old Testament, but then added, "But I say unto you". For us now this is the new "Law" and it is the Law of Love. The Mosaic Law only dealt with committed sin. Jesus went deeper and went for the root or the cause for these sins. As we have already seen, women were counted as nothing under the rabbinical attitude towards them. Jesus came to a male dominated Jewish society and for all intents and purposes, it was a man's religion. Women were severely repressed and dominated by men. These Pharisees, Scribes, and Doctors of the Law had what was called "the tradition of the elders", their teachings on the Talmud, and the Apocrypha, which were seen as having greater authority than the Scriptures themselves. Jesus was constantly at war with these religious zealots who cared more about the outward side of man than the heart of man. But God always looks on the heart (I Samuel 16:7).

In Jesus' ministry, He allowed women to touch Him and He touched them, which was strictly forbidden. He included women among His disciples. Actually they appear to be the ones who really supported Him and His ministry financially. Some of His closest friends were women. He also asked them to be the very first evangelists. His whole attitude toward women was bold, daring, and definitely revolutionary. He literally changed the way men (and people in general) should look and treat women. Jesus came to redeem all mankind, not just men! So in this chapter we want to explore in depth, Jesus' ministry and attitude toward women.

I.   Jesus is God – So whatever Jesus does, it means that the Father would have done the same thing!

A.   Scriptures

1.   John 1:1-3, 14 – "*¹In the beginning was the Word, and the Word was with God, and the Word was God. ²The same was in the beginning with God. ³All things were made by him; and without him was not any thing made that was made...¹⁴And the Word was made flesh, and dwelt among us, (and we beheld his glory, the glory as of the only begotten of the Father,) full of grace and truth."*

2.   Hebrews 1:8 – "*But unto the Son he saith, Thy throne, O God, is for ever and ever: a sceptre of righteousness is the sceptre of thy kingdom."*

3.   Colossians 1:12-19 – "*¹²Giving thanks unto the Father, which hath made us meet to be partakers of the inheritance of the saints in light: ¹³Who hath delivered us from the power of darkness, and hath translated us into the kingdom of his dear Son: ¹⁴In whom we have redemption through his blood, even the forgiveness of sins: ¹⁵Who is the image of the invisible God, the firstborn of every creature: ¹⁶For by him were all things created, that are in heaven, and that are in earth, visible and invisible, whether they be thrones, or dominions, or principalities, or powers: all things were created by him, and for him: ¹⁷And he is before all things, and by him all things consist. ¹⁸And he is the head of the body, the church: who is the beginning, the firstborn from the dead; that in all things he might have the preeminence. ¹⁹For it pleased the Father that in him should all fulness dwell;"*

4.   Isaiah 9:6 – "*For unto us a child is born, unto us a son is given: and the government shall be upon his shoulder: and his name shall be called Wonderful, Counseller, The mighty God, The everlasting Father, The Prince of Peace."*

5.   Jude 25 – "*To the only wise God our Saviour, be glory and majesty, dominion and power, both now and ever. Amen."*

6.   I Timothy 3:16 – "*And without controversy great is the mystery of godliness: God was manifest in the flesh, justified in the Spirit, seen of angels, preached unto the Gentiles, believed on in the world, received up into glory."*

7.   Matthew 1:18-23 – "*...²¹And she shall bring forth a son, and thou shalt call his name JESUS: for he shall save his people from their sins. ²²Now all this was done, that it might be fulfilled which was spoken of the Lord by the prophet, saying, ²³Behold, a virgin shall be with child, and shall bring forth a son, and they shall call his name Emmanuel, which being interpreted is, God with us."*

8. I John 5:20 – "*And we know that the Son of God is come, and hath given us an understanding, that we may know him that is true, and we are in him that is true, even in his Son Jesus Christ. This is the true God, and eternal life.*"

9. Isaiah 44:6 – "*Thus saith the LORD the King of Israel, and his redeemer the LORD of hosts; I am the first, and I am the last; and beside me there is no God.*"

10. Hebrews 1:3 – "*Who being the brightness of his glory, and the express image of his person, and upholding all things by the word of his power, when he had by himself purged our sins, sat down on the right hand of the Majesty on high;*"

11. Colossians 1:15-18 – "*15Who is the image of the invisible God, the firstborn of every creature: 16For by him were all things created, that are in heaven, and that are in earth, visible and invisible, whether they be thrones, or dominions, or principalities, or powers: all things were created by him, and for him: 17And he is before all things, and by him all things consist. 18And he is the head of the body, the church: who is the beginning, the firstborn from the dead; that in all things he might have the preeminence.*"

12. John 3:31 – "*He that cometh from above is above all: he that is of the earth is earthly, and speaketh of the earth: he that cometh from heaven is above all.*"

13. John 8:58 – "*Jesus said unto them, Verily, verily, I say unto you, Before Abraham was, I am.*"

B. The Father delivered everything into Jesus' hands.

1. Matthew 11:27 – "*All things are delivered unto me of my Father: and no man knoweth the Son, but the Father; neither knoweth any man the Father, save the Son, and he to whomsoever the Son will reveal him.*"

2. John 1:18 – "*No man hath seen God at any time; the only begotten Son, which is in the bosom of the Father, he hath declared him.*"

3. John 3:35 – "*The Father loveth the Son, and hath given all things into his hand.*"

4. John 5:16-24, 26-27, 30-32, 36-40, 43

5. John 6:27, 32-40, 46-51, 57

6. John 8:16-19, 10:30-32

7. John 14:6-12 – "*6Jesus saith unto him, I am the way, the truth, and the life: no man cometh unto the Father, but by me. 7If ye had known me, ye should have known my Father also: and from henceforth ye know him, and have seen him. 8Philip saith unto him, Lord, shew us the Father, and it sufficeth us. 9Jesus saith unto him, Have I been so long time with you, and yet hast thou not known me, Philip? <u>he that hath seen me hath seen the Father</u>; and how sayest thou then, Shew us the Father? 10Believest thou not that I am in the Father, and the Father in me? the words that I speak unto you I speak not of myself: but the Father that dwelleth in me, he doeth the works. 11Believe me that I am in the Father, and the Father in me: or else believe me for the very works' sake. 12Verily, verily, I say unto you, He that believeth on me, the works that I do shall he do also; and greater works than these shall he do; because I go unto my Father.*"

8. John 16:15 – "*All things that the Father hath are mine: therefore said I, that he shall take of mine, and shall shew it unto you.*"

C. Jesus always did what pleased the Father

1. Mark 14:36 – "*And he said, Abba, Father, all things are possible unto thee; take away this cup from me: nevertheless not what I will, but what thou wilt.*"

2. John 8:29 – "*And he that sent me is with me: the Father hath not left me alone; for I do always those things that please him.*"

3. John 10:15-18

4. John 14:31

So we know from these passages that Jesus was always acting as the Father would.

II. A Deeper Look At Jesus' Ministry To And With Women

A. His real attitude

    1. Galatians 3:28 – "*There is neither Jew nor Greek, there is neither bond nor free, there is neither male nor female: for ye are all one in Christ Jesus.*"

    2. Luke 13:14-16 – "*14And the ruler of the synagogue answered with indignation, because that Jesus had healed on the sabbath day, and said unto the people, There are six days in which men ought to work: in them therefore come and be healed, and not on the sabbath day. 15The Lord then answered him, and said, Thou hypocrite, doth not each one of you on the sabbath loose his ox or his ass from the stall, and lead him away to watering? 16And ought not this woman, being a daughter of Abraham, whom Satan hath bound, lo, these eighteen years, be loosed from this bond on the sabbath day?*"

B. His genealogy – There are both Hebrew and Gentile names throughout Jesus' genealogy, showing His grace. Judaism would never even record their names.

    1. Matthew 1:3 – Tamar (Genesis 46:12)

    2. Matthew 1:5 – Rahab (Hebrews 11:30-31)

    3. Matthew 1:5 – Ruth (Ruth 2-4)

    4. Matthew 1:6 – Bath-sheba (I Samuel 12:24)

    5. Matthew 1:16 – Mary (Matthew 1:20-21)

C. Those that followed Him – Many women followed Jesus throughout His earthly ministry and it seems they were the ones who ministered to all His needs.

    1. Luke 8:1-3 – "*1And it came to pass afterward, that he went throughout every city and village, preaching and shewing the glad tidings of the kingdom of God: and the twelve were with him, 2And certain women, which had been healed of evil spirits and infirmities, Mary called Magdalene, out of whom went seven devils, 3And Joanna the wife of Chuza Herod's steward, and Susanna, and many others, which ministered unto him of their substance.*"

    2. Mark 14:1-10 – "*3And being in Bethany in the house of Simon the leper, as he sat at meat, there came a woman having an alabaster box of ointment of spikenard very precious; and she brake the box, and poured it on his head. 4And there were some that had indignation within themselves, and said, Why was this waste of the ointment made? 5For it might have been sold for more than three hundred pence, and have been given to the poor. And they murmured against her. 6And Jesus said, Let her alone; why trouble ye her? she hath wrought a good work on me. 7For ye have the poor with you always, and whensoever ye will ye may do them good: but me ye have not always. 8She hath done what she could: she is come aforehand to anoint my body to the burying. 9Verily I say unto you, Wheresoever this gospel shall be preached throughout the whole world, this also that she hath done shall be spoken of for a memorial of her...*"

    3. Matthew 27:55-56 – "*And many women were there beholding afar off, which followed Jesus from Galilee, ministering unto him: Among which was Mary Magdalene, and Mary the mother of James and Joses, and the mother of Zebedee's children.*"

    4. Mark 15:40-41 – "*There were also women looking on afar off: among whom was Mary Magdalene, and Mary the mother of James the less and of Joses, and Salome; (Who also, when he was in Galilee, followed him, and ministered unto him;) and many other women which came up with him unto Jerusalem.*"

    5. Acts 1:3-16, Acts 2:1-4

D. Some interesting women in the life of Jesus – These women are mentioned because they were important people in His life.

    1. Troubling widow – Luke 18:1-8

    2. Pilate's wife – Matthew 27:17-19

    3. Poor widow – Mark 12:41-44

4. Mary at the tomb – John 20:11-18
5. Woman anointing Jesus' head – Matthew 26:6-13
6. Woman anointing His feet – Luke 7:37-50

7. First evangelists being women

   a. Matthew 28:1-10
   b. Luke 24:1-11, 22-24
   c. Mark 16:1-8
   d. John 20:1-10

8. Women who stood by Jesus to the end

   a. John 19:25-27
   b. Luke 23:27-28, 49, 55-56
   c. Matthew 27:55-61

9. Those whom Jesus ministered to going against the tradition of the elders

   a. Mark 10:6-12
   b. Mark 5:24-34
   c. Luke 10:38-42
   d. John 4:7-42
   e. John 8:2-11
   f. Matthew 8:14-17
   g. Matthew 19:18-25
   h. Matthew 15:22-28 (Mark 7:25-30)
   i. Luke 7:12-16

10. Those who witnessed His burial in the tomb – Luke 23:55-56
11. Those who confirmed His Messiahship – Anna (Luke 2:36-38), Mary (Luke 2:41-52)

12. Women used in the parables of Jesus

    a. Leavened mean – Matthew 13:33
    b. Two women grinding – Matthew 24:41
    c. Wise and foolish virgins – Matthew 25:1-13
    d. Lost coin – Luke 15:8-10
    e. Unjust judge – Luke 18:1-8
    f. Travailing woman – John 16:21-24

13. Jesus' family (mother, sisters, aunt, cousin)

    a. Luke 1:36
    b. Mark 6:3
    c. John 19:25

14. His birth through a virgin – Luke 1:26-38
15. Women worshipping at His birth – Luke 1:45-55

III. All The Instances In Scripture Where Jesus Dealt With Women Listed By Gospel

A. In the book of Matthew

1. Woman with the issue of blood – Matthew 9:20-22
2. Jarius' daughter – Matthew 9:18-19, 23-26
3. Canaanite woman – Matthew 15:21-28
4. Woman anointing Jesus' head – Matthew 26:5-13

B. In the book of Mark

1. Simon's mother-in-law – Mark 1:29-31
2. Woman with the issue of blood – Mark 5:24-34
3. Syrophenician woman – Mark 7:24-36
4. Anointing Jesus – Mark 14:3-9
5. Gospel commission – Mark 16:15-16

C. In the book of Luke

1. Jesus as young boy – Luke 2:41-52
2. Widow of Nain – Luke 7:11-17
3. Luke 7:36-50
4. Women blessing Him – Luke 11:27-28
5. Woman with spirit of infirmity – Luke 13:10-17
6. Mary and Martha – Luke 10:38-42
7. Remember Lot's wife – Luke 17:32

D. In the book of John

1. Wedding at Cana – John 2:1-11
2. Samaritan woman – John 4:4-42
3. Woman taken in adultery – John 8:1-11
4. Resurrection of Lazarus – John 11:25
5. Mary anoints Jesus – John 12:1-8
6. Jesus giving his mother to John – John 19:25-28

Lesson 25
The Principle Of Barrenness In Women

As we continue in our study of women, in this lesson we will discover a very important principle of women who were barren in the Scripture. It was not originally God's will for women to be barren. This is found in Old Testament Law. Nonetheless, God allowed some women to be barren for a greater purpose: to show His miraculous power in them and through them. In each case, a special son or manchild was born that ultimately God used mightily in the earth as deliverers, judges, prophets, etc. We will look at all these women and their stories and then see how their barrenness before birthing a child of great importance speaks to our own lives personally.

All of us will experience times of barrenness in our lives. The Scripture calls it the wilderness or desert experience. It is simply a time in our lives when God changes our character through His dealings. Jesus set this pattern for us during His life on earth for no sooner than Jesus was filled with the Holy Ghost, the Spirit of God led Him into the wilderness. The same pattern was seen in the nation of Israel for no sooner than God redeemed and delivered them out of Egypt, God led them into the wilderness as well. This is true with so many others such as Moses, John the Baptist, Paul the Apostle, and Joseph the last patriarch. Immediately upon being delivered, saved, or after they were called to ministry, they spent great amounts of time in the wilderness. So we find here a pattern that God uses barrenness in His specially called servants. He does this to prepare them for their ministry. In this lesson, we will look at these women who were barren, how they endured, and seeing they ultimately brought forth a child and by seeing what happened in their lives, we can then apply it to our own.

I.   It Was Not God's Original Intent For Women To Be Barren

A woman's number one purpose in being is to be fruitful. She was created for that purpose. In olden times it was counted as being a disgrace to be childless. Some might even call it a curse. But our great God, who does nothing without purpose had His reasons for these particular women to be barren. He allowed it in their lives for a higher purpose. As they went through the disgrace, the reproach, and the chiding of others, God used it so that we might learn more about His ways and His eternal purposes. But in the beginning it was not so.

A.   Scriptures

1.   Exodus 23:26 – *"There shall nothing cast their young, nor be barren, in thy land: the number of thy days I will fulfil."*
2.   Deuteronomy 7:14 – *"Thou shalt be blessed above all people: there shall not be male or female barren among you, or among your cattle."*
3.   Proverbs 30:15-16 – *"The horseleach hath two daughters, crying, Give, give. There are three things that are never satisfied, yea, four things say not, It is enough: The grave; and the barren womb; the earth that is not filled with water; and the fire that saith not, It is enough."*
4.   I Timothy 2:15 – *"Notwithstanding she shall be saved in childbearing, if they continue in faith and charity and holiness with sobriety."*
5.   Genesis 1:22 – *"And God blessed them, saying, Be fruitful, and multiply, and fill the waters in the seas, and let fowl multiply in the earth."*
6.   Deuteronomy 28:4 – *"Blessed shall be the fruit of thy body, and the fruit of thy ground, and the fruit of thy cattle, the increase of thy kine, and the flocks of thy sheep."*
7.   Psalms 127:3 – *"Lo, children are an heritage of the LORD: and the fruit of the womb is his reward"*

God does not dwell in confusion. He allowed barrenness for a reason, for a higher purpose. It is used to train and disciple His servants. All true ministries will pass through it.

B.   Definitions of Barren

1.   Hebrew words

       a.   *Aqar* – sterile; from a root, *aqar* – to pluck up by the roots, to hamstring, to exterminate, dig down, root up.

       b.   *Shakkuwl* – bereaved, robbed of children; from a root, *shakal* – to miscarry, suffer abortion; this word is also translated *deprived, childless, robbed, and bereaved*

   2.   Greek words

       a.   *Steiros* – sterile, stiff and unnatural; from a root, *steros* – stiff, solid, stable; from a root, *histemi* – to stand, abide, establish, hold up, stand still, continue, covenant.

       b.   *Argos* – inactive, unemployed, lazy, useless, idle, slow

   3.   Dictionary definition – incapable of producing offspring, unproductive, unfruitful, bereft, lacking

C.   A list of many barren women in Scripture

   1.   Sarah – Genesis 11:30, 16:1
   2.   Rebekah – Genesis 25:21
   3.   Rachel – Genesis 29:31
   4.   Hannah – I Samuel 2:5
   5.   Elisabeth – Luke 1:7
   6.   Manoah's wife – Judges 13:2-3

As we have already looked at Elisabeth in detail, we shall look at the other five and trust that God will give us revelation that can help and bless us by seeing why they were barren but ultimately fruitful.

D.   Barrenness as a judgment from God

   1.   II Samuel 6:23 – *"Therefore Michal the daughter of Saul had no child unto the day of her death."*
   2.   Job 24:13-21
   3.   Leviticus 20:20-22

E.   Other Scriptures on barrenness

   1.   Proverbs 30:15-16 – *"The horseleach hath two daughters, crying, Give, give. There are three things that are never satisfied, yea, four things say not, It is enough: The grave; and the barren womb; the earth that is not filled with water; and the fire that saith not, It is enough."*
   2.   II Peter 1:2-8 – *"...8For if these things be in you, and abound, they make you that ye shall neither be barren nor unfruitful in the knowledge of our Lord Jesus Christ."*
   3.   Psalms 113:5-9 – *"5Who is like unto the LORD our God, who dwelleth on high, 6Who humbleth himself to behold the things that are in heaven, and in the earth! 7He raiseth up the poor out of the dust, and lifteth the needy out of the dunghill; 8That he may set him with princes, even with the princes of his people. 9He maketh the barren woman to keep house, and to be a joyful mother of children. Praise ye the LORD."*

II.   All of Us However Are Called To Go Through A Wilderness Experience

A.   Word definitions for Wilderness

   1.   Hebrew word, *Midbar* – a driving, like a cattle drive, a pasture; from a root, *dabor* – to arrange.

   2.   Greek words

       a.   *Tahum* – to lie waste, a desolation of surface

b. *Eremia* – solitude, desert; from a root, *eremos* – lonesome, waste, desert, desolate, solitary.

Both the Hebrew and Greek words for "desert" are translated "wilderness". So the wilderness experience and the desert time that God brings to His people are one and the same.

B. An experience intended for all of us

    1. Scriptural examples

        a. Exodus 3:18 – *"And they shall hearken to thy voice: and thou shalt come, thou and the elders of Israel, unto the king of Egypt, and ye shall say unto him, The LORD God of the Hebrews hath met with us: and now let us go, we beseech thee, three days' journey into the wilderness, that we may sacrifice to the LORD our God."* – The children of Israel

        b. Exodus 3:1 – *"Now Moses kept the flock of Jethro his father in law, the priest of Midian: and he led the flock to the backside of the desert, and came to the mountain of God, even to Horeb."* – Moses

        c. Matthew 4:1 – *"Then was Jesus led up of the Spirit into the wilderness to be tempted of the devil."* – Jesus

        d. Luke 1:80 – *"And the child grew, and waxed strong in spirit, and was in the deserts till the day of his shewing unto Israel."* – John the Baptist

        e. II Corinthians 11:26 – *"In journeyings often, in perils of waters, in perils of robbers, in perils by mine own countrymen, in perils by the heathen, in perils in the city, in perils in the wilderness, in perils in the sea, in perils among false brethren;"* – Ministers of the gospel

        f. Song of Solomon 8:5 – *"Who is this that cometh up from the wilderness, leaning upon her beloved? I raised thee up under the apple tree: there thy mother brought thee forth: there she brought thee forth that bare thee."* – The body of Christ

God arranges to drive us through these desolate places of solitude, waste, and dealings to mold us and make us into His image. Every major figure in the Word had his time in these places. It is a rite of passage for all who would be called sons. It is both necessary and essential to us growing up and becoming like our God. It is the only path to perfection. It is one of the ways God chooses to mature us.

        g. Isaiah 64:9-12 – *"⁹Be not wroth very sore, O LORD, neither remember iniquity for ever: behold, see, we beseech thee, we are all thy people. ¹⁰Thy holy cities are a wilderness, Zion is a wilderness, Jerusalem a desolation. ¹¹Our holy and our beautiful house, where our fathers praised thee, is burned up with fire: and all our pleasant things are laid waste. ¹²Wilt thou refrain thyself for these things, O LORD? wilt thou hold thy peace, and afflict us very sore?"* – Please remember that all of these things (fire, pleasant things laid waste, afflictions) are sent to change us, to mold us into His image, and not to hurt us or to simply be mean to us.

        h. Isaiah 51:3 – *"For the LORD shall comfort Zion: he will comfort all her waste places; and he will make her wilderness like Eden, and her desert like the garden of the LORD; joy and gladness shall be found therein, thanksgiving, and the voice of melody."* – Our return to paradise is through the dealings of God.

        i. Psalms 72:9 – *"They that dwell in the wilderness shall bow before him; and his enemies shall lick the dust."* – In the wilderness, we learn to be humble and learn that He is God.

        j. I Samuel 17:28 (I Samuel 16:11) – *"And Eliab his eldest brother heard when he spake unto the men; and Eliab's anger was kindled against David, and he said, Why camest thou down hither? and with whom hast thou left those few sheep in the wilderness? I know thy pride, and the naughtiness of thine heart; for thou art come down that thou mightest see the battle."* – The wilderness is a place of preparation and a place of learning to care for others.

        k. Hebrews 11:38-39 – *"(Of whom the world was not worthy:) they wandered in deserts, and in mountains, and in dens and caves of the earth. And these all, having <u>obtained a good report</u> through faith, received not the promise:"* The world is not worthy of those who go through the wilderness experience.

l. Psalms 107:1-8 – "*¹O give thanks unto the LORD, for he is good: for his mercy endureth for ever. ²Let the redeemed of the LORD say so, whom he hath redeemed from the hand of the enemy; ³And gathered them out of the lands, from the east, and from the west, from the north, and from the south. ⁴They wandered in the wilderness in a solitary way; they found no city to dwell in. ⁵Hungry and thirsty, their soul fainted in them. ⁶Then they cried unto the LORD in their trouble, and he delivered them out of their distresses. ⁷And he led them forth by the right way, that they might go to a city of habitation. ⁸Oh that men would praise the LORD for his goodness, and for his wonderful works to the children of men!*"

m. Song of Solomon 3:6 – "*Who is this that cometh out of the wilderness like pillars of smoke, perfumed with myrrh and frankincense, with all powders of the merchant?*" – It is here we take on His nature.

n. Song of Solomon 8:5 – "*Who is this that cometh up from the wilderness, leaning upon her beloved? I raised thee up under the apple tree: there thy mother brought thee forth: there she brought thee forth that bare thee.*" – we learn here that it is by His grace we will become anything in Him. We also learn on Him and He becomes our <u>all in all</u>.

C. The wilderness is a place to mature

1. Isaiah 35:1-10

"*¹The wilderness and the solitary place shall be glad for them; and the desert shall rejoice, and blossom as the rose. ²It shall blossom abundantly, and rejoice even with joy and singing: the glory of Lebanon shall be given unto it, the excellency of Carmel and Sharon, they shall see the glory of the LORD, and the excellency of our God. ³Strengthen ye the weak hands, and confirm the feeble knees. ⁴Say to them that are of a fearful heart, Be strong, fear not: behold, your God will come with vengeance, even God with a recompence; he will come and save you. ⁵Then the eyes of the blind shall be opened, and the ears of the deaf shall be unstopped. ⁶Then shall the lame man leap as an hart, and the tongue of the dumb sing: for in the wilderness shall waters break out, and streams in the desert. ⁷And the parched ground shall become a pool, and the thirsty land springs of water: in the habitation of dragons, where each lay, shall be grass with reeds and rushes. ⁸And an highway shall be there, and a way, and it shall be called The way of holiness; the unclean shall not pass over it; but it shall be for those: the wayfaring men, though fools, shall not err therein. ⁹No lion shall be there, nor any ravenous beast shall go up thereon, it shall not be found there; but the redeemed shall walk there: ¹⁰And the ransomed of the LORD shall return, and come to Zion with songs and everlasting joy upon their heads: they shall obtain joy and gladness, and sorrow and sighing shall flee away.*"

2. Isaiah 41:19 – "*I will plant in the wilderness the cedar, the shittah tree, and the myrtle, and the oil tree; I will set in the desert the fir tree, and the pine, and the box tree together:*"

D. Examples of how God uses the wilderness to expose His people

1. Exodus 14:10-14 – "*¹⁰And when Pharaoh drew nigh, the children of Israel lifted up their eyes, and, behold, the Egyptians marched after them; and they were sore afraid: and the children of Israel cried out unto the LORD. ¹¹And they said unto Moses, Because there were no graves in Egypt, hast thou taken us away to die in the wilderness? wherefore hast thou dealt thus with us, to carry us forth out of Egypt? ¹²Is not this the word that we did tell thee in Egypt, saying, Let us alone, that we may serve the Egyptians? For it had been better for us to serve the Egyptians, than that we should die in the wilderness. ¹³And Moses said unto the people, Fear ye not, stand still, and see the salvation of the LORD, which he will shew to you to day: for the Egyptians whom ye have seen to day, ye shall see them again no more for ever. ¹⁴The LORD shall fight for you, and ye shall hold your peace.*"

2. Exodus 16:7 – "*And in the morning, then ye shall see the glory of the LORD; for that he heareth your murmurings against the LORD: and what are we, that ye murmur against us?*"

3. Numbers 14:1-10

E. The Call to Aloneness

All true ministers will experience great times of aloneness (barrenness). It drives us to seek God. It keeps us humble. It also helps us relate to the people to whom we will be ministering to. It is not easy at all but it is necessary.

1. Isaiah 51:2 – "...*Abraham your father...for I called him alone, and blessed him, and increased him.*"

    a. Genesis 12:1
    b. Hebrews 11:8-9

2. Jeremiah 15:17 – "...*I sat alone because of thy hand...*" – Other translations:

    a. "...*I sat alone, under thy hand...*"
    b. "...*with your hand on me, I held myself aloof...*"
    c. "...*I sit alone beneath the hand of God...*"

Jeremiah sat alone because of what was found in verse 16, His Word.

3. Psalms 102:7 – "*I watch, and am as a sparrow alone upon the house top.*" – Other translations:

    a. "...*been like a solitary bird on a housetop.*"
    b. "...*like a lonely bird on the roof.*"
    c. "...*lonely as a single sparrow on the housetop.*"

4. Lamentations 3:26-28 – "...*He sitteth alone and keepeth silence, because he hath borne it upon him.*" – Other translations:

    a. "...*just burden, in solitude, and silence, justly borne.*"
    b. "...*let him sit alone uncomplaining and silent in hope, because God has laid the yoke upon him.*"
    c. "...*let him sit alone and sigh, if it is heavy upon him.*"

5. II Timothy 4:16-17 – "*At my first answer no man stood with me, but all men forsook me...*" – Other translations:

    a. "*At my first defense, I had no one at my side...*"
    b. "*At my first appearance in court, no one came to help me...*"
    c. "*At my first meeting with my judges, no one took my part...*"

6. Exodus 24:2 – "*And Moses alone shall come near the LORD...*"
7. Micah 7:14-16 – "*Feed thy people...which dwell solitarily in the wood...*"
8. Luke 4:1, 14 – "...*was led by the Spirit into the wilderness...*"
9. Luke 9:36 – "*And when the voice was past, Jesus was found alone...*"
10. Genesis 32:24-32 – "*²⁴And Jacob was left alone; and there wrestled a man with him until the breaking of the day...*"
11. John 6:15 – "*When Jesus therefore perceived that they would come and take him by force, to make him a king, he departed again into a mountain himself alone.*"

III. God's Promise To Bless The Barren

As we will see, God allowed barrenness in some women, even though it wasn't supposed to happen to God's people (Exodus 23:26, Deuteronomy 7:14, Malachi 3:11). He allowed it to work a greater and nobler purpose in these women. Ultimately though, He blessed all of them. These situations are a type to us personally of what we may have to go through in our own lives, barrenness before birthing, humility before exultation, death before life. The church as a whole is represented here also of what God will allow before a manchild is born (the perfect church, the remnant, etc).

A. The Scriptures declare this.

1. Psalms 113:9 – *"He maketh the barren woman to keep house, and to be a joyful mother of children. Praise ye the LORD."* – Other translations:

    "He gives the childless woman a family…"
    "He gives children to the woman who has none…"
    "He honors the childless wife…"

2. Isaiah 54:1-10 – *"¹Sing, O barren, thou that didst not bear; break forth into singing, and cry aloud, thou that didst not travail with child: for more are the children of the desolate than the children of the married wife, saith the LORD…"* – Other translations:
    "Let your voice be loud and good, O woman without children…"
    "Shout for joy, O barren one…"
    "Sing of childless woman…"

3. I Samuel 2:5 – *"They that were full have hired out themselves for bread; and they that were hungry ceased: so that the barren hath born seven; and she that hath many children is waxed feeble."* – Other translations:

    "…even the barren gives birth to seven…"
    "…the childless woman now has seven children…"
    "…truly, she who had no children has become the mother of seven…"
    "…so that the barren hath borne many…"

4. Malachi 3:11 – *"And I will rebuke the devourer for your sakes, and he shall not destroy the fruits of your ground; neither shall your vine cast her fruit before the time in the field, saith the LORD of hosts."* – Other translations:

    "…your vine field shall not fail to bear…"
    "…your vine will not lose its fruit before harvest time…"
    "…nor miscarry to you doth the vine in the field…"
    "…your vine in your field will not be barren…"

5. Song of Solomon 4:2 – *"Thy teeth are like a flock of sheep that are even shorn, which came up from the washing; whereof every one bear twins, and none is barren among them."* – Other translations:

    "…none is missing among them."
    "…not one of them is missing."
    "…none has lost her young."
    "…not one of them is bereaved."
    "…and there is none without young."

IV. A Closer Look At Some Of The Barren Women In Scripture

A. Sarai

1. Genesis 11:29-30
2. Genesis 15:1-4 – God's promise
3. Genesis 16:1-11 – Ishmael is produced because of their presumption; Ishmael's name means – he will hear God, he will be heard of God, God hears. He is a type of the flesh (Genesis 16:12 – *"And he*

will be a wild man; his hand will be against every man, and every man's hand against him; and he shall dwell in the presence of all his brethren.")

4. At this time neither Abram nor Sarai had their names (character) changed. They had to go through this process of barrenness and failure and eventually overcome to receive God's blessing.

5. Their names changes

   a. Genesis 17:1-5 – Abram means – exalted father, a high father, high and lofty thinker; Abraham means – father of a multitude, father of mercy, a father of many nations.
   b. Genesis 15:21 – Sarai means – contentious, my ruler, my princess, quarrelsome; Sarah means – princess, noble woman, chieftainness, and comes from a root meaning – a princess, a noble lady, to lead, to fight.

6. Genesis 18:1, 9-14 – Their unbelief
7. Genesis 21:1-7 – Promise fulfilled (Hebrews 11:11 – "*Through faith also Sara herself received strength to conceive seed, and was delivered of a child when she was past age, because she judged him faithful who had promised.*")

B. Rebekah

1. Her name means – a rope with a noose, to tie firmly, captivating; from a root, a hitching place.

2. Family History

   a. Her father, Bethuel means – virgin of God, separated of God, a relation of God, abode of God, dweller in God.
   b. Her grandmother, Milcah means – queen, counsel
   c. Her grandfather, Nahor means – snorting, breathing hard, slayer, inflamed, heated
   d. Her brother, Laban means – white, glorious; from a root – to be white, to be clean.

3. Her story

   a. Genesis 24:1-10 – Abraham's request for a bride for Isaac
   b. Genesis 25:20-21 – Her barrenness, "*20And Isaac was forty years old when he took Rebekah to wife, the daughter of Bethuel the Syrian of Padan-aram, the sister to Laban the Syrian. 21And Isaac intreated the LORD for his wife, because she was barren: and the LORD was intreated of him, and Rebekah his wife conceived.*" Forty is the number for testing and trial; God answer's Isaac's prayer. Isaac's name means – laughter

   c. Genesis 25:22-23 – Her birthing, "*22And the children struggled together within her; and she said, If it be so, why am I thus? And she went to inquire of the LORD. 23And the LORD said unto her, Two nations are in thy womb, and two manner of people shall be separated from thy bowels; and the one people shall be stronger than the other people; and the elder shall serve the younger.*" – This speaks to us of our own struggles within us, the flesh and the spirit fighting for supremacy. Below are Scriptures of this struggle.

      1) Matthew 26:41 – "*Watch and pray, that ye enter not into temptation: the spirit indeed is willing, but the flesh is weak.*"
      2) Romans 8:5-14
      3) John 1:17
      4) Galatians 4:22-31
      5) Romans 6:1-18, Ephesians 4:21-24, Ephesians 2:1-6
      6) Romans 7:4-6, 14-15

175

C. Manoah's Wife

1. Judges 13:2-5, 24-25 – "*2And there was a certain man of Zorah, of the family of the Danites, whose name was Manoah; and his wife was barren, and bare not. 3And the angel of the LORD appeared unto the woman, and said unto her, Behold now, thou art barren, and bearest not: but thou shalt conceive, and bear a son. 4Now therefore beware, I pray thee, and drink not wine nor strong drink, and eat not any unclean thing: 5For, lo, thou shalt conceive, and bear a son; and no rasor shall come on his head: for the child shall be a Nazarite unto God from the womb: and he shall begin to deliver Israel out of the hand of the Philistines...24And the woman bare a son, and called his name Samson: and the child grew, and the LORD blessed him. 25And the Spirit of the LORD began to move him at times in the camp of Dan between Zorah and Eshtaol.*"

    a. Manoah's name means – rest, quiet, consolation or parents
    b. She was the mother of Samson, God's deliverer
    c. Samson's name means – little sun, splendid sun, strong, distinguished

D. Elisabeth

1. Luke 1:5-7, 9-17, 24-25, 36-37, 40-45, 57-60
2. Elisabeth's name means – God is her oath, a worshipper of God, God of the covenant
3. John's name means – Jehovah has been gracious, Jehovah has graciously given

E. Anna

1. Luke 2:36-39 – "*36And there was one Anna, <u>a prophetess</u>, the daughter of Phanuel, of the tribe of Aser: she was <u>of a great age</u>, and had lived with an husband seven years from her virginity; 37And she was a widow of about fourscore and four years, <u>which departed not from the temple</u>, but <u>served God with fastings and prayers night and day</u>. 38And she coming in that instant <u>gave thanks</u> likewise unto the Lord, and <u>spake of him to all them that looked for redemption in Jerusalem</u>. 39And when they had performed all things according to the law of the Lord, they returned into Galilee, to their own city Nazareth.*"

    a. Anna means – grace
    b. She was the daughter of Phanuel which means – vision of God, the face of God
    c. She was of the tribe of Aser (Asher) which means – fortunate, happy
    d. Her purpose was to reveal the Messiah. Her barrenness resulted in the birthing of our Saviour.

F. Hannah

1. I Samuel 1:1-2 – "*1Now there was a certain man of Ramathaim-zophim, of mount Ephraim, and his name was Elkanah, the son of Jeroham, the son of Elihu, the son of Tohu, the son of Zuph, an Ephrathite: 2And he had two wives; the name of the one was Hannah, and the name of the other Peninnah: and Peninnah had children, but Hannah had no children.*"

    a. Hannah's name means – grace, mercy, favor, gratuitous gift
    b. Peninnah means – coral, place of dead fish
    c. Elkanah – God has redeemed, possession of God
    d. Ramathaim-zophim – double eminence, high place, watchmen
    e. Ephraim – two fold increase, doubly fruitful

G. Great Woman (Shunammite)

1. II Kings 4:8-36 – This great woman was full of substance and ministered to the man of God Elisha.

Rise Up Ye Women

Isaiah 32:7-20 – *"The instruments also of the churl are evil: he deviseth wicked devices to destroy the poor with lying words, even when the needy speaketh right.⁸But the liberal deviseth liberal things; and by liberal things shall he stand.⁹ Rise up, ye women that are at ease; hear my voice, ye careless daughters; give ear unto my speech.¹⁰ Many days and years shall ye be troubled, ye careless women: for the vintage shall fail, the gathering shall not come.¹¹ Tremble, ye women that are at ease; be troubled, ye careless ones: strip you, and make you bare, and gird sackcloth upon your loins.¹² They shall lament for the teats, for the pleasant fields, for the fruitful vine.¹³ Upon the land of my people shall come up thorns and briers; yea, upon all the houses of joy in the joyous city:¹⁴ Because the palaces shall be forsaken; the multitude of the city shall be left; the forts and towers shall be for dens for ever, a joy of wild asses, a pasture of flocks;¹⁵ Until the spirit be poured upon us from on high, and the wilderness be a fruitful field, and the fruitful field be counted for a forest.¹⁶ Then judgment shall dwell in the wilderness, and righteousness remain in the fruitful field.¹⁷ And the work of righteousness shall be peace; and the effect of righteousness quietness and assurance for ever.¹⁸ And my people shall dwell in a peaceable habitation, and in sure dwellings, and in quiet resting places;¹⁹ When it shall hail, coming down on the forest; and the city shall be low in a low place.²⁰ Blessed are ye that sow beside all waters, that send forth thither the feet of the ox and the ass."*

What a passage of Scripture! Meditate with me and consider what God is saying. Women have been put down for so long, they have allowed the traditions of men to become their belief. They have been lulled to sleep! Verse 10 says many days and years shall be troubled, the vintage shall fail, and the gathering shall not come. What is he talking about? In the natural sense, he is speaking of a harvest, but we know that there is a spiritual interpretation that relates to us. The gathering Isaiah is speaking of is the same one found in Genesis 49:10. It is the gathering of the people of God unto Himself! This is the gathering that will not take place as long as women are at ease! When women are put down and not allowed to come forth in ministry, we prolong the coming of the Lord. What is vintage? Vintage is the fruit of the earth. He says it has been lost. Why? Because women have been at ease, they've been asleep! This harvest is lying waste because there are not enough laborers. The fields are white unto harvest, but the laborers are few. Women have believed that *"You are not a laborer, neither can you labor"* far too long.

Do you realize the literal meaning for the word "religion"? It means *"to bind"*. Women have been bound by religion for years. We're not talking about "women's lib" or the feminist movement, but about releasing women to obey the call of God on their lives. The Lord is saying in this hour, *"Rise up, ye women! Hear My voice!*

God is not pleased with the fact that women have not been allowed to minister. It is grievous to Him because His eyes have been upon the nations. He sees the places we cannot see, where there are people willing to sacrifice their lives to know about Jesus. Yet the fruit is going to waste, the harvest is rotting. Why? It is because of the traditions of men, the fears of men and because of error.
In the last great move of God that is yet to come upon the earth, God is going to unleash to the world the ministry of women. Men have not been able and will never be able to win the world for Jesus without the ministry of women!

Solomon said, *"Cease my son to hear the words that cause thee to err."* Cease to hear them! Don't listen to words that are going to keep you from heeding the call of God.

Rise up, ye woman that have been lulled to sleep! Be stirred in your spirits and begin to come forth and obey the Lord. The gathering unto Him will not come until you do! Jesus never said women couldn't minister. It is a traditional viewpoint birthed from the fear that men have of women who are stirred in God. Women that have heard from the Lord can't be quiet. Amos says *"the lion has roared, who can help but prophesy?"*

If you are in a place where women are not allowed to minister, come out of Babylon and get in a place where you can come forth in the Lord. Verse 11 says, *"Tremble ye women"* because there should be a trembling of fearfulness that you <u>might miss it!</u> Now is the time to enter into the things of God.

Verses 12 -14 speak of the waste, the palaces forsaken and the multitude of cities left. Forts and towers shall be for dens. Scripturally speaking, a den is the place where wild animals live. This speaks of demons. Do you know there are churches with wild animals in their midst? They have kept women suppressed and oppressed and ignorant of God's Word too long.

Sisters, have you been lulled to sleep by the words of men? Are you at ease? Some of us love Jesus with all of our hearts, but the fire is not burning. We are complacent and apathetic in relation to the Lord and His call on our lives. Isaiah tells us God seeks men and women who will stir themselves up. Stir yourselves up, rise up and take your place boldly and confidently knowing it is right for you to minister God's word. Don't let the vintage fail; don't hinder the gathering from coming! Jesus and all of creation are waiting for you to RISE UP!

Dr. Samuel Greene, Ph.D.
www.nwmin.org

Dr. Samuel Greene is president and founder of Narrow Way Ministries International (nwmin.org), an outreach missionary arm of the body of Christ seeking to disciple and teach believers everywhere foundational truths and sound doctrine helping the body of Christ grow up into Jesus in all things. Brother Sam was saved at the young age of fifteen and he has walked with the Lord now for over forty five years. He was ordained into the ministry in 1976 and has pastored all over the United States as well as started churches and Bible Schools all over the world. Dr. Greene has also written over fifty books to help solidify and found the body of Christ in basic sound doctrine as well as revelational truths about the coming Kingdom of God as well as the doctrine of the remnant. God spoke to him at the age of fifteen and said he was going to teach the doctrine to the remnant in the last days. Not knowing what this meant, he simply began to search the Scriptures as God brought into his life many men and women of God who taught him faithfully. Dr. Greene's guiding passion is for God to bring forth His people into the bride of Christ that He has called her to be with His image carrying His glory all over the earth.

For information on obtaining **WOMEN IN MINISTRY AUDIO** to accompany this study manual, please contact us at **www.nwmin.org**

www.ingramcontent.com/pod-product-compliance
Lightning Source LLC
LaVergne TN
LVHW061333060426

835512LV00017B/2668